WOMEN IN BUDDHIST TRADITIONS

WOMEN IN RELIGIONS

Series Editor: Catherine Wessinger

Women in Christian Traditions
Rebecca Moore

Women in New Religions
Laura Vance

Women in Japanese Religions
Barbara R. Ambros

Theories of Women in Religions
Catherine Wessinger

Women in Buddhist Traditions
Karma Lekshe Tsomo

Women in Buddhist Traditions

Karma Lekshe Tsomo

NEW YORK UNIVERSITY PRESS
New York

NEW YORK UNIVERSITY PRESS
New York
www.nyupress.org

References to internet websites (URLs) were accurate at the time of writing. Neither the author nor New York University Press is responsible for URLs that may have expired or changed since the manuscript was prepared.

Library of Congress Cataloging-in-Publication Data
Names: Karma Lekshe Tsomo, 1944– author.
Title: Women in Buddhist traditions / Karma Lekshe Tsomo.
Description: New York : New York University Press, 2020. | Series: Women in religions | Includes bibliographical references and index.
Identifiers: LCCN 2020016535 (print) | LCCN 2020016536 (ebook) | ISBN 9781479803415 (cloth) | ISBN 9781479803422 (paperback) | ISBN 9781479803446 (ebook) | ISBN 9781479803453 (ebook)
Subjects: LCSH: Women in Buddhism. | Buddhist women.
Classification: LCC BQ4570.W6 K343 2020 (print) | LCC BQ4570.W6 (ebook) | DDC 294.3082—dc23
LC record available at https://lccn.loc.gov/2020016535
LC ebook record available at https://lccn.loc.gov/2020016536

New York University Press books are printed on acid-free paper, and their binding materials are chosen for strength and durability. We strive to use environmentally responsible suppliers and materials to the greatest extent possible in publishing our books.

Manufactured in the United States of America

10 9 8 7 6 5 4 3 2 1

Also available as an ebook

CONTENTS

Note on Transliteration and Pronunciation of Names and Terms vii

Introduction: Why Study Women in the Buddhist Traditions? 1

1. Women in Early Indian Buddhism 17

2. Buddhist Women in South and Southeast Asia 38

3. Buddhist Women in East Asia 54

4. Buddhist Women in Inner Asia 69

5. Buddhist Women in the West 92

6. Women's Ordination across Cultures 108

7. Grassroots Revolution: Buddhist Women and Social Activism 132

Conclusion 149

Acknowledgments 167

Questions for Discussion 169

For Further Reading 175

Notes 177

Works Cited 193

Index 211

About the Author 223

NOTE ON TRANSLITERATION AND PRONUNCIATION OF NAMES AND TERMS

A discussion of women in Buddhist traditions necessarily includes words in the original languages of those traditions. The Theravāda Buddhist traditions are based on scriptures recorded in the Pāli language, whereas the Mahāyāna Buddhist traditions are based on scriptures written in Sanskrit. In this book, the standard transliterations of words in those two South Asian languages include diacritical marks to indicate pronunciation. The reader will note in the text that either Pāli or Sanskrit words are used depending on the tradition and the language of the relevant scriptural sources being discussed. The Mahāyāna Buddhist traditions in China, Tibet, Korea, Japan, and elsewhere are based on the Mahāyāna scriptures, many of which have been translated into their own languages, so Sanskrit terms are used when discussing Mahāyāna Buddhist traditions, in addition to terms in those languages. Some chapters alternately use Pāli and Sanskrit versions of the same word or name, especially when discussing the earliest sources on the life of the Buddha and his teachings, because later written texts were preserved in both these languages.

In transliterations of Pāli or Sanskrit words, a macron (a straight bar) over a vowel indicates an elongated sound. Pāli and Sanskrit words are often similar. For example, the word for a fully ordained nun in Pāli is *bhikkhunī* and in Sanskrit, *bhikṣuṇī*. The word for "action" is *kamma* in Pāli and *karma* in Sanskrit. Other words, such as "Buddha," are the same in both Pāli and Sanskrit. The *th*, *dh*, *ph*, and *bh* sounds are aspirates, not sibulants. Theravāda, for example, is pronounced with a hard *t* as in "town," not a dental, as in "thank." The transliterated letters *ś* and *ṣ* are both close to the "sh" sound in English. The Sanskrit *ṃ* is pronounced as a nasalized *n*. The Sanskrit consonants *ṇ* and *ḍ* are pronounced as nasalized versions of *n* and *d*.

The transliteration of Tibetan words follows the Wylie system developed by Turrell V. Wylie in the 1950s, still commonly used today, which avoids diacritical marks. Chinese words are romanized following the Pinyin system. In romanized Japanese words, a macron over a vowel, such as *ō*, indicates a long vowel.

In the case of names of people, institutions, and places, the transliteration generally follows the phonetic equivalent without diacritics, or the preference of the person or institution. The exception is that diacritical marks are used in the transliterated names of persons mentioned in Buddhist scriptures. For example, Mahāprajāpatī Gautamī is the name in Sanskrit of the Buddha's aunt and foster mother, while her name in Pāli is Mahāpajāpatī Gautamī.

Although the use of diverse languages may be a bit confusing or inconvenient, it is also a useful reminder that these Buddhist traditions have long histories and spread over a vast geographical expanse. Through these linguistic distinctions, we can appreciate the uniqueness of these traditions as well as their continuity over many centuries.

Introduction

Why Study Women in the Buddhist Traditions?

The story of women in Buddhism is complex, because the world's Buddhist traditions and the roles of women within them are richly diverse. From India to Japan, Sri Lanka to Russia, each tradition has its unique history, culture, religious life, and cultural mores for women. Moreover, new refractions of each Asian Buddhist tradition are now developing in countries outside of Asia. It may be tempting to slip into simplistic stereotypes about Asian and non-Asian Buddhist women, but Buddhist societies span a multitude of different cultural heritages, geographical settings, and social strata, making it impossible to accurately characterize Buddhist women as a whole. In studying women in Buddhist traditions, therefore, we encounter a major challenge. Is it possible to identify patterns of Buddhist thought and behavior that influence gender roles or reinforce existing patterns of thought and behavior in such a wide spectrum of cultures and societies?

The Buddhist traditions extend over a period of twenty-five centuries, with roots in ancient Indian culture and branches extending to almost every corner of the globe. Not only did Buddhism put down roots over an extensive geographical area, but also these traditions have continued to evolve over a very long period of time, a process that is clearly in evidence throughout the world today. To complicate matters, wherever Buddhist teachings put down roots, they found themselves on soil that was already home to a multitude of indigenous cultures with their own religious traditions. These traditions inevitably influenced, and continue to influence, the ways in which Buddhist ideas and practices are understood and adapted. Tracing the branches and fruits of these culturally specific transmissions and adaptations is as fascinating as it is challenging.

With few early historical materials to work with and countless cultural variations and interpretations, getting a clear picture of women's roles in the Buddhist traditions is not an easy task. Moreover, as in other religious traditions, women have often been neglected or erased in existing accounts. Nevertheless, after nearly three decades of research on Buddhist women by dedicated scholars in many disciplines, there is more information available today than ever before. In 1987 when, almost by accident, I began doing ethnographic research on Buddhist women, I discovered that very little had been written on the topic. The major study available was I. B. Horner, *Women under Primitive Buddhism*, published in 1930.

Horner's work was remarkable for its time and is influential even today, but it surprised me that Buddhist women's history and ideas had subsequently received so little attention. In many contemporary surveys of Buddhism, the topic of women appears to be simply an add-on. Fortunately, many new books, book chapters, and articles have appeared in the last few decades. Although certain areas of study, such as Buddhist feminist hermeneutics, have barely begun, we have far more information on women in Buddhism available today than ever before.

What can we learn from a study about women in Buddhist traditions? The task here is to provide a broad overview of women in Buddhist societies, taking examples from diverse cultures and communities, to learn what women value in the Buddhist teachings and what obstacles they face in putting those teachings into practice. Our focus will be not on specific social customs but on gaining a broad understanding of the status and self-understanding of women in societies that identify as Buddhist. The objective is not to frame a definitive picture, an impossible task, but to pique readers' interest in Buddhist women and raise questions for further reading and research. The study of women in Buddhist cultures provides not only a window on the religious lives of women but also a vantage point from which to learn more about Buddhist philosophy, psychology, culture, and society. Despite the variety and complexity of the Buddhist traditions, we can learn a great deal about them through the lives of women.

History in the Mirror

We can begin with the hypothesis that the teachings of the Buddha ("the awakened one"; ca. 563–483 BCE) offered women a new outlook on life and greater independence in charting the course of their lives. The *brāhmaṇa* social class in India was the most prestigious of the four primary social classes of that time. Although *brāhmaṇas*[1] were not necessarily priests, many *brāhmaṇa* men were priests, and they were the scholars and teachers of the Vedic scriptures composed in Sanskrit and conveyed orally for thousands of years. The worldview conveyed by the *brāhmaṇas* that was prevalent alongside Buddhism during the first millennium of its development on the Indian subcontinent included the *āśramas*, the four stages of an ideal life for a male (student, householder, retiree, and renunciant, that is, one who renounces household life to pursue the spiritual path). The *brāhmaṇa* worldview included four aims of life (*puruṣārthas*) for a male belonging to the first three *varṇas*, or social classes: sensual pleasure in marriage, prosperity, moral values, and liberation.

The Buddhist traditions trace their roots to Buddha Śākyamuni, who was born Siddhārtha Gautama sometime during the fifth or sixth century BCE in a park known as Lumbini, just north of what is today the border between Nepal and India. According to the traditional narrative, when he was just seven days old, his mother Mahāmāyā passed away and he was nursed and nurtured by her sister, Mahāprajāpatī, who proved to be an extremely kind foster mother. As a scion of the Śākya clan and the designated heir of his father's principality, Siddhārtha grew up in relative luxury, enjoying all the pleasures of palace life, including innumerable courtesans. When he was sixteen years old, he married a beautiful cousin named Yaśodharā, who was also sixteen. After many years, she gave birth to a son, Rāhula.

Around that time, Siddhārtha's prodigious curiosity led him to venture beyond the palace walls, where he discovered sickness, old age, death, and a calm, introspective renunciant. Because of his sheltered upbringing, he had not been exposed to the ancient Indian tradition of *śrāmaṇas*, seekers who renounce householder life in order to engage in contemplative practices and pursue spiritual goals. After the shock of encountering suffering for the first time, he was deeply impressed by the serene countenance of this homeless wanderer. These experiences led the young prince to abandon his luxurious life, his wife, and his newborn son Rāhula in favor of the spiritual path. He spent six years learning different philosophical perspectives and engaging in strenuous religious practices, including extreme fasting and other arduous feats, but he remained unconvinced and unfulfilled, so he sat down to meditate under a tree and resolved not to arise until he had discovered the true meaning of life. After six days of intensive meditation, he awakened to the true nature of things "as they are": the problematic nature of human existence, the root causes of suffering, the possibility of ending suffering, and the way to achieve that goal. Gods, humans, and the earth itself acknowledged his discoveries. The Buddha (the Awakened One) spent the remaining forty-five years of his life sharing these discoveries with audiences all over northern India. It is believed by Buddhists that Buddha Śākyamuni, who lived during the present historical era, was not the only person to become awakened; there have been countless *buddhas* in previous eras, and there are many yet to come.

Buddha Śākyamuni ("sage of the Śākya clan") taught a path to liberation from suffering and dissatisfaction that was open to all who wished to purify the defilements of their minds. His followers included women and men of all ages, social classes, and backgrounds. Although the Buddha probably did not intend to be a social activist, the path of wisdom and compassion that he taught was quite revolutionary at the time. In place of the worship of gods and performance of rituals, which were restricted to male religious specialists of the *brāhmaṇa* class, he taught an ethical interpretation of the law of cause and effect and an empirical method of self-discovery that could be practiced by everyone. The Buddha verified the prevailing belief in rebirth and the causal connection between actions and their consequences during meditation under the *bodhi* tree just prior to his awakening. He began to share his insights on the urging of divine beings and spent forty-five years teaching throughout northern India. He taught that mental defilements such as desire, hatred, ignorance, pride, and jealousy are the causes of repeated rebirth within the cycle of existence (*saṃsāra*). Rebirth inevitably entails suffering and dissatisfaction, and the only way to become free of suffering is to achieve freedom from rebirth. After gaining insight into these teachings and the contemplative practices that facilitate understanding, his disciples were sent out far and wide "in the four directions" to spread his teachings, and thousands of men and women achieved the state of freedom from suffering and dissatisfaction. They became known as *arhats*, beings who are free from mental defilements and hence liberated from suffering and the bondage of rebirth in the wheel of birth and death.

Based on the insights he gained during meditation, the Buddha explained that sentient beings take different forms in *saṃsāra*, the wheel of repeated becoming, and there is nothing indelible, intrinsic, or enduring about these identities. Accordingly, a person may be born in a different body—male or female—in different circumstances from lifetime to lifetime. The circumstances of being reborn in a female body were thought to be more difficult and so a male rebirth was thought to be preferable. Female bodies were considered more difficult because, for example, women experience the sufferings of menstruation, childbirth, and menopause. Women are vulnerable to sexual harassment and rape and, at the time of the Buddha, were thought to require protection. At marriage, a woman had to leave her natal home and go to live with her husband's family, so daughters were often considered a liability—another mouth to feed until their marriage, which often required a large dowry.

In the patriarchal social milieu that prevailed in northern India at that time, women faced many limitations and difficulties. Aristocratic women such as the Buddha's stepmother Mahāprajāpatī and wife Yaśodharā were subject to many restrictions, as were women of other social classes. In this context, the Buddha's declaration that women and men alike were capable of liberating themselves from suffering and from the cycle of rebirth was revolutionary. On a practical level, his decision to allow women to enter the monastic community (Pāli: *saṅgha*; Sanskrit: *saṃgha*) offered women an alternative to domestic life and the socially prescribed roles of wife and mother. The verses of some of the earliest Buddhist nuns, recorded in the *Therīgāthā*, are testimony to the spiritual achievements and freedom these awakened women experienced.

From India, the teachings of the Buddha spread in many directions and, at various points in history, became the dominant worldview in many parts of Asia. The main branches of Buddhism that developed were Theravāda and Mahāyāna. The Theravāda branch prevailed primarily in South and Southeast Asia, while the Mahāyāna became dominant in North and East Asia. Social customs and family practices vary widely in Buddhist societies, influenced by earlier cultures. Tracing the links and divergences among Buddhist beliefs, social practices, and religious institutions will be key to our understanding of attitudes toward women.

Buddhist Principles, Social Practices

In the social views disseminated by the *brāhmaṇas*,[2] a woman was expected to marry and follow the dictates of her husband—indeed, she was taught to view her husband as god (*pati* means "god" and also "husband") and be totally devoted to him.[3] By contrast, a Buddhist woman could decide, if she wished, to leave the household life and become a nun. If women from Buddhist families preferred to marry, they generally had more freedom than most to select their own partners. The Buddha gave advice about how to live a happy married life, but there are no religious laws that pertain to marriage in Buddhism.[4] Marriage is a civil contract, in which religion plays little role. Monks or nuns may be invited to recite prayers or impart blessings, but marriage alliances are not sacred or sanctified by any higher power. There are no religious strictures against premarital sex or widow remarriage. Buddhists are encouraged to live by five lay precepts, which include abstaining from sexual misconduct, but these are personal choices, not divinely sanctioned obligations. The closest thing to a Buddhist legal code is the *vinaya*, a collection of texts that explain the precepts for monastics.

Customs regarding marriage, divorce, and property rights are culture specific. In Buddhist cultures, religious authorities generally prefer to leave family matters to the discretion of those concerned, giving counsel according to the Buddha's teachings when it is sought, and avoiding what are deemed "affairs of this world." In most Buddhist societies, clerics are celibate monks and nuns.[5] Although they may have been previously married (like Buddha Śākyamuni himself), celibate monastics are not expected or encouraged to take part in worldly matters. They are to abide by Buddhist values including generosity, ethical conduct, patience, mindfulness, wisdom, and loving-kindness. Religious values and the exemplary conduct of well-restrained monks and nuns undoubtedly influence Buddhist decision-making and interpersonal relationships, but monastic institutions have no jurisdiction over the lives of laypeople and no influence or particular interest in marriage practices, except to impart blessings and wish everyone peace and happiness.[6]

In the Buddhist view, violence against any sentient being, including animals, is never religiously sanctioned. Although some Buddhists may condone violence in a life-or-death situation, the first precept is to abstain from taking life and is widely interpreted to mean refraining from harming any sentient being. In the family, especially, because it is the environment for the nurturing of children, violence in any form is discouraged. Instead, the Buddha taught his followers to live with loving-kindness and compassion for all in thought, word, and deed. Meditations on loving-kindness focus especially on loved ones and then extend to all living beings. Although teaching nonharm as a moral principle does not ensure that all Buddhist families are havens of domestic peace and harmony, Buddhists value nonviolence and generally try their best to live up to this ideal.

Buddhist thought and social custom are often interwoven and influenced by beliefs and practices that predate the introduction of Buddhism. Gender hierarchies that privilege men over women, especially in politics and religion, are evident in all Buddhist societies. Although according to the Buddhist understanding of karma, the natural law of cause and effect, social and economic inequalities may be the result of a person's actions in the past, injustices cannot be justified by Buddhist teachings. The Buddha admitted seekers from all social and economic backgrounds into his community; in fact, the original Buddhist monastic community may be the earliest documented example of democratic governance.[7] Still, socially embedded customs tend to give priority to males. These customs may reflect local practices or early Indian values, but the privileged place of males in Buddhist families, organizations, and societies may also be influenced by the privileged place of monks in Buddhist monastic institutions. In Buddhist societies even today, boys are more likely to get their parents' blessing and encouragement to enter a monastery. Boys are encouraged to become monks, in part to create merit (good karma) for their parents, but it is rare for girls to receive similar encouragement to become nuns. Until recently at least, the higher status of monks over nuns has contributed to a general preference for boys over girls. As a result, monks have traditionally far outnumbered nuns in Buddhist societies.

Relationships between monks and nuns are prescribed in the monastic codes, influenced especially by the "eight weighty rules" (Pāli: *garudhamma*; Sanskrit: *gurudharma*) in the *vinaya* that assign monks a superior status in the monastic ordering. Although the rules for monastics do not apply to laypeople, this gender differential in the monastic community seems to have been influenced by gendered social norms and to have perpetuated certain gender-specific social practices, preconceptions, and expectations that give priority to men over women.

For example, at the time of the Buddha, monks outnumbered nuns, so the teachings that have been preserved are often directed to monks. As a first step in overcoming self-grasping, the Buddha advised his followers to visit graveyards and cremation grounds and to meditate on the nature of the human body.[8] Through meditation, he taught, one can see things "as they are" and thus cut through ignorance and delusion. By understanding that all human beings are equally subject to death and decay, one can see through the illusion of a separate, independently existent self. By understanding the true impermanent nature of things, one can see that although human bodies may appear attractive on the outside, inside they are full of many disgusting substances. Insight into the true nature of the body thus helps to free one from sensual attachment and the disappointments that arise from that attachment. Because the Buddha was addressing an audience of celibate monks, he used the unpleasant qualities of the female body as an example. The Buddha presumably used the "foul" nature of the female body as an example to help his audience of celibate monks cut through desire and maintain their commitment to renunciation, but the teaching may have perpetuated preconceptions about the impurity of women in patriarchal culture. If the Buddha had been addressing an audience of celibate nuns, he would presumably have used the unpleasant qualities of the male body as an example. Unfortunately, out of context, the references to the disgusting nature of the female body have been interpreted to imply that the male body is somehow superior to the female body.

Such scriptural passages contributed to the impression that a male rebirth is preferable to a female rebirth.[9] In Buddhist societies, one frequently hears that "being born as a woman is the result of bad karma," even though there is no evidence that the Buddha said such a thing. How do these teachings on the impure nature of the human body affect women, who are frequently associated with the body due to their unique reproductive capability?

The Buddhist scriptures include many positive representations of women, for example, extolling the love of mothers for their children, but the texts are inconsistent. One narrative describes the Buddha as being reluctant to admit women to his new mendicant community and portrays him as admitting Mahāprajāpatī only after she agrees to accept the eight weighty rules that subordinate nuns to monks.[10] In this narrative, the Buddha is shown as predicting the decline and disintegration of his teachings, the Dharma, within five hundred years as a result of admitting women to the *saṅgha*, the monastic order.[11] These narratives reflect the patriarchal gender relationships and expectations that existed in Indian society at the time. Despite the liberating nature of the Buddha's teachings and the practical alternative of monastic life for women, these stories have helped to reinforce patriarchal norms in Buddhist societies. Gradually, literary references to nuns' active, public participation in Buddhist activities became less frequent; the contributions of monks became the central focus, and often women are absent from Buddhist narratives altogether. This declining visibility of women in the scriptures seems to be linked with the socially and scripturally sanctioned subordination of women. Reinforced by unequal educational opportunities, gender inequalities in the *saṅgha* seem to mirror ambivalent attitudes toward women in society in general. As a consequence, in the Buddhist texts there are both powerful images of highly realized women and also passages that tend to diminish and disparage them.[12]

The story of women in Buddhist traditions is multifaceted, varying over many centuries and a huge geographical expanse. The interrelationships among the Buddhist traditions are also complex and fluid, transfigured with the spread of Buddhism to other Asian countries and now all over the world. In these pages, we will identify commonalities in the experiences of Buddhist women, keeping in mind that the histories and cultural developments of the Buddhist traditions make each one unique. In the coming years, as scholars uncover more materials about these traditions and women's roles within them, we will certainly need to revise our thinking beyond this introductory survey. For now, we will trace Buddhist women's history in its early stages in India, and then expand to later periods of historical development in selected Asian and non-Asian contexts. This history will include stories of Buddhist women who live celibate lives as nuns, women who live family lives as wives and mothers, and women practitioners who do not fit neatly into either of these categories. The stories of Buddhist renunciant women will include those who observe the more than three hundred precepts of a fully ordained nun (Sanskrit: *bhikṣuṇī*; Pāli: *bhikkhunī*), as well as nuns who observe various enumerations of five, eight, nine, or ten Buddhist precepts. We will discuss whether and how these distinctions affect women's spiritual practice, education, social acceptance, and the economic support they receive from the lay community. We will mark the significant characters and turning points in Buddhist women's history, including recent developments that parallel the globalization of Buddhism.

The Buddha taught a path to the goal of awakening, attained by abandoning all mental defilements or destructive emotions. Awakening is therefore a quality of consciousness or awareness, and consciousness has no sexual markers or gender. In the course of re-becoming, over many lifetimes, sentient beings take different forms and different sexes. Lacking any intrinsic essence, beings also lack any intrinsic gender. The celibate ideal, which is perceived to be the ideal lifestyle for abandoning desire, is also ultimately devoid of any intrinsic gender identity. The celibate, renunciant state as well as the liberated state can therefore be conceived as beyond gender distinctions. Yet gender distinctions remain on the conventional level, retained in rituals, personal perceptions, everyday interactions, and practical matters in daily life. In Buddhist monasteries, monks and nuns are typically segregated. Celibate monastics are not free from gender identities or from gender discrimination.

It is common to hear apologists say that there is no gender discrimination in Buddhism and that awakening is beyond the distinctions of male and female. Claims of gender equality are contradicted, however, by numerous examples of inequality in the perceptions and treatment of women. Pollution taboos that prohibit women from entering religious sites while menstruating are still found in some Buddhist societies even today, for example, in Bhutan, Burma, Ladakh, and Thailand.[13]

Gender distinctions may also be conceived in a positive light. For example, today the choice to identify with a specific gender or elsewhere on the gender spectrum—non-binary, non-gender conforming, or no gender at all—is considered by many to be a human right. Although the notion of erasing or going beyond gender identity may be held forth as a means of eliminating gender discrimination, erasing gender distinctions altogether is a contested ideal, especially for those who have struggled with gender identity and finally embraced a preferred gender.

In the modern era, with greater sexual freedom, some also challenge the traditional assumption that celibacy (*brahmacarya*, "the pure life") is the ideal lifestyle for achieving liberation.

When Buddha Śākyamuni presented his teachings on liberation from suffering, he taught a path of mental purification and transformation of consciousness that was equally accessible to women and men, both lay and monastics. Yet throughout much of Buddhist history, the experiences of women have most often been confined to prescribed familial and monastic institutions, and women's own ideas, preferences, and contributions have often been dismissed, repressed, or overlooked. Today, many Buddhist scholars are drawing attention to the scriptures and legends that helped to shape attitudes toward women and are rethinking the complex interactions of religion, culture, and society that affect Buddhist women's lives and choices. Especially in recent decades, with a growth of interest in Buddhist and feminist ideas internationally, new questions are being raised about the status of women in Buddhist societies and also about the assumptions that underlie contemporary narratives about them. These studies illuminate the diverse spiritual paths that women have taken in this major wisdom tradition.

The Buddha taught that all beings have the potential to purify their minds and become free from mental defilements, suffering, and rebirth. As the various Buddhist traditions developed, a woman could aspire to the highest goal envisioned by her tradition, whether to become an *arhat* (a liberated being), a *bodhisattva* (a being on the path to perfect awakening), or even a fully awakened Buddha. Even if the path was described as arduous, especially in a female body, a woman could achieve the highest goal her tradition had to offer, in theory at least. In the tradition known today as Theravāda ("path of the elders"), prevalent in South and Southeast Asia, the goal is to become an *arhat*, one who is liberated from cyclic existence. In the tradition known as Mahāyāna ("great vehicle"), prevalent in North and East Asia, the goal is to advance on the *bodhisattva* path to become a fully awakened *buddha*. Many statements denying that a woman can become a *buddha* appear in both Theravāda and Mahāyāna texts, but the existence of numerous female *arhats* during the time of the Buddha is ample evidence that women were able to achieve that specific goal. In the Mahāyāna tradition, it is believed that all sentient beings not only are capable of becoming *buddhas* but also will eventually become *buddhas*. It follows that women have the potential to become fully awakened *buddhas*. However, according to the Sūtrayāna branch of the Mahāyāna tradition, although it is possible for a woman to practice on the *bodhisattva* path and stages in a female body and eventually become a *buddha*, in her final lifetime she must appear in a male body, like Buddha Śākyamuni. In the Vajrayāna branch of the Mahāyāna tradition, which teaches practices of visualizing oneself in the form of a fully awakened being, it is said that a woman can become a *buddha* in female form. The classic example is Tārā, an exceptional woman who generated a strong determination to achieve full awakening in female form for the benefit of sentient beings, and successfully did so.[14]

Only the Mahīśāsaka, an early Buddhist school of thought, in which phenomena are regarded as existing only in the present moment, taught that a woman cannot become a fully awakened *buddha*, but this school died out in India long ago.[15]

In actuality, many women in Buddhist cultures do not aspire for these lofty attainments. Instead, they tend to pursue devotional practices quietly and to support the spiritual endeavors of men, who dominate the social and religious hierarchies. Nevertheless, throughout history there have been extraordinary women practitioners who challenged social norms and emerged from the silence, giving testimony to their courage and exemplifying Buddhism's liberative promise. Through the power of these stories, beginning with accounts of the first female *arhats* in ancient India, Buddhist women have glimpsed their own potential and gained inspiration to persevere on the path to awakening. In contemporary Buddhist feminist circles, these accounts, both in history and legend, are being highlighted as models for women's realization (direct insight into the Buddha's teachings) and spiritual liberation.

Buddhist texts and communities convey divergent representations of women. The presentation of women as the seducers and corrupters of men is epitomized in the story of the Buddha's temptation by the voluptuous "daughters of Māra" the night before his enlightenment. (See figure I.1.)

Some of the less favorable portrayals and attitudes toward women may be traced to the pervasive patriarchal bias that characterized ancient Indian society during the early centuries of Buddhism's development,

Figure I.1. Painting of the future Buddha tempted by the seductive power of women while meditating under the *bodhi* tree, by Tiffani Gyatso, at Centro de Estudos Budistas Bodisatva, Caminho do Meio, Viamão, Brazil. Credit: Photo by Karma Lekshe Tsomo.

but these attitudes may also be traced to the Buddha's alleged reluctance to admit women to the *saṅgha*, the eight weighty rules that he reportedly imposed upon Mahāprajāpatī, and predictions of resultant decline. The eight rules, which legislate monks' authority over nuns, may have contributed to persistent gender bias in Buddhist religious structures that have given priority to monks and ensured the continuity of the *bhikkhu saṅgha* (community of monks) but not the *bhikkhunī saṅgha* (community of nuns) in Theravāda Buddhism. Even if women in Buddhist societies are aware that female *arhats* existed in Buddhist history, they may easily become discouraged by the meager support contemporary nuns receive toward their requisites: meals, robes, medicines, and dwellings. They may also become discouraged by the lack of validation and encouragement for women, especially those who opt out of the culturally preferred roles for women as wives and mothers.

Gender discrimination in Buddhism is not a phenomenon that applies only to some bygone era. Even today, Buddhist women in many countries, including Western countries, may encounter ingrained prejudices and assumptions about women's nature and capabilities, perpetuated by women and men alike. These prejudices and assumptions become clear if, for example, a woman decides to remain single, to not give birth to children, or to become a nun. Learning more about the variety of roles women have played in Buddhist traditions illuminates the ways in which women in diverse cultures have navigated the expectations of society, by either accepting, ignoring, or transforming them.

Revolutionizing the Future

In a global community that is strongly influenced by democratic ideals of justice and equality, gender discrimination is generally no longer seen as justifiable and is associated with many social problems, including domestic violence, sex trafficking, and the neglect of girls' health and education. In the eyes of much of the world, archaic religious structures that put women at a disadvantage—materially, psychology, socially, and spiritually—run counter to a new global ethic of gender equity and seem sadly out of step with the times. Assumptions about women's supposed karmic inferiority and the reality of their often invisible roles in Buddhist institutions—patterns that have been taken for granted for centuries—are now coming under scrutiny both in Buddhist societies and internationally. Discriminatory attitudes and patriarchal structures not only appear contradictory to the liberating teachings of the Buddha but also may cause people to question the value of pursuing Buddhist practice in today's world, especially beyond Asia.

A dramatic increase in interest in the topic of women in Buddhism has generated a wave of new scholarship. Some studies focus on women in specific cultures or at different stages in Buddhist historical development, while others are literary analyses of the conflicting portrayals of women, as a category, that are found in Buddhist texts. As yet, however, there has been no updated introduction to women in Buddhism that offers an adequate treatment of the topic overall.

Tracing the path of Buddhism's historical and cultural development, this book begins with a discussion of Buddhist women in the early

Indian context—the Buddha's mother, stepmother, wife, and earliest female disciples. It then moves to the lives, challenges, and achievements of women in other cultural contexts and periods of Buddhist history, up to the present day. In recounting the struggles and attainments of a range of realized and ordinary women, we will explore several salient themes, including the ways in which Buddhist teachings have been spiritually liberating for women, and also the ways in which certain teachings have been used to reinforce women's subordination within patriarchal social structures and Buddhist institutions. Using selected examples from a variety of Buddhist cultures, we will investigate women's unique roles within specific Buddhist societies and trace common threads among them. A transformation of Buddhist attitudes is currently taking place to envisage what social, religious, psychological, and ideological changes are needed to revolutionize Buddhist societies and institutions, and create a truly egalitarian society.

Buddhist teachings and traditions are increasingly transnational, and many antiquated attitudes are up for review. One major issue is the seeming contradiction between the internally egalitarian organizational structures modeled by the early *bhikkhu* and *bhikkhunī saṅghas* and the hierarchical structures of many Buddhist institutions today. Buddhist texts and teachings provide solutions to many forms of suffering, but they do not explicitly address the structural inequalities that underlie many forms of suffering and injustice. The ultimate goal of Buddhist practice—the achievement of liberation—is said to be beyond gender, but on a practical level gender matters very much. Without conducive circumstances for Buddhist learning and practice, the goal of liberation is merely a dream for many women. Liberation as a theoretical ideal needs to be aligned with conditions on the ground. In reality, women disproportionately experience the misfortunes of everyday life. Poor, illiterate, uneducated, and overworked, millions of women find little leisure time for Buddhist practice.

It is heartening that a revolutionary new vision of Buddhism includes a sincere concern for women and the benefits that awakened women can offer society. This new vision has spurred a vibrant transnational movement to work for Buddhist women, to allow access to all kinds of education and all levels of monastic ordination. Buddhist scholars, practitioners, and scholar/practitioners are engaged in efforts to understand the roots of gender inequities and to analyze critically the texts and unexamined assumptions that have perpetuated myths of women's inferiority. With new research methodologies and a broader knowledge base, scholars aspire to apply these tools to a thorough reinterpretation of texts and traditions, and to uncover more information about the contributions that women have made to Buddhist thought and practice. Transcending cultural differences, new modes of communication facilitate creative and mutually beneficial international exchanges. A Buddhist feminist movement that began in the 1980s stretches across cultural boundaries to investigate the gender-specific presuppositions and limitations that not only persist in Buddhist cultures but also confine many human minds. The Buddhist feminist imagination is both a natural historical development, spurred by the global women's movement, and an intensely personal journey for many Buddhist women, nurturing self-awareness and establishing solidarity with other women and male allies. Awakening, both as an attainment beyond gender, available to all, and as an awareness born of women's experience, holds the promise of liberating and revolutionizing humanity.

1

Women in Early Indian Buddhism

According to Buddhist tradition, throughout his life, the Buddha was surrounded by exemplary women. The legends about his life begin with his mother, Mahāmāyā Gautama, portrayed as an exemplar of purity. She conceived the young prince in a dream of a white elephant who carried a white lotus in his trunk and entered her right side. The Buddha's miraculous birth took place when Queen Mahāmāyā, traveling to her natal home, stopped in a beautiful grove of blossoming fruit trees at Lumbini. As the queen reached up for a tree branch for support, the infant emerged fully formed from her right side, and then stood and took seven steps. The *devas* (gods) rejoiced, and the child was given the name Siddhārtha Gautama. His father, King Śuddhodana of the Śākya clan, is cast as a ruler with high hopes that his son would grow up to succeed him. Siddhārtha is described as growing up in his father's capital, Kapilavastu. Queen Mahāmāyā is portrayed as an ideal woman for her role in giving birth to a special, male child, which perfectly matched the expectation for women in the social and cultural milieu of ancient India. Although she passed away when the young prince was barely a week old, she is framed in this portrait as the perfect woman in perpetuity, and images of her giving birth to the future Buddha are ubiquitous throughout Asia (see figure 1.1). Indeed, without Mahāmāyā, the young prince would never have been born and hence there would have been no Buddha Śākyamuni, and no teachings, disciples, or Buddhist traditions.

After Queen Mahāmāyā died, her sister, Mahāprajāpatī Gautamī (Pāli: Mahāpajāpatī), who was also married to King Śuddhodana, became Siddhārtha's loving foster mother. She displayed archetypal selfless maternal devotion, nurturing the young prince as if he were her own offspring. Later, after the prince became a fully awakened Buddha, she demonstrated her intelligence, commitment, and courage by leading some five hundred women of the royal Śākya clan to petition him to allow women to enter the *saṅgha* ("community," monastic order).

Figure 1.1. Image of Mahāmāyā, mother of the future Buddha, who died a week after he was born, at Dharmakirti Vihar, Kathmandu, Nepal. Credit: Photo by Karma Lekshe Tsomo.

When Siddhārtha grew to adulthood, he married the beautiful princess Yaśodharā, who exemplified the role of the perfect wife, bearing his son and never forsaking him, not even after he abandoned both her and their child. The fourth key female figure is a young woman named Sujātā, identified as Rādhā in some texts. At the nadir of Siddhārtha's spiritual search, when he was totally emaciated by hunger and thirst, Sujātā appeared and demonstrated selfless compassion by providing food to nurture his awakening. Gradually, as women became part of the early monastic community, thousands received the Buddha's teachings and through diligent practice became *arhats*.

The Buddha attracted a wide range of followers during his lifetime, some of whom wished to follow his example and renounce the householder life. After the Buddha had achieved perfect awakening, he went to the Deer Park in Sarnath near Varanasi on the Ganga River, where five of his ascetic companions were staying. These five young *śrāmaṇas* (renunciants) had followed him as he pursued the path of austerity and abandoned him after he lost faith in extreme asceticism and broke his fast by accepting milk rice from a maiden named Sujātā near Bodhgaya. When these five ascetics met up with the Buddha again in the Deer Park after his awakening (*bodhi)* while sitting under a peepul (*ficus religiosa* or *bodhi*) tree, they at first shunned him but then recognized that he had become realized and asked what goal he had achieved. The Buddha told them that he had attained the state of deathlessness, or liberation (Sanskrit: *nirvāṇa*; Pāli: *nibbāna*). They bowed at his feet and resolved to similarly reach the goal of liberation. As he uttered the phrase "Come here," these five disciples became the first Buddhist monks and thus began the *bhikṣu saṅgha*, the community of ordained monks. As the number of *bhikṣus* grew and mistakes were made, the Buddha began to set forth rules of behavior, which gradually grew into a body of monastic precepts that were later recorded in the *vinaya* texts. These became the guidelines for the Buddhist monastic order (*saṅgha*), reportedly the world's oldest continuous organization.

When the Buddha began teaching soon after his awakening, countless women followed him and became respected communicators of Buddhist knowledge. However, the accomplishments of women were greatly enhanced when Mahāprajāpatī initiated the *bhikṣuṇī saṅgha*, the community of fully ordained Buddhist nuns, the world's oldest documented women's organization. She achieved liberation and provided skilled leadership for countless accomplished women for the rest of her very long life.

Buddhist studies scholar Kathryn R. Blackstone has compiled a list of the renowned female *arhats* credited with composing the verses of liberation included in the *Therīgāthā* (Verses of the Elder Nuns), expressing the insights and attainments of seventy senior nuns who lived at the time of the Buddha.[1] These verses, preserved in Pāli, document both the obstacles and the achievements of these pioneering women who transcended cultural stereotypes to become nuns and effect their own freedom. Indologist Ria Kloppenborg has identified stereotypes of women that appear in the verses and seem to have been common characterizations at the time: women as stupid, as devoted daughters, as obsessed with their bodies and adornments, as temptresses, as obsessed with childbearing, and as old ugly hags.[2] Images of the liberated women who transcended these stereotypes have served as inspiration for innumerable practitioners across cultures.

To understand the full significance of women's successful practice and contributions in Buddhism, we must consider the context in India, the land where the Buddha first taught and where his teachings and community first took root. During the sixth to fifth centuries BCE, India was primarily agricultural, but society was becoming increasingly urbanized. Small kingdoms and principalities were developing across northern India, and trade was generating prosperity for the entrepreneurial class. The prevailing society was decidedly patriarchal, and women's activities were often highly restricted.[3] Negative stereotypes of women were commonplace in South Asian societies at the time. After marriage, women were often treated with contempt until they gave birth to a son; then they were treated with greater respect.[4] If the boy died, the mother might lose her privileged status and be castigated or rejected. At the same time, countless female deities were worshiped and revered. The spiritual creative power (*śakti*) of the universe was understood to be female and embodied in goddesses. Although women had *śakti*, the emphasis was on the need to control women so they did not conceive a child out of wedlock. The dichotomy between the divine feminine and ordinary embodied women creates a profound ambivalence that is evident even today in Hindu society.

Buddhist Women at the Beginning

According to the *Therī-apadāna*, a compilation of biographies of eminent early Buddhist nuns, Buddha Śākyamuni, like countless *buddhas* before him, established a fourfold community (*cāturdisa-saṅgha*) consisting of monks (Pāli: *bhikkhu*; Sanskrit: *bhikṣu*), nuns (Pāli: *bhikkhunī*; Sanskrit: *bhikṣuṇī*), laymen (*upāsaka*), and laywomen (*upāsikā*).[5] It follows that each of these *buddhas* instituted full monastic ordination for women. According to the oldest texts, the ideal Buddhist society is composed of these four groups. Together, they create a stable foundation for the social order, with each of the four sectors serving as a pillar to maintain an ideal, balanced, harmonious society. Buddha Śākyamuni considered nuns to be an essential element in this configuration. In a significant statement in the Pāli version of the *Mahāparinibbāṇa Sutta*, the Buddha says, "I will not pass away until I have nun disciples who are wise, well trained, self-confident, and learned."[6] Like the Buddha's other disciples, the nuns were charged to act as examples of discipline, ethics, and learning, to transmit the teachings, and to inspire others on the path. Not only was the task of embodying and sharing the teachings of the Buddha entrusted to the fourfold *saṅgha*, but also the flourishing and even the continued existence of the teachings in the world depended on it.

The Buddha taught a path to liberation—freedom from the delusions of the mind, from suffering, and from rebirth in cyclic existence—that was accessible to all. He reportedly gave teachings publicly to people of all ages, genders, and social backgrounds, without discrimination. His teachings (Pāli: Dhamma; Sanskrit: Dharma) explaining the path or process for achieving liberation were considered revolutionary in rejecting caste hierarchy and priestly authority. As we have seen, he also admitted women to the *saṅgha*, albeit on an unequal footing according to the texts preserved and transmitted by Buddhist monks. These texts describe women's travails and the joys of liberation, some in the words of liberated nuns themselves. Their stories are found in the *vinaya*, the monastic codes, and in other texts that were eventually transmitted to China, Korea, Tibet, and many other countries. The transmission of these stories about women who achieved liberation were part of a process of appropriation, adaptation, and reconfiguration of Indian Buddhist philosophy, practice, and institutional structures that flourished for centuries.

A number of texts recount the achievements of illustrious women at the time of the Buddha.[7] Several centuries intervened between the period when these women lived and the time that their stories were committed to writing, but the monk narrators had prodigious memories and as youth had been trained to memorize oral texts. In addition to narratives about the Buddha's stepmother and wife, the Buddhist texts abound with stories about other accomplished women of this early generation. Rūpanandā, the Buddha's half-sister, was acknowledged as being foremost in meditation; Soṇā was most "strenuous in effort"; Sakulā was most highly attained in divine insight; Bhaddā Kuṇḍalakesā was swiftest in attaining higher insight; Bhaddā Kapilānī was foremost in remembering her past lives; Bhaddā Kaccānā was most skilled in remembering innumerable eons; Sigālamātā was foremost in faith; and Kisāgotamī was renowned for her asceticism and for wearing garments woven of rough fibers.[8] Paṭācārā and Sukkhā were acknowledged as great teachers. Laywomen such as Visākhā, Mallikā, and Ambapalī were renowned for their virtue and generosity. These stories served to teach Buddhist principles and values, and to inspire women on the path. For example, the *Therī-apadāna* (Biographies of elder nuns) describes the lives of numerous eminent women at the time of the Buddha, including the story of Khemā, Uppalavaṇṇā, Paṭācārā, Bhaddā Kuṇḍalakesā, Kisāgotamī, Dhammadinnā, and Visākhā. These seven women in a previous lifetime had been the daughters of a king named Kikī who did not allow them to become nuns. After cultivating virtue for thousands of lifetimes, they were reborn at the time of Buddha Śākyamuni and were among his leading disciples.[9] Stories about Uppalavaṇṇā can be found in the *Manorathapūrani*, the *Therīgāthā*, and a commentary on the *Dhammapada*, texts that were written down in Pāli in Sri Lanka sometime between the third and sixth centuries CE but apparently were based on orally transmitted stories dating back to the time of Buddha Śākyamuni.[10]

Certain Buddhist texts clearly state that women have the potential to achieve liberation and become free from mental defilements, suffering, and further rebirth.[11] Many also include the names of exemplary nuns who did so. By comparison, however, the number of monks who reportedly achieved liberation is far greater. For example, in the Dīgha Nikāya in the Pāli canon, the complete collection of Theravāda scriptures, the *Mahāpadāna Sutta* states that there were 6,800,000 *arhat* monks in one assembly of a previous *buddha* named Vipassī, but no *arhat* nuns are mentioned.[12] This demonstrates that the gender imbalance in Buddhism is a very old problem indeed. Monks are more prominently represented in the texts and also in the various Buddhist cultures and communities that evolved over time.

Indian Buddhist texts and commentaries describe a Buddha as being unique in having the thirty-two major physical characteristics (*lakṣaṇa*) of a great person (*mahāpuruṣa*) that attest to the extraordinary spiritual attainments of a fully awakened being.[13] The salient point here is that the body of a Buddha is explicitly described as being male, by virtue of possessing a sheathed penis "like a royal stallion."[14] It therefore follows that the ultimate state attainable by a human being is envisioned in a male body. Buddhist scholar José Cabezón points out two competing discourses regarding the Buddha's sexuality. Prior to his renunciation, he is portrayed as a virile, sexual being: "His masculinity and heterosexual prowess are evidenced by the fact that he showed interest in women, married, and begat a son."[15] After his awakening, however, when his sexual virility is under control, "the Buddha's genitals are depicted as retracted into his abdomen or pelvis, 'enclosed in a sheath like those of a fine elephant or stallion.'"[16]

Not everyone aspires to become a fully awakened Buddha, however; many aspire to become an *arhat*, a being who is liberated from cyclic existence. The Buddha himself affirmed that the liberation of an *arhat* is possible for women and men alike. The story of highly accomplished women in Buddhism is therefore a saga of trial and triumph, prominence and erasure, testimony and silence. Fortunately, the voices of some of these women have been preserved, and remarkable women continue to express their realizations even today.

Representations of Women in Early Buddhist Texts

The Buddhist canon is quite unique in including the voices of women, especially the voices of women who renounced household and family in favor of the renunciant life. Buddhist scholar Alice Collett points out that a significant number of Buddhist texts were composed by or about women, including the *Therīgāthā*, the *Apadānas* (biographies of the Buddha's disciples, including forty women), the *Avadānaśataka* (stories of realization, including a number of women), and the Aṅguttara Nikāya (containing stories of eminent nuns and laywomen).[17] She acknowledges the valuable work of pioneering feminist scholars of Buddhism in the West, notably Caroline Rhys Davids (1857–1942), Mabel Bode (1864–1922), and I. B. Horner (1896–1981), in bringing to light the spiritual accomplishments of women in these texts. At the same time, she argues that Western studies of women in Buddhist literature have emphasized certain texts over others (namely, the *Therīgāthā* and the Pāli *vinaya*),[18] and suggests that a detailed study of all available literature is needed in order to gain a fuller understanding of women in ancient Indian Buddhism.

In India at the time of the Buddha, women were associated with fecundity and reproduction, which stand in direct contrast to the Buddhist goals of renunciation and liberation. We find scriptural evidence of the preconceptions that celibacy and independence are not natural states for women, that motherhood is a woman's natural inclination, and that women are happy under men's protection and dominance. We find no parallel preconceptions about men's inherent inclination to reproduce or to seek happiness under women's protection. Women are portrayed as sexually avaricious and therefore threatening to the virtue of men, especially male renunciants. However, contradicting the common stereotypes of women as temptresses and seducers of men, in the Buddhist canon and commentaries we also find stories portraying women as utterly disinterested in sexual exploits and fully confident in rebuffing the advances of men. The most vivid story tells of the beautiful nun Subhā Therī who, when accosted by an admirer, plucks out her eye and presents it to her erstwhile seducer.[19] Her eye is later restored in the presence of the Buddha, suggesting the power of the spiritual attainments of both the Buddha and Subhā Therī. Indeed, there are many stories that portray the piety, virtue, and spiritual attainments of women, contradicting popular preconceptions and expectations of women in that day.[20]

It is important to acknowledge the historical and cultural context within which texts were composed and to be aware of a tendency to read back into times past our own modern egalitarian biases. Even so, from a gender studies perspective, admittedly a vantage point that is newly developed even within Western scholarship, historical and cultural context cannot be used to erase or diminish questions of gender. Female exemplars of realization appear in Buddhist accounts but may be portrayed as prepubescent eight-year-olds, sparing them the pollution of menstruation. Physical beauty is the result of virtuous actions created in the past, but it can be dangerous for women, who are seen as the snares of men, whereas good looks pose no such disadvantage for men.[21] In the *Lotus Sūtra*, an influential Mahāyāna text that affirms women's potential for awakening, and the *Mahāratnakūṭa*, women are portrayed transforming themselves into men to attest to their awakened state, reinforcing the assumption of male superiority.[22] Even when women implicitly challenge male spiritual privilege and powerfully transform their gender identities, they are shown manifesting their spiritual attainments in male form.[23] For example, in the *Candrottādārikāparipṛcchā*, a Mahāyāna text from the third or fourth century CE, Candrottā, the stunningly beautiful and precocious daughter of the famed Buddhist scholar-practitioner Vimalakīrti, miraculously transforms her female body into a male body in order to demonstrate the nondual nature of enlightenment. These gender-shifting feats demonstrate that all forms are ultimately empty and therefore beyond gender. However, stories illustrating the nondual nature of awakening do not explain or justify contradictions between theoretical equality and the predilection to portray awakening as requiring a male body that runs through Buddhist texts, rituals, and societies.

Gender identities appear to have been understood as fluid and mutable at the time of the Buddha. In the course of innumerable lifetimes, sentient beings take rebirth in countless different life forms and different genders.[24] Further, gender transformation might be possible even in one lifetime; shifting between male and female gender identities seems to have been a commonly accepted concept.[25] For example, according to a well-known legend, when Buddha Śākyamuni descended to earth from the Heaven of the Thirty-Three Gods (Trāyastriṃśa) after giving teachings to his mother Queen Mahāmāyā residing there, a nun named Utpala (Pāli: Uppalavaṇṇā; Sanskrit: Utpalavarṇā) transformed herself into a (male) *cakravartin* ruler in order to get the first glimpse of him.[26] The exceptionally beautiful daughter of a wealthy merchant, Utpala opted out of marriage, became a nun, swiftly achieved the state of an *arhat*, and was recognized by the Buddha as foremost among the nuns in the attainment of supernormal powers (Pāli: *iddhi*; Sanskrit: *siddhi*). As religion scholar Serinity Young puts it, according to the Buddhist texts, the achievement of supernormal powers not only allows one insight into the mutability of gender but also gives one the power to "enact this mutability" by transforming one's sexual characteristics.[27]

Although sexual identities in Buddhist scriptures were depicted as mutable, changes from lifetime to lifetime were not so frequent, due to habitual affinities with one gender or another. Rebirth in a female body was assumed to involve much greater suffering than rebirth in a male body and was therefore regarded as less desirable.[28] It was but a small step from there to regarding a female rebirth as the result of unwholesome actions (*karma*) in the past and a male rebirth as the result of wholesome actions. Consequently, it is a common belief in Buddhist societies that a female rebirth is the result of bad *karma*. A strong preference for male offspring may not be surprising in patriarchal Indian society, but it is surprising to see a strong preference for male identity against the background of Buddhism's relatively egalitarian principles.

Buddhist texts also contain stories about women who were capable of high spiritual and intellectual mastery; numerous exceptional female practitioners were lauded by the Buddha. Dhammadinnā, for example, was a nun who became an *arhat* and gained renown as the foremost *bhikṣuṇī* in teaching Dharma.[29] Dhammadinnā had been married to a merchant named Visākha who became a monk, so she decided to become a nun. In the story, Visākha prostrates to Dhammadinnā and asks her a number of both simple and thorny questions, to which she responds with distinction. When she then reiterates the conversation to the Buddha, he confirms her understanding and assures her that he would have replied in the same manner. As an outstanding teacher, Dhammadinnā serves as an inspiration and positive role model for other women, as do the many other women of awakening.

Mahāprajāpatī's Going Forth

A major historical juncture for women in Buddhism was when Mahāprajāpatī Gautamī, the Buddha's foster mother and aunt, asked the Buddha's permission to renounce the household life in order to follow his teachings and the monastic discipline. It is said that Mahāprajāpatī received her ordination directly from the Buddha when she became the first Buddhist nun (see figure 1.2).[30] As the story goes in the *vinaya* portion of the Pāli canon, five or six years after the Buddha's five companions became the first *bhikkhus*, Mahāpajāpatī expressed a wish to join the newly created order. When the Buddha hesitated, presumably out of

Figure 1.2. Painting of Mahāprajāpatī Gautamī, foster mother of the future Buddha, who became the first Buddhist nun, at Hue Lam Temple, Ho Chi Minh City, Vietnam. Credit: Photo by Karma Lekshe Tsomo.

concern for the safety of the aspiring female renunciants, Mahāpajāpatī led hundreds of noblewomen on foot across northern India in what was mostly likely the first women's liberation movement in history. After repeated urging by Ānanda, his male cousin and attendant, the Buddha agreed to the admission of women, and the *bhikkhunī saṅgha* began. The *saṅgha* ("assembly" or monastic order) that the Buddha established thus consisted of both male and female ordained renunciants who had reached the age of twenty and had made a commitment to observe specific precepts, or rules of training. The categories of novice monks (Pāli: *sāmaṇera*; Sanskrit: *śrāmaṇera*) and novice nuns (Pāli: *sāmaṇerī*; Sanskrit: *śrāmaṇerika*) were established as a period for training in the precepts in preparation for the rite of higher ordination (*upasampadā*). A woman is required to spend two years as a probationer (Pāli: *sikkhamāṇā*; Sanskrit: *śikṣamāṇā*) before receiving full ordination as a *bhikkhunī* (Sanskrit: *bhikṣuṇī*).

As noted earlier, when Mahāpajāpatī requested to live the homeless life, the Buddha reportedly agreed on the condition that she observe the eight weighty rules. According to the version of this event included in the *Madhyama-āgama*, a collection of medium-length discourses of the Buddha in the Pāli canon, she made her first request to him during the rainy season retreat at Kapilavastu, the Buddha's hometown, where she and the other Śākya women mentioned in this text lived:

> At that time Mahāpajāpatī Gotamī approached the Buddha, paid homage with her head at the Buddha's feet and, standing back to one side, said: "Blessed One, can women attain the fourth fruit of recluse-ship? For that reason, [can] women in this right teaching and discipline leave the household out of faith, becoming homeless to train in the path?"
>
> The Blessed One replied: "Wait, wait, Gotamī, do not have this thought, that in this right teaching and discipline women leave the household out of faith, becoming homeless to train in the path. Gotamī, you shave off your hair like this, put on ochre robes and for your whole life practice the pure holy life."
>
> Then, being restrained by the Buddha, Mahāpajāpatī Gotamī paid homage with her head at the Buddha's feet, circumambulated him thrice and left.[31]

Mahāpajāpatī is depicted as approaching the Buddha with this request on three separate occasions, once more in Kapilavastu, and again in another town, receiving the same answer each time. Before the third occasion recounted in the *Madhyama-āgama*, Mahāpajāpatī is described as following the Buddha "together with some elderly Sakyan women" to the next location where he stopped.[32] After the Buddha declined her request the third time, Ānanda intervened on her behalf:

> The venerable Ānanda saw Mahāpajāpatī Gotamī standing outside the entrance, her bare feet soiled and her body covered with dust, tired and weeping with grief. Having seen her, he asked: "Gotamī, for what reason are you standing outside the entrance, your bare feet soiled and your body covered with dust, tired and weeping with grief?"
>
> Mahāpajāpatī Gotamī replied: "Venerable Ānanda, in this right teaching and discipline women do not obtain the leaving of the household out of faith, becoming homeless to train in the path."
>
> The venerable Ānanda said: "Gotamī, you just wait here, I will approach the Buddha and speak to him about this matter.
>
> "Blessed One, can women attain the four fruits of recluse-ship? For that reason, [can] women in this right teaching and discipline leave the household out of faith, becoming homeless to train in the path?"
>
> The Blessed One replied: "Wait, wait, Ānanda, do not have this thought, that in this right teaching and discipline women leave the household out of faith, becoming homeless to train in the path. Ānanda, if in this right teaching and discipline women obtain the leaving of the household out of faith, becoming homeless to train in the path, then this holy life will consequently not last long."[33]

Ānanda then is described as reminding the Buddha of the kindness of Mahāpajāpatī, who suckled and raised him after his birth mother passed away, and recounted her accomplishments in faith, ethical development, and learning. The Buddha then agreed that Mahāpajāpatī could enter the homeless life if she agreed to observe the eight weighty rules for life. In the *Madhyama-āgama* recension of the story, these weighty rules require a woman seeking *bhikkhunī* ordination to receive ordination from monks as well as nuns, and once she is ordained to request instruction from monks every half month, spend the rainy season in a place where there are monks, report to both the communities of monks and nuns at the end of the rainy season retreat, refrain from posing unwanted questions to monks, refrain from exposing monks' offenses, perform penance for infractions before both assemblies, and pay homage even to junior monks.[34]

There are several notable contradictions in both the content and chronology of the eight rules that assign a subordinate status to nuns and elevated authority to monks. First, there are contradictions in the method of ordination. During the early days of the Buddha's dispensation, monks were ordained with a simple declaration: "Come, *bhikṣu*." Gradually, this was replaced by the recitation of the declaration of taking refuge in the Awakened One, his teachings, and the renunciant community: "I go for refuge to the Buddha; I go for refuge to the Dharma; I go for refuge to the Saṅgha."[35] The recitation of the refuge formula was later replaced by a somewhat more elaborate ordination procedure. Several texts show nuns being ordained with a simple declaration by the Buddha, "Come, *bhikṣuṇī*." If the Buddha imposed the eight weighty rules on Mahāprajāpatī, why did he revert to a simple declaration for other nuns later on? Second, there are inconsistencies among various recensions of this story and the nature of the eight rules. Third, there are logical incongruities in all recensions related to chronology. How could the Buddha have required Mahāprajāpatī to agree to receive ordination from both the *bhikṣu* and the *bhikṣuṇī saṅghas* when the *bhikṣuṇī saṅgha* had not yet been founded? Again, how could he have required her to go before both assemblies to be absolved of transgressions when there was as yet no *bhikṣuṇī saṅgha*?

The story as recounted in these texts raises other questions too. Ānanda is portrayed as convincing the Buddha to admit women to the *saṅgha*. Upon reflection, it appears odd that the Buddha needed to be convinced. The German Theravāda monk-scholar Bhikkhu Anālayo contends that it was not Ānanda's advocacy for the women's request that caused the Buddha to change his mind but rather the women's determination to live the homeless life: "Now, according to a range of sources the Buddha's initial decision to teach the Dharma at all was based on surveying the potential of human beings to reach awakening. Thus, he would have been well aware that women do have such potential, without needing a reminder."[36] In fact, the Buddha readily admitted as much when he declared that women were capable of achieving the four fruits of the path: stream-enterer, once-returner, non-returner, and liberated being (*arhat*).

According to the Aṅguttara Nikāya in the Pāli canon, Ānanda was later castigated by some elder monks and made to confess to a wrongdoing for having advocated the admission of women to the *saṅgha*. Undaunted, he stated unapologetically that it was appropriate to allow women to join the *saṅgha*. Further, it was not Ānanda who established the *bhikkhunī saṅgha* but the Buddha himself. In the face of these controversial passages, Anālayo advances an alternative view, using evidence elsewhere in the texts to argue that, once the Buddha had made a decision, he was not easily dissuaded by others.[37] Based on the evidence, it appears likely that the eight rules were developed later and have been inserted into earlier narratives of Mahāpajāpatī's admission to the order.

The Buddha's concern for nuns living a mendicant life is clear in a number of places in the texts. For example, due to incidents of sexual harassment and rape, the Buddha declared that nuns were no longer required to sleep under trees. Instead, they were required to live together in communities for their own safety and to construct their monasteries in towns rather than in more isolated locations; according to Buddhist studies scholar Gregory Schopen, nuns "found themselves in, quite literally, a very different position from that of monks."[38] One of the *gurudharmas* requires nuns to stay for their rainy season retreat in a place where there are monks, which may be based on a concern for the nuns' safety.

To a contemporary sensibility, it is difficult to justify those rules that place nuns under the authority of the monks, but in ancient times and up to the present day it has not been uncommon for women to relinquish their independence in exchange for security. Regardless of the provenance and chronology of the eight *gurudharmas*, it is likely that over time the disparity in status between nuns and monks reflected in these rules worked to diminish the status of both laywomen and nuns relative to laymen and monks. The presupposition that women are less capable, less inclined to spiritual attainment, and more enmeshed in worldly affairs has led to gender inequalities, in both religious and secular spheres, in all Buddhist societies.

In Western scholarship, a great deal of ink has been devoted to the Buddha's hesitation to admit women to the *saṅgha*. Anālayo notes that in the *Madhyama-āgama*, as well as in *vinaya* texts of two of the Buddhist schools that developed after the Buddha's death—the Mahīśāsaka and (Mūla-)Sarvāstivāda Schools, whose *vinaya* texts are extant in Chinese translations—the Buddha had already agreed to allow women to shave their heads, don robes, and live a renunciant life, but in the home rather than as homeless wanderers, because becoming homeless posed a danger to the women and left them vulnerable to sexual assault. It was presumably for this reason that the Buddha suggested women should shave their heads, wear robes, and practice "the pure holy life" (celibacy) in their homes without seeking full ordination.[39] The Mahīśāsaka School was a precursor to the Dharmaguptaka School of *vinaya* that has been practiced in China, Korea, Taiwan, and Vietnam, up to the present day.

Anālayo points out that in the *vinaya* texts of four other Buddhist schools, including the *Cullavagga* in the Theravāda *vinaya*, a different story is told about how the Śākya women shaved their heads and put on ochre robes.[40] According to this account, Mahāpajāpatī and her five hundred Śākya female companions took the initiative and decided to shave their heads, put on robes, and walk a vast distance with many hardships to find the Buddha and once again request going forth "from home into homelessness."[41] The contrast between the two narratives is significant. If the Buddha had already concluded that the queen and her retinue were indeed capable of leading a renunciant life, and had given them permission to shave their heads, put on ochre robes, and live the renunciant life at home, his hesitation to grant Mahāpajāpatī's request that they be permitted to enter into the homeless life may have been prompted by worries about whether these aristocratic women could cope with the dangers and difficulties of living as homeless wanderers. Rather than expressing doubts as to whether they were capable of liberation, his reluctance may well have been based on a sincere concern to protect nuns from harassment and abuse.[42]

Anālayo constructs a cogent narrative from the diverse texts about the founding of the *bhikkhunī saṅgha* in which Mahāpajāpatī and her followers were advised by the Buddha to shave their heads, don the robes of renunciants, and practice at home rather than adopting the lifestyle of homeless wanderers.[43] Not satisfied by this compromise, they subsequently proved their determination to live the homeless life by shaving their heads, donning the robes, and walking barefooted to find the Buddha to request again that they be permitted to live the renunciant lifestyle; the Buddha then relented and allowed them to join the monastic order, which at that time consisted of wandering mendicants.[44] For two and a half millennia, Buddhist women have continued to prove their determination on the path to liberation, despite countless obstacles.

The Prediction of Decline

In addition to the matter of the eight weighty rules, a number of Buddhist texts record a prediction by the Buddha that the ordination of nuns would decrease the duration of pure Buddhism to five hundred years. As noted above, in the *Madhyama-āgama*, the Buddha is quoted as saying that, if women were permitted to live the homeless life, the teachings would not endure. This utterance indicates a concern that homeless wandering would pose a danger to the nuns' celibacy and safety. Later in the passage, the Buddha says, "Ānanda, if in this right teaching and discipline women had not obtained the leaving of the household out of faith, becoming homeless to train in the path, then this right teaching would have remained for a thousand years."[45] This utterance lends itself to quite a different interpretation than the former: it becomes a prediction that the Dharma will disappear as a result of women's admission to the monastic order. However, since women subsequently did not live a literally homeless life but instead settled in urban areas, the danger to both the nuns and the Buddhist teachings was successfully averted.[46] Now, more than 2,500 years later, the Buddhist teachings are still alive and well, despite women's admission to the *saṅgha*. Comparative philological analysis makes it clear that variations in the texts express different attitudes toward women. It is difficult to assess whether these different attitudes reflect the intentions of those responsible for recounting the teachings or reflect attitudes prevalent in society at the time. Regardless, it is likely that the attitudes toward women expressed in the texts subsequently influenced the ways in which women, their character, and their spiritual capabilities were regarded in societies for generations to come.

In comparing parallel versions of an account of the teachings of the monk named Nandaka in the Pāli canon, Anālayo points out significant differences in gender relations. These include differences in the way nuns are introduced (for example, by mentioning their fame and greatness), the degree of deference indicated in the postures they adopt, whether the Buddha spontaneously teaches the nuns, whether the Buddha replies to a nun's request, the type of response he makes, the degree of thoughtfulness with which he makes them, the degree of respect that nuns show to monks, descriptions of the nuns' insights and attainments, and other markers.[47] Such indicators convey important information about social customs at the time, about what was considered appropriate or inappropriate conduct for monastics, and also about attitudes toward women in general. Moreover, when Anālayo compares parallel versions of the story of Nandaka delivering a discourse to the community of nuns in the Pāli canon, he finds certain discrepancies, both subtle and significant, among the accounts. Some early accounts seem to express a greater respect for nuns and portray them in a more favorable light than others. Taken together, these discrepancies give the impression that attitudes of the monks toward the capabilities and attainments of nuns may have not only changed over time but also differed among redactors and commentators. In other words, whether a text speaks of thirteen outstanding nuns or five hundred fully awakened nuns may reflect the attitudes and opinions of those who recited and thus transmitted the texts orally for several hundred years before they were committed to writing.[48] Internal inconsistencies among the texts, even among different redactions of the Pāli texts, seem to indicate that changes occurred over time that may reflect the preferences of the reciters. In reading the *Nandakovāda Sutta*, Anālayo concludes that less favorable attitudes toward nuns in later texts may have influenced certain Theravāda texts. This conclusion challenges a prevalent assumption that the Theravāda texts are more misogynistic and that the Mahāyāna texts are more women friendly.[49]

There are also inconsistencies in accounts between Mahāprajāpatī's initially joyful acceptance of the weighty rules and her later plea to the Buddha to revoke the rule that establishes the seniority of all *bhikkhus*, no matter how junior, to all *bhikkhunīs*, no matter how senior.[50] Anālayo suggests that the rules were an attempt to keep the nuns under control, given the uncertain future of the Buddhist *saṅgha* after the Buddha's passing, and reflected the patriarchal nature of Indian society in that day.[51]

Women Disseminating the Dharma

The Buddha's teachings traveled beyond India quite early, perhaps even during the Buddha's lifetime, and women played pivotal roles in the transnational dispersion of Buddhism. According to the *Mahāvaṃsa*, the teachings were transmitted to the island of Lanka (now Sri Lanka), off the southeast coast of India, as early as the third century BCE. Just six months after Emperor Aśoka's son Bhikkhu Mahinda traveled to Lanka to teach and ordain the first monks of the Sinhalese *bhikkhu saṅgha*, Aśoka's daughter Bhikkhunī Saṅghamittā traveled there to teach and ordain the first nuns, initiating the Sinhalese *bhikkhuṇī saṅgha*.[52] Legend has it that Mahinda reached the island 236 years after the Buddha passed away. There, he delighted King Paṇḍuvāsadeva and forty thousand followers with the Buddha's teachings. When Princess Anulā, wife of the king's brother, asked Mahinda's permission to join the order, he explained that he was not permitted to perform the ordination of a *bhikkhuṇī* without the participation of the *bhikkhuṇī saṅgha*.[53] Instead, he recommended that the king invite his sister Saṅghamittā to come from India for the ordination.[54]

Saṅghamittā sailed to Lanka in the company of a large retinue and brought with her a sapling of the *bodhi* tree, under which the Buddha achieved awakening, in a golden vase (see figure 1.3). Once she arrived and the tree took root, Princess Anulā received ordination along with a thousand other women.[55] The account is full of wondrous miracles that inspire awe in the minds of the faithful. It follows a storyline similar to that of the Buddha: men are admitted to the order first, and women are allowed to join soon thereafter. Both as the bearer of the venerated *bodhi* tree and as the founder of the *bhikkhuṇī saṅgha* on the island of Lanka, Saṅghamittā was a key figure in the early transmission of the Buddha's teachings. In contemporary Sri Lanka, her courage and contributions are commemorated every year on Saṅghamittā Day on the full moon of December, the only national holiday in the world named in honor of a woman.[56]

The next famous episode in women's dissemination of the teachings began with the voyage of Bhikkhunī Devasārā (Tessara) from Lanka to China in the fifth century CE. The story is recounted in *Lives of Eminent Nuns* by Baochang (Pao-ch'ang), a Chinese scholar monk who lived between the fourth and sixth centuries CE and compiled the biographies of 485 eminent monks and 65 eminent nuns in China.[57] The nuns described were known for their devotion, discipline, meditation practice, and abilities to elicit responses from the *buddhas* and *bodhisattvas*. Throughout Chinese history, Buddhist nuns have made significant contributions to Buddhism. Preserving the lineage (unbroken transmission) of full

Figure 1.3. Saṅghamittā, daughter of Emperor Aśoka, who traveled with a *bodhi* tree sapling to Sri Lanka, where she performed the first ordination of Buddhist nuns in the country. Belanvilla Maha Vihara, Colombo, Sri Lanka. Credit: Photo by Shravasti Dhammika.

ordination for women, and transmitting it to Korea, Taiwan, and Vietnam, is one example. Another example is the exceptional achievements of Buddhist nuns in meditation practice. For instance, historical documents record the name of Zhiyuan Xinggang (1597–1654), a master in the practice of Linji Chan Buddhism, which was subsequently transmitted to Japan (Rinzai Zen) and other countries.[58] Buddhist nuns continue to make significant contributions up to the present day through social activism, as can be seen in the work of Bhikṣuṇī Cheng Yen and Bhikṣuṇī Chao Hwei in Taiwan[59] and others around the world.

Lamps of Liberation

Many early texts tell the story of Mahāprajāpatī's going forth and the establishment of the monastic order for women (*bhikṣuṇī saṅgha*). Many of these accounts include very positive evaluations of the nuns' spiritual cultivation. Buddha Śākyamuni himself established the *bhikṣuṇī saṅgha*, upon Mahāprajāpatī's request, and women have been active participants in the practice and transmission of the Buddha's teachings from the beginning until today. It could even be argued that without the *bhikṣuṇī saṅgha* the Buddha's teachings might have been lost to subsequent generations.

From the outset, the achievements of the *bhikkhuṇīs* were undoubtedly major factors in generating women's interest in the Buddha's teachings. The inspiration that laywomen gained from the nuns' achievements surely motivated their own practice and encouraged them to pass the teachings on to their children. It also motivated laywomen to support the Buddhist teachings and the *saṅgha* through generous almsgiving. The *Therīgāthā*, a collection of seventy-three verses ascribed to seventy female *arhats*, is said to be "the *first* anthology of women's literature in the world."[60] It expresses liberal views by and about women who clearly demonstrated women's potential through their spiritual achievements. The importance of this text is revealed in the report that Ānanda recited these inspiring verses at the First Council, a communal recitation of the Buddha's teachings that was held soon after his passing away. From the variant cadences of the verses it can be assumed that the collection was cherished and continued to develop over a period of several centuries.[61]

Countless nuns and laywomen have distinguished themselves in the study, practice, and dissemination of the Buddha's teachings over many centuries. However, as we have seen, gradually literary references to women's active, public participation in Buddhist societies became less frequent. Whether this decline was linked with the socially sanctioned subordination of women, unequal educational opportunities, or issues of authority within the monastic community, women became virtually invisible in written accounts throughout much of Buddhist history. Unfortunately, even today some Buddhist societies are missing one of the four essential pillars of the ideal Buddhist society: the *bhikṣuṇī saṅgha*. Without *bhikṣuṇīs* to ensure balance and help elevate the status of women, the spiritual potential of all levels of society is diminished. The contemporary movement for full ordination for women aims to restore the balance by nurturing the potential for awakening among all human beings in both the renunciant and lay communities. Ensuring greater equity is one effort among many in the world today whereby Buddhists can help relieve the sufferings of sentient beings.

2

Buddhist Women in South and Southeast Asia

Buddhism has had a major impact on South and Southeast Asian cultures for hundreds of years, but references to women in the Buddhist annals of these regions are few and far between. In spite of women's active participation in Buddhist religious life from the start, until recently their stories have rarely been told. Like women elsewhere in the world, Buddhist women have been, and often still are, excluded from both Buddhist and secular education and from male-dominated religious institutions. They have typically been directed toward the responsibilities associated with marriage and family, defined by and expected to comply with the patriarchal status quo. As practitioners of Theravāda Buddhism, they are dedicated to achieving liberation from the cycle of birth and death, but in actual practice, women's spiritual path to liberation is significantly influenced by gendered social constructs and preconceptions that affect not only the education and self-perceptions of female and male practitioners but also the religious aspirations, confidence, and even the living conditions of nuns and monks. Generally, women's contributions to religious life have been made quietly, even surreptitiously. For example, it has recently come to light in Thailand that an important treatise titled *Thammanuthamma-patipatti* (published 1932–34) that had been attributed to a Thai monk named Luang Pu Mun Bhuridatta (1870–1949) was in fact written by a woman named Khunying Yai Damrongthammasan (1882–1944).[1] Women are taught to embody the virtue of humility to the extent that their contributions have most often been unacknowledged.

Nowadays, Theravāda Buddhist women practitioners are becoming more visible and women's monastic communities are becoming active and respected centers for learning, practice, and achievement.[2] While having more opportunities in the secular sphere, a new generation of women is voicing deep-rooted spiritual aspirations, especially for intensive meditation, religious literacy, and full ordination. Theravāda Buddhist women represent diverse cultures with distinct histories, languages, and cultural traditions. Although there are remarkable similarities in their Buddhist values and cultural narratives, and they may all chant the refuge prayer in Pāli, Theravāda Buddhist women do not speak with one voice, may not share a common language, and do not all concur on every issue, including the issue of full ordination for nuns as *bhikkhunīs*. For example, today more than two thousand nuns in Sri Lanka have chosen to receive *bhikkhunī* ordination, while around two thousand other nuns practice as *dasasilmātās*, observing ten precepts.[3] This chapter traces historical and contemporary unifying developments that connect Southeast Asian Buddhist women regionally, using meditation, education, and ordination as rubrics for understanding their experiences and interactions. The lives of women in Burmese Buddhism are described as an example, because they represent a strong living tradition of learning and practice, and have the largest percentage of nuns of any Theravāda Buddhist country.

Engendering Connections: Women in Theravāda Buddhism

In Myanmar (Burma), Cambodia, Laos, Sri Lanka, and Thailand, an overwhelming majority of the population follows the Theravāda tradition of Buddhist practice. This tradition is based on the Pāli recension of the Buddhist texts in the *tipiṭaka* (Sanskrit: *tipiṭaka*, "three baskets"): *suttas* (Sanskrit: *sūtras*, the discourses of the Buddha), *vinaya* (codes of monastic discipline), and *abhidhamma* (Sanskrit: *abhidharma*, "higher teachings," systematic commentary). In Hong Kong, Malaysia, and Singapore, the Chinese Mahāyāna style of practice predominates, but in recent years there has been increasing interest in the Theravāda approach, especially among the younger, English-educated generation. In Vietnam, the Theravāda tradition is strong in the southwestern part of the country among the Khmer Krom people, while Mahāyāna is dominant in the rest of the country. In Bangladesh, India, Indonesia, Malaysia, and Nepal, the Theravāda form of Buddhism is strong among a small percentage of the total population.[4] As in many pluralistic societies, Buddhists from diverse traditions may intermingle socially, exchange ideas, and participate in each other's rituals and celebrations. Inevitably, Buddhist beliefs and practices both influence and are influenced by the religion of the majority.

Use of the term "Theravāda" (School of the Elders) began relatively late, but its roots can be traced to the Sthaviravāda tradition—one of perhaps eighteen schools that developed during the early centuries of Buddhist history, and emphasized strict observance of the monastic precepts (Pāli: *sīla*; Sanskrit: *śīla*), or rules of ethical conduct. Laymen and laywomen ideally observe five precepts: to refrain from (1) taking life, (2) taking what is not given, (3) telling falsehoods, (4) engaging in sexual misconduct, and (5) taking intoxicants. On special days, such as full moon and new moon days (*uposatha*), they may observe eight precepts: the five precepts (substituting no sexual activity for sexual misconduct), plus (6) not eating solid food after noon; (7) not engaging in singing, dancing, or other entertainments, or wearing cosmetics, perfumes, or jewelry; and (8) not sitting or sleeping on high or luxurious seats or beds. Novice monks (Pāli: *sāmaṇera*; Sanskrit: *śrāmaṇera*) and novice nuns (Pāli: *sāmaṇerī*; Sanskrit: *śrāmaṇerika*) observe these precepts on a daily basis, with the seventh one divided into two precepts, plus one more, not handling silver and gold, in addition to numerous rules of deportment (*sekhiya*). In the Theravāda tradition, fully ordained monks (*bhikkhus*) observe 227 precepts and fully ordained nuns (*bhikkhunīs*) observe 311.

Overall, Theravāda Buddhist accounts have focused primarily on the achievements of men, particularly male monastics. Looking at history through the lens of gender in human society overall, this is not so surprising. The surprising part is that the omission of women in Theravāda accounts conflicts with the egalitarian ideals expressed in the same early Buddhist scriptural accounts. In contrast to the patriarchal ethos of India at the time, early texts record that the Buddha accepted women as renunciants, initiated an order of nuns (the *bhikkhunī saṅgha*), and explicitly affirmed women's equal spiritual potential. He even put guidelines in place to protect nuns from exploitation. Unfortunately, not long after his death, patterns of male domination reemerged, not only in the monastic orders, but also in the surrounding lay communities that supported them.

Over the course of Buddhist history, we find many examples of both ordinary and exceptional female practitioners who supported the preservation and flourishing of the Buddhist teachings. In recent years, however, rather than remaining in the shadows of history, communities of nuns have become reinvigorated, and both laywomen and nuns have begun taking more visible roles in religious life. Today, the changing spiritual aspirations of women are having an increasingly important impact on the direction and social relevance of Theravāda Buddhism.[5]

The histories and cultures of Theravāda Buddhists in South and Southeast Asia are richly diverse, yet the lives and experiences of Buddhist women in these countries are notably similar. For example, in accordance with time-honored Buddhist cultural traditions of generosity and devotion, for many centuries women have honored the Buddha with offerings of flowers and fruits, supported the construction of monasteries (*vihāras*) and meditation centers, and regularly donated alms to monastics. Women participated in the activities of their local temples and, through stories and example, encouraged their children and neighbors to abide by good ethical principles. And yet, until recently, women could not be ordained as *bhikkhunīs* and be part of the *saṅgha* (monastic order), because the Theravāda *bhikkhunī* lineage came to an end centuries ago. For most women in these countries, receiving higher ordination is not a major concern, because institutional status is considered unrelated to their ultimate goal of achieving *nibbāna*. Coincidentally or not, the number of nuns is far fewer than monks in Theravāda countries, and they occupy no official position in the religious hierarchy. Many women aspire to take rebirth as males in future lives, so they may become monks.

Most women in Theravāda traditions agree on the ultimate goal of *nibbāna* (Sanskrit: *nirvāṇa*), but they do not necessarily agree on every issue affecting women. As a reference point for understanding Buddhist women's diverse religious, cultural, and social contexts, it is useful to identify certain unifying features and trends that connect women regionally and transnationally, most notably meditation, education, and ordination.

Revival of lay meditation practice is a unifying trend that has swept Buddhist countries throughout the region. Although there has been a renaissance of meditation practice among laypeople in Theravāda Buddhist countries in the twentieth century, lay meditation practice is not new. Examples of lay meditators, especially women, have been noted since early times. Ten-day meditation courses taught by teachers in the Burmese lineages of Ledi Sayadaw (1846–1923), U Ba Khin (1899–1971), Mahasi Sayadaw (1904–82), Pa-Auk Tawya Sayadaw (b. 1934), S. N. Goenka (1924–2013), and so on, have become commonplace, and women are enthusiastic participants. In Burma, workers may apply for leave from their jobs, shave their heads, and check into a meditation center for a month of intensive practice. In meditation retreats like these, which are also popular in Cambodia, Indonesia, Laos, Malaysia, Thailand, and Vietnam, women comprise the majority of practitioners. Through intensive retreats and daily meditation practice, women not only further their spiritual practice but also gain confidence, a sense of independent agency, a strengthened sense of religious identity, and a renewed commitment to their Buddhist heritage. Some dedicated women practitioners travel to meditation centers of good repute throughout Southeast Asia to attend retreats and learn from specific teachers. In the process, they meet other women practitioners, share information, and tacitly or explicitly inspire each other in their practice. At present, most meditation teachers are male, but it is only a matter of time before a critical mass of female meditation teachers will begin to emerge.

The second unifying trend is a growing interest among women to seek out Buddhist education programs. Many eight- or ten-precept nuns (*thilashin*) in Burma and eight- or ten-precept nuns (*mae chee*) in Thailand now study Pāli, and nuns are becoming teachers of Pāli and Buddhist studies. Some nuns in Malaysia, Nepal, Sri Lanka, and Vietnam are pursuing advanced degrees in Buddhist studies, and some nuns are becoming Dharma teachers and university professors. In contrast to traditional methods of gaining access to Buddhist learning orally, through memorization,[6] Southeast Asian women now have greater access to a wide selection of print resources about Buddhism written in their own languages and online access to Buddhist texts and commentaries. Many nuns are acclaimed teachers of Pāli and *abhidhamma*, and many are teachers of monks. Buddhist laywomen and nuns meet at retreats, workshops, professional gatherings, and conferences such as the Sakyadhita (Daughters of the Buddha) International Conferences on Buddhist Women, where they share their ideas and insights (see figure 2.1). These dynamic events serve as forums for women to discover the empowering effects of knowledge, meditative experience, and solidarity.

The third trend, the contemporary movement that seeks to create opportunities for full ordination for women as *bhikkhunīs*, is both unifying and highly controversial. Some monks who oppose the increasing presence of *bhikkhunīs* in the region claim that the issue is divisive, even

Figure 2.1. Indonesian Buddhist women at the opening ceremony of the 14th Sakyadhita International Conference on Buddhist Women held in 2015 in Yogyakarta, Indonesia. Credit: Photo by Olivier Adam.

to the extent of creating a schism in the *saṅgha*. This opposition has had a dampening effect on many nuns who might otherwise welcome the opportunity to receive higher ordination. No matter what position one may take, there is no denying that the full ordination issue is being widely discussed. In predominantly Mahāyāna countries such as Korea, Malaysia, Singapore, Taiwan, and Vietnam, which have substantial numbers of fully ordained nuns, the issue is more or less moot. Even in Theravāda countries such as Burma, Cambodia, and Laos where there are few, if any, *bhikkhunīs*, and the possibility of higher education for nuns is not supported by the dominant male *saṅgha*, there is a greater awareness that such a category of women's ordination exists and that full ordination for women is now a real possibility in other countries. Nuns from Indonesia, Thailand, and Vietnam who prefer to take ordination in the Theravāda tradition have been traveling to Sri Lanka and returning home, where they may eventually pass the ordination on to other women. Many women in the Theravāda traditions continue to ordain as eight- or ten-precept nuns, often on a temporary basis;

however, there is a growing awareness that there are now more options. Buddhists in Theravāda countries increasingly recognize that vibrant *bhikṣuṇīs* are thriving in Mahāyāna countries such as Korea, Taiwan, and Vietnam, and many would like to improve conditions for ordained women in their countries. *Bhikkhunīs* are in the news, and they are not going away.

All these factors are significantly changing the face of Buddhism in South and Southeast Asia. With expanding educational opportunities, greater knowledge about Buddhism, and increasing opportunities for intensive meditation practice, many of the limitations women previously faced are melting away. Many women in traditionally Buddhist communities still regard offering alms to monks as the highest means of accumulating merit, but gradually they are also beginning to value the presence of nuns and to appreciate their commendable discipline and dedication. In an era of highly publicized scandals involving monks, some lay followers are losing faith in monastic institutions altogether, but others are coming to realize that the nuns are a treasure hidden in plain sight. With the easier communications and travel opportunities that are now available, the preconceptions Theravāda women once had about other Buddhist traditions are breaking down and new bonds of friendship are developing across lines of difference. The international Buddhist women's movement, encouraged by the Sakyadhita International Association of Buddhist Women, is having a ripple effect in many directions, breaking down stereotypes and fostering working relationships among women across cultures. These expanding connections and interactions among Buddhist women, lay and ordained, are creating a new sense of community, solidarity, insight, and social activism that transcends previously imagined boundaries.

Buddhist Women as Householders and Renunciants

As noted, for many centuries, women in the Theravāda traditions have not had access to full ordination as *bhikkhunīs*. Since the eleventh century CE, the lineage of *bhikkhunī* ordination disappeared in India and Sri Lanka, and was never transmitted to Burma, Cambodia, Laos, or Thailand. Fortunately, as documented in the Chinese sources, the *bhikkhunī* lineage was transmitted from India to Sri Lanka (third century BCE) and from Sri Lanka to China (fifth century CE), whence it spread to East Asia. As we have seen, recently nuns in the Theravāda traditions have gradually begun to access ordination in a lineage preserved in China, Korea, Taiwan, and Vietnam by traveling to these countries, or by being ordained in Sri Lanka or India. Starting in 1996, the lineage has been restored by nuns who received ordination abroad and returned to Sri Lanka to revive the tradition. Yet, as noted, this revival of *bhikkhunī* ordination in the Theravāda traditions is not welcomed by all.

A number of important issues remain to be considered in what may appear to be a simple matter of reinstituting a lost lineage. For example, some nuns do not have the means to travel to Sri Lanka or another country, and the Sri Lankan *bhikkhunī saṅgha* only has the capacity to ordain a certain number of nuns each year. A *bhikkhunī* ordination is a rather elaborate affair, requiring preceptor masters of both female and male orders (*ubato saṅgha*) to confer the precepts. A quorum of ten preceptors is required for conferring a *bhikkhu* ordination, while twenty (ten female and ten male) are required for a *bhikkhunī* ordination; that is, whereas a male candidate may be ordained as a *bhikkhu* by a quorum of ten *bhikkhus*, for a female candidate to be ordained as a *bhikkhunī*, a quorum of ten *bhikkhunīs* and ten *bhikkhus* is needed. In addition, some nuns do not feel comfortable receiving the *bhikkhunī* precepts without permission from their teachers, who may be either monks or ten-precept nuns (*dasasilmātā*). If a junior nun receives permission from her ten-precept nun teacher, she may hesitate to receive *bhikkhunī* ordination, since she would then become senior, outranking her teacher in the traditional monastic hierarchy, which creates an awkward situation. Another important issue to consider is that many nuns are simply not interested in receiving higher ordination.

Some orthodox interpreters use the English word "nun" to refer only to fully ordained *bhikkhunīs*, but if we use the term to mean a female renunciant or celibate monastic, it would also apply to the novice nuns (Sanskrit: *śrāmaṇerika*; Tibetan: *getsulma*) of the Tibetan tradition who observe thirty-six precepts; the ten-precept nuns (*dasasilmātās*) of Sri Lanka; the eight-, nine-, or ten-precept *thila shin* of Burma, the *mae chee* of Thailand, the *don chee* of Cambodia, and the *mae khao* of Laos; and the nuns of Japan who live a celibate renunciant lifestyle while observing the *bodhisattva* precepts of the *Brahmajāla Sūtra*. Although this broad application of the term "nun" oversimplifies the differences among these categories, it seems reasonable to refer to all Buddhist renunciant women as nuns and proceed to distinguish the differences among their histories, precepts, and lifestyles. Even though complete and accurate histories of women's ordination in many Buddhist countries are yet to be recovered, and it is doubtful whether they ever will be, contemporary interest in the ordination of women warrants a discussion of the varied lineages of ordination for women.

Women in Theravāda communities are not generally encouraged to become nuns and may be actively discouraged from doing so by their families and social circles. Whereas monks are typically revered and boys and young men are praised and rewarded for receiving ordination, even temporarily, it is assumed that the proper role for a young woman is to marry and give birth to children, hopefully sons. As a result, most women in Buddhist societies opt for family life. As householders, women assume the important role of nurturing their extended families and are likely to contribute to the family income by working in various occupations outside the home. Devout Buddhist women often regard their roles as supporters of male monastics and their institutions as their primary religious practice. As women, they take pride in providing alms to monks and in seeing their sons become monks, even for a short time. Many older women, often after having experienced great suffering, take robes after their husbands die and their children are grown. In Vietnam, for example, many women gained insight into the Buddha's teachings on suffering while witnessing the horrors of war. In Cambodia, many women sought shelter in monastic life after losing their entire families during the unimaginable suffering of the Khmer Rouge years (1975–79).[7] Some women have been ordained after suffering years of domestic violence.

Today, in communities where there are no *bhikkhunīs*, nuns typically receive their precepts from a *bhikkhu*, in a simple ritual similar to that of the Buddha's ordination of Mahāprajāpatī, thus symbolically continuing the Buddha's lineage.[8] These nuns wear white robes (pink in Burma), shave their heads, and observe careful renunciant behavior, guided by seventy-five rules of deportment. Although they strive to adhere to the exacting precepts of a *bhikkhunī*, they are not recognized as *bhikkhunīs* because they do not receive the *upasampadā* or full ordination. Eight-to ten-precept holders are not regarded as members of the *saṅgha* and therefore are not eligible for the benefits of full monastic membership. Some laypeople deny that female renunciants are nuns, reserving that term for fully ordained *bhikkhunīs*; some even regard them as laywomen with shaved heads.

Monks are regarded as a "field of merit," meaning that a layperson's donations to monks are praiseworthy due to their superior religious and social status. Because *bhikkhus* observe many more precepts and protocols, making offerings to them is believed to be a karmically fruitful action that results in prosperity in this and future lives. The social identity of eight- to ten-precept nuns is less well defined; they are recognized as having renounced household life, and yet, lacking full ordination, they occupy a median position somewhere between the laity and the *saṅgha*. Even though nuns voluntarily observe many of the same precepts as the monks and live very ascetic lives, making offerings to nuns is not viewed as equally meritorious, and nuns' access to Buddhist education is limited or nonexistent. When lay followers offer donations to monasteries and monastics, they strongly prefer to support monks rather than nuns—according to anecdotal evidence, in a ratio of about five to one. Nevertheless, a recent study of the interrelationships between the nuns, monks, and laity, especially pertaining to almsgiving, reveals complementary networks that are mutually beneficial,[9] in what some have called "an economy of merit."[10] When the preferential treatment of male monastics is pointed out to nuns, they tend to make light of it, asserting that their motive for religious practice is liberation, not social status or material gain. The fact remains that Theravāda nuns are often unable to benefit their communities fully because they are educationally and economically disadvantaged.

Buddhists in Southeast Asia tend to laud the achievements of monks, and hence few renunciant women have been publicly recognized for their spiritual attainments. Many lay Buddhists, both female and male, presume that a genuine religious vocation is the purview of monks, not nuns. Disparities in the levels of education and training between monks and nuns are both the cause and the result of this presumption. Few young women have had sufficient confidence and determination to pursue a monastic vocation, due to the lack of educational opportunity as well as social approbation. The few who have persevered in their aspiration live quiet lives with few resources, few mentors, no official recognition, and little encouragement. In Cambodia and Laos, until recently, religious education has been available only to monks, and meditation instruction for female practitioners was also difficult to come by.[11] Nuns renounced worldly attachments but were rarely invited to give blessings or perform funerals and other religious services. Renunciant women might count themselves fortunate to be able to live in a corner of a monastic compound in exchange for cooking and cleaning for monks. To serve monks is fulfilling for many nuns but is time consuming and often leaves them exhausted.

In recent years, both laywomen and nuns have initiated new directions in social transformation. There have been attempts to get nuns more actively involved in community service and social welfare work. Nuns in Sri Lanka are now involved in hospital chaplaincy, for example, and frequently conduct classes in Dhamma (Sanskrit: Dharma) for children. Grassroots initiatives in leadership training and counseling for survivors of gender-based trauma are being developed in Burma and Thailand.[12] In Thailand, nuns have been active in temple programs to educate youth about the ill effects of smoking and drugs. In Cambodia, some nuns have been trained in community health, HIV/AIDS awareness, and counseling survivors of torture and other traumas. There have even been efforts to mobilize the services of elderly nuns to promote breastfeeding.[13]

These efforts to engage women renunciants in social service have had considerable success, but women who enter monastic life generally do so because they are interested in learning and practicing Buddhism, not because they wish to do social work. In fact, Buddhism is often associated with social disengagement and for disavowing worldly involvements, a critique that is not wholly undeserved. Many nuns experience an ongoing tension between two conflicting ideals: the contemplative life and the life of altruistic service to society. Some understand service to the community not as in conflict with the contemplative life but as a natural expression of the qualities and ideals cultivated in meditation. After all, compassionate counseling and mediation skills have been the purview of Buddhist monastics since earliest times. Others decline to become involved in social service activities such as these, saying, "We did not become nuns to do social welfare work. We became nuns to achieve liberation. If we wanted to be social workers, we could have gone that direction. But we became nuns so that we can practice the Dhamma, eradicate the defilements of the mind, and become free from *saṃsāra*." Most nuns are happy to recite *paritta* (verses of protection and blessing) for the benefit of the lay community, and many are actively engaged in meditation practices. Some nuns are engaged in all these activities, also taking the opportunity to study texts whenever the opportunity arises.

Women in Burmese Theravāda Buddhism

In Myanmar, previously known as Burma, where around 75 percent of the population identifies as Theravāda Buddhist, women enjoy a relatively high social standing. Women are generally educated, skilled in business, and entrusted with the family finances. As Buddhist followers, they engage in daily devotional practices, make frequent offerings to monks and temples, and do their best to live according to the five lay Buddhist precepts. These days, many women also participate in intensive meditation retreats held at countless meditation centers throughout the country. With the exception of a few highly acclaimed meditation teachers who enjoy great currency, such as Mahasi Sayadaw and S. N. Goenka, Burma was effectively cloistered from the international community for the second half of the twentieth century by its military dictatorship. In the interim, meditation centers flourished, and women were their most active patrons. Both women and men may ordain temporarily, often during the three-month rainy season retreat (*vassa*), as a way to acquire merit, repay the kindness of their parents, and pay respect to deceased relations.

Every Burmese male is expected to ordain at least once in his lifetime and thereby gains immediate access to free religious education and other privileges. Men are said to possess *bhun* (Pāli: *bhaga*), a certain special power or good fortune that is weaker in women. This gendered cultural disparity in spiritual power is reflected in male privilege and superior ranking in the religious sphere. Monks are venerated and their presumed virtue is liberally rewarded in material ways. The status of monks and lay donors are interrelated, as influential people vie to donate liberally to high-ranking monks.[14]

Burmese Buddhist women may practice as a layperson or they may take eight, nine, or ten Buddhist precepts and live as *thila shin* ("possessors of virtue"), either on a temporary basis or as a lifetime commitment. While attending meditation retreats, lay practitioners (*yogis*) generally wear a white blouse, a brown *longyi* (sarong), and a brown stole under the right arm and over the left shoulder. Nuns wear pink robes with an orange *longyi* and a rust-colored stole, perhaps symbolic of the outer robe of a *bhikkhu*, placed over their left shoulder. *Thila shin* generally take eight precepts, or sometimes ten, as a means of accruing merit for their parents and themselves. There is a preference for "virgin nuns" (*ngebyu*), that is, nuns who have not been married or sexually active before taking the precepts of a nun, implying a kind of symbolic purity.[15] *Thila shin* are recognized as enacting a religious identity that parallels the identity of the monks. Although the status of monks is indisputably superior, each distinct renunciant identity may be regarded as equally valid in its own right. Some argue that the nuns' exclusion from the traditionally recognized *saṅgha* marginalizes renunciant women and places them at a disadvantage. Others argue that the nuns' ambiguous status allows them greater freedom of movement and institutional autonomy, without the constraints of the 227 precepts of the *bhikkhus*' discipline and without coming under the *bhikkhus*' authority.

According to social anthropologist Hiroko Kawanami, "In 2010, there were a total of 3,165 independent nunneries registered with the Department of Religious Affairs in Myanmar."[16] These include several hundred nunneries (*kyaung*) with 5,746 nuns located in the Sagaing Hills, a veritable "kingdom of monasteries." It is estimated that there may be as many as sixty thousand *thila shin* in Burma today, though there may be more who are not registered with the government. The nuns are organized into ten Tilashin Councils at the state/divisional level and 206 at the township level, ultimately under the supervision of the Supreme Sangha Council (of monks) since the early 1990s and in close cooperation with local government officials.[17] All nuns over the age of twelve are required to register with the Department of Religious Affairs.

Burmese monks are expected to go for alms every morning and receive cooked food, in accordance with the *vinaya*. For women, offering alms is a way to express devotion to the *saṅgha*, accumulate merit, and interact with the monastic community. In Burma, monks may

Figure 2.2. Nuns in the dining hall at Sakyadhita Thilashin Nunnery School, Sagaing, Myanmar. Credit: Photo by Liên Bui.

also collect alms from the nuns. The practice of mendicancy (going for alms) secures the monks' status as sources of merit for the laity—the renunciation of ordinary desires symbolized by living on alms, thereby dissociating them from the secular world of sense desires. In contrast, the nuns are only allowed to go for alms on certain days, whether individually or in organized groups, and are prohibited from receiving cooked food; instead, they collect raw rice and money.[18] This inversion of the renunciant symbology obliges the nuns to buy and cook their own food—contradicting the expected behavior for monastics and thereby reinforcing the association between women and the secular world of attachments.[19] Although nuns are prohibited from accepting cooked food as alms and must prepare their own meals, nuns such as those at Sakyadhita Thilashin Nunnery School in Sagaing collectively practice mindful eating, observing "noble silence" (see figure 2.2).

Theravāda Buddhism spread through Burma during the Pagan Dynasty (849–1287), as attested in stone inscriptions. In the inscriptions from Pagan, many women of different classes of society are mentioned as donors, including many who were extremely wealthy. Epigraphs that mention *bhikkhunīs* have been found in southern Burma, but their status, history, and what happened to them is unclear. According to G. H. Luce, a prolific scholar of Burmese culture, women were ordained in Burma in early times, up to the fifteenth century. Barbara Watson Andaya, professor of Southeast Asian studies, cites a British envoy's report as saying, "Burmese nuns had once worn the yellow robes of the *bhikkunī* [*sic*], but that the order had been abolished in order to encourage population growth."[20] In the 1930s, a Burmese monk named Shin Adicca advocated for the full ordination of nuns but was unsuccessful in gaining sufficient acceptance for the idea. In the 1950s, a teacher of *vipassanā* (Sanskrit: *vipaśyanā*; insight) meditation named Jetavana Sayadaw (1868–1955), who was a teacher of Mahasi Sayadaw, strongly endorsed the restoration of *bhikkhunī* ordination in his commentary to the *Milindapañha* but was not able to gain support for this idea. In 1970, a Burmese woman applied to the government seeking full ordination, but her petition was not successful. In a disturbing case, Saccavadi (b. 1965), a Burmese nun with a *dhammācariya* ("teacher of dhamma") degree who ordained as a *bhikkhunī* in Sri Lanka in 2003, was imprisoned in Burma in 2005 for refusing to disavow her decision to become fully ordained.[21] After seventy-six days of incarceration, she returned to Sri Lanka and lived there until 2008, when she disrobed due to the trauma she had experienced in Burma, and now lives in the United States.[22]

Most nuns in Burma today are content to practice as *thila shin*, embodying their renunciant identity in everyday life, and few are interested in challenging the monastic authorities' decision to bar them from the *saṅgha*. As *thila shin*, nuns in Burma today have many opportunities for intensive meditation practice and religious education. There are a number of institutes where nuns may study Pāli and *abhidhamma*, and nuns take a significant role in teaching Buddhism, or "propagating the *sāsana* (teaching)." Each year the government recognizes the most accomplished scholars among the nuns as well as the monks. Women are discouraged from taking public roles, however, and nuns tend to stay out of the limelight to avoid public scrutiny. Nuns do not ordinarily give public teachings, even though some are very good scholars and many have passed the same exams as the monks. Nuns are rarely invited to preside over religious rituals, even when they are capable of doing so.

Thilashin may attend a three-year course leading to the *dhammācariya* degree, which enables them to teach in nunneries, but currently the only academic option is the Sitagu International Buddhist Academy established in Sagaing in 1994. Plans are afoot to build an Institute for Higher Buddhist Education with campuses in Sagaing and Rangoon that will potentially be open to nuns.

Meanwhile, a number of exceptional women in Burma have exceeded the limitations imposed on them, excelling in scriptural studies, teaching, meditation, social service activities, and recently politics. Hiroko Kawanami tells the stories of several prominent nuns who were pioneers in Buddhist studies in Burma.[23] A number of nuns established nunnery schools (*sathin-daik*) that offer exemplary programs in both *pariyatti* (study) and *paṭipatti* (practice). Others became accomplished teachers. For example, after completing her *dhammācariya* studies, Daw Yusanda began teaching Dhamma regularly at Shwedagon Pagoda in Yangon in 1976, and gained renown throughout the country as an articulate, engaging speaker.[24] An example of a nun involved in social engagement is Daw Aggañānī, who founded Sasana Ramsi Dhamma School in 2010. Beginning with just nine young girls in a bamboo hut, the school now has more than seventy students, most of whom are orphans or semi-orphans and from very poor families. The school provides them with a residential education through high school to give them a better chance in life. Perhaps the most globally renowned Buddhist woman today is Aung San Suu Kyi (b. 1945), a *vipassanā* meditation practitioner best known for her political engagement, who has risen to become the de facto head of state in Myanmar.

3

Buddhist Women in East Asia

Beginning in the early centuries CE, Buddhism became a significant feature of the religious landscape in China, from where the teachings were also transmitted to Korea, Japan, Taiwan, and Vietnam. As the Buddha's teachings came from India across both land and sea to China, they influenced, merged with, and competed with the Confucian, Daoist, and ancestral traditions. Buddhists in these countries generally follow the Mahāyāna branch of Buddhism, based on texts that emerged several hundred years after the Buddha passed away. Texts such as the *prajñāpāramitā* ("perfection of wisdom") literature expound the *bodhisattva* path to becoming a fully awakened Buddha, in contradistinction to the *śrāvaka* ("hearer") path to becoming an *arhat* that is preserved in the Pāli canon. Among the early pioneering figures who came from India to China, we find no reference to nuns, but we do discover that many women in China became devoted followers and eventually some also became nuns.

Altogether the texts of six schools of monastic discipline (*vinaya*) were translated into Chinese. Of these, the earliest ordinations in China were based on the Dharmaguptaka school, which developed out of the earlier Mahīśāsaka school. From the Tang Dynasty onward, the Dharmaguptaka became the dominant (eventually the only) school of *vinaya* that was followed in China.[1] The Dharmaguptaka lineage has 250 precepts for *bhikṣus* and 348 for *bhikṣuṇīs*, and is still practiced today in China, Korea, Taiwan, and Vietnam. It is the only living lineage of full ordination for women and is therefore especially important for the contemporary movement to restore the *bhikṣuṇī* lineage in countries where it did not previously exist.

Women's Responsibilities and Renunciation in Early Chinese Buddhism

The first nuns who are known to have initiated Buddhist practice communities in China did so without the benefit of the rules they were expected to live by.[2] There is no conclusive evidence that any Indian nuns visited China or that any Chinese women traveled to India. The *bhikṣuṇī prātimokṣa* (the code of monastic conduct for fully ordained nuns) reportedly appeared in China around the middle of the third century CE, but it remains unclear what school of *vinaya* it belonged to. At the beginning of the fourth century, a woman named Jingjian Zhu (ca. 292–36), along with twenty-four others, received the ten precepts of a novice nun (*śrāmaṇerī*) from a monk.[3] Later, in the middle of the fourth century, Jingjian Zhu and four companions took *bhikṣuṇī* ordination from *bhikṣus* in accordance with the Mahāsāṃghika *vinaya* and became the first *bhikṣuṇīs* in China. The ordination was conducted by *bhikṣus* alone, however, because there were no *bhikṣuṇīs* in China at the time to complete the required quorum of ten *bhikṣuṇīs* needed to train the candidates and ask them twenty-four personal questions, for example, whether they were free from family impediments and physical infirmities.[4] The fact that the nuns were embarrassed to answer these personal questions in the presence of *bhikṣus* is the reason given for requiring *bhikṣuṇī* preceptors in addition to *bhikṣu* preceptors, the so-called dual ordination. Thus, the nuns ordained in China in the fourth century were not ordained in full compliance with the *vinaya*. It was not until the fifth century that the complete texts of four *vinaya* schools became available in Chinese and it became clear that Jingjian and her four companions had not met all the requirements, because there had been no quorum of ten fully ordained nuns to perform the formal acts of the monastic community, such as ordinations.

In 429 CE, a group of nuns arrived in southern China by ship from Lanka, but they had an insufficient number to conduct ordinations.[5] In 434 CE, when a second group of nuns arrived from Lanka, a fully constituted quorum was able to perform the first known duly authorized ordination for more than three hundred Chinese nuns at Nanlin Monastery, in what is today Nanjing. In this way, a lineage of *bhikṣuṇī* ordination was officially established in China and has continued until today. By the early eighth century, due to the influence of the Chinese monk Dao'an (312–85), the Dharmaguptaka *vinaya* had become the standard throughout the land.

Biographies of Buddhist Nuns, compiled in the early sixth century by the monk Baochang (Pao-ch'ang), contains sixty-five biographies of Chinese nuns who lived during the fourth to early sixth centuries.[6] He extolled the virtues of these renunciant women with remarkable enthusiasm:

> These nuns, then, whom I offer as models, are women of excellent reputation, paragons of ardent morals, whose virtues are a stream of fragrance that flows without end. . . . Such virtue as theirs is like the deep ocean or the lofty peak—like the harmonious music of bronze and jade bells. Indeed, they are like models of virtue in an autumnal age, reliable guides in a decadent time.[7]

The text briefly describes their family backgrounds, their motivations for renouncing worldly life, the spiritual practices they pursued, their attainments, and other aspects of their lives and deaths. The stories in the *Biographies of Buddhist Nuns* extol the nuns both for their extraordinary piety and for ascetic practices such as self-immolation or abstaining from food. Austerities such as fasting and offering one's body to the Buddha through auto-cremation were regarded as meritorious; letting go of the body was interpreted as letting go of the self.[8] Neither of these practices is sanctioned in the early Buddhist texts, which reject extreme asceticism, but they seem to have been regarded as markers of sanctity during the early centuries of Buddhist transmission to China, perhaps due to Daoist influence. From a modern sensibility, this raises serious questions, but nevertheless the biographies are notable in recounting stories of the nuns' attainments in meditation, teaching, and miraculous powers.

About a century after these biographies were compiled, some highly regarded male *vinaya* masters painted unflattering portraits of nuns in their writings, which influenced attitudes toward female renunciants for generations to come.[9] For example, according to Daoxuan, an influential seventh-century *vinaya* scholar monk, all past and future *buddhas* concur that women can practice just as well at home, so they need not become nuns. He refers to an obscure *vinaya* text that sets out ten reasons to blame Ānanda for advocating for Mahāprajāpatī, the first woman to request ordination and be admitted to the *saṅgha*, suggesting that the monks would have gotten more respect and donations and the Dharma would have lasted far longer if the women had stayed home.

History has belied this point, since the Dharma has long outlived the canonical prediction of its demise.[10]

In the Confucian scheme of family and society, women's roles were well defined and, from a contemporary feminist perspective, restrictive. Buddhism needed to adapt to the Chinese cultural environment to be accepted, and that meant coming to terms with Confucian beliefs and social mores. Filial piety (*xiào*), which historian Bret Hinsch considers "the preeminent virtue of pre-Buddhist China and the most fundamental organizing principle of Chinese society,"[11] requires allegiance to the family, social harmony, marriage, and procreation. These requirements were quite at odds with the Buddhist ideals of *saṅgha* (monastic community), individual liberation, renunciation, and celibacy. Not only was the new religion foreign to China, but also it promoted shaving one's head and cremating the body after death—both affronts to the ancestors. To be accepted, the Buddhists needed to find ways to resolve these apparent contradictions. Women were especially challenged to find solutions to this ethical and social dilemma, since their social identity was closely associated with home and family. Eventually devoted Buddhist women came to see Buddhist practice as a way to provide spiritual care for their extended families. Through rites of repentance, generosity, and moral purity, they accumulated merit that could then be dedicated on behalf of their ancestors. In this way, they not only protected the health and well-being of their families and clans but also forged new spiritual identities and expanded the scope of their benevolence beyond the family to all living beings. One nun named Ling-shou (early fourth century) countered her father's accusations of being unfilial with this retort: "My mind is concentrated on the work of religion, and my thought dwells exclusively on spiritual matters. Neither blame nor praise moves me; purity and uprightness are sufficient in themselves. Why must I submit thrice [to father, husband, and son], before I am considered a woman of propriety?" Her father thereupon accused her of thinking only of herself, to which she responded: "I am setting myself to cultivate the Way exactly because I want to free all beings from suffering. How much more, then, do I want to free my two parents!"[12]

As Buddhist texts and teachings gradually seeped into Chinese literature and consciousness, Buddhist thought and culture became transformed in ways that were largely consistent with Indian Buddhist tradition, yet with a flavor that was distinctively Chinese. The literature portrays women as being especially devout. Over the centuries, and especially during the Tang Dynasty (618–905), dedicating images and copying Buddhist texts became popular ways for women to gain merit. At Lanfeng Shan (Misty Peak Mountain), in Henan Province, there is an especially rich collection of tributes to dedicated women practitioners carved in stone memorials.[13] However, even after the introduction of Buddhism, Confucian ideology continued to have a strong impact on Chinese society, influencing family life, ethics, politics, and social relations, including gender relations. Mirroring the emperor, who wielded the Mandate of Heaven—divinely sanctioned rulership—the male head of household wielded inordinate power over other members of the family. With the exception of peasant women who were engaged in manual labor in the fields and forests, women were largely confined to the domestic sphere and rewarded for serving and obeying. The autonomy of women was limited by social customs such as foot binding and widow chastity. Entering a Buddhist monastery was one of the few alternative paths a woman could follow.

As feminist scholars have pointed out since at least the 1980s, there are tensions and contradictions between the philosophically egalitarian promise of Buddhism—that *all* sentient beings have the potential for awakening—and the patriarchal conventions reflected in Buddhist texts and the subordinate status of women in both Indian and Chinese societies. On one hand, Buddhist monasteries afforded women an alternative to marriage and childbearing, and also served as a refuge for abused wives and widows. On the other hand, not every woman who wished was allowed to fulfill her aspiration to become a full-time practicing renunciant. Many parents, including many who professed to be Buddhist, actively discouraged or prevented a daughter from joining a monastery, believing that women had a filial duty to their in-laws to produce offspring. Even today, it is not uncommon to meet nuns who had to wait until after their parents died to receive ordination. Although parents in Chinese societies may be similarly reluctant to allow a son to become a monk, the preconception that women have a natural predilection and responsibility for childbearing is difficult to dispel.

Enlightenment in Female Form in China

In China, a question that continues to arouse debate is whether women can become enlightened and, if so, under what circumstances and through what processes. Equally as provocative is the question of whether women can become enlightened in female form. In the Mahāyāna traditions, questions arise about whether women can be born in a Pure Land (*kṣetra-śuddhi*), the abode of a fully awakened being. In these traditions, upon awakening, a *buddha* manifests three forms, known as the three bodies of a *buddha* (*trikāya*): a formless body of awakened awareness (*dharmakāya*), an enjoyment body (*saṃbhogakāya*) that manifests in a Pure Land, and an emanation body (*nirmāṇakāya*) that appears in the world. The Pure Lands are the abodes of *buddhas* in *saṃbhogakāya* form created by the merit of their awakening. In such an auspicious environment, *bodhisattvas* may take teachings from the *buddha* of that Pure Land and thereby advance swiftly on the path to full awakening. There are disparities in the texts about whether it is possible to take birth in a Pure Land in a female body or only in a male body.[14] These questions are controversial, and the texts tell different stories.

Buddhism in China developed a vibrant Pure Land tradition, in which devotees aspire to take rebirth in the Sukhāvatī ("full of delight") Pure Land of Amitābha Buddha, the *buddha* of infinite light and life. According to the *Larger Sukhāvatī-vyūha-sūtra*, the thirty-fifth vow of Amitābha Buddha famously says, in a roundabout fashion, that if a woman has faith in Amitābha, aspires to awakening, and spurns her female body, she will never again be born as a woman. Paul Harrison, a scholar of Chinese Buddhism, notes that in the earliest recension of the *Larger Sukhāvatī-vyūha-sūtra*, a woman with faith in Amitābha Buddha who aspires to awakening and spurns a female body can avoid being born again as a woman, *if she wishes*.[15] Moreover, there appear to be no gender distinctions in the Pure Lands, implying that the beings in residence there (who are all *buddhas* and *bodhisattvas*) are nongendered and presumably asexual. On the contrary, however, as Buddhist studies scholar Gregory Schopen and others have pointed out, certain texts explicitly state that the *buddha* fields (Pure Lands) are devoid of women or even the sound of the word "woman."[16] Influenced by such gender bias, both in the texts and in their social conditioning, it is quite common to hear women in Buddhist societies aspiring to become male in their next life. The assumption is that, for achieving enlightenment, being born in a male body is preferable.

From a sociological perspective, in patriarchal societies, males are preferred and given all manner of privileges, including the preferential treatment of monks over nuns, and it therefore stands to reason that some women may wish to take a male rebirth. Harrison argues that the bias against women that is evident in many early Mahāyāna texts seems to have become softened as time went on, yet it clearly influenced attitudes toward women and their spiritual potential. Buddhist studies scholar Serinity Young reminds us that in the texts of the enormously popular cult of Amitābha Buddha, those who aspire to rebirth in Sukhāvatī Pure Land are taught to despise their female form, which will ensure that they will never take rebirth in female form again.[17] Although the Mahāyāna tradition is often regarded as egalitarian and woman friendly, it appears that women's best hope in the Pure Land tradition is to take a male rebirth, work toward awakening in male form, and embody the final goal of awakening in male form. Certain other Mahāyāna texts, such as the *Bodhisattvabhūmi* by the fourth-century Indian monk and philosopher Asaṅga, also unequivocally express a deprecating view of women as weak in intelligence and full of defilements. Some texts, such as the noncanonical *Meritorious Virtue of Making Images*, explicitly state that unwholesome actions can result in a female rebirth and wholesome actions can result in a male rebirth.[18] James Dobbins, a scholar of Japanese Buddhism, terms this the "disjunction between ideal and practiced religion."[19]

In China, Avalokiteśvara, known as the *bodhisattva* of compassion, gradually evolved into female form as Guanyin, who "hears the cries of the world" (see figure 3.1). The symbolic value of an embodiment of perfect enlightenment in female form, one whose wish-fulfilling compassion reaches all segments of society, cannot be overestimated. Although images of Avalokiteśvara in male guise endured, especially the form with a thousand hands and a thousand eyes to see the sufferings of sentient beings, by the twelfth century, Guanyin in her distinctively female form had become ubiquitous.[20] The transition from a male embodiment of compassion as Avalokiteśvara in India to a female embodiment as Guanyin in China occurred gradually over a period of hundreds of years, and the reasons for

Figure 3.1. Image of the *bodhisattva* Guanyin at Dorje Chang Institute, Auckland, New Zealand. Credit: Photo by Karma Lekshe Tsomo.

the change are a matter of speculation. Perhaps the images of enlightenment imported from India were simply too exclusively male, in contrast to the indigenous mother goddesses that abounded in China. Perhaps people naturally associated the virtue of compassion with women, especially as the mother image. Regardless of the reasons for Guanyin's miraculous transformation, she remains the most accessible image of enlightenment for millions of people in East Asia even today—whether or not they identify as Buddhist—on display and ready to provide succor in homes and restaurants as well as in temples of every variety.

Buddhist Women of Korea

Buddhism was brought to Korea in the fourth century CE, during the Three Kingdoms period, by monks who had studied in China. Although indigenous shamanistic traditions remained strong in Korea, Buddhist culture was embraced by the ruling classes and soon had a significant impact on the literature, art, medicine, and religious life of the people. Women's practice and achievements were rarely recorded, but it is well known that an order of fully ordained nuns was established alongside an order of fully ordained monks. Later, during the Koryŏ period (982–1392), Korean queens and women of means flocked to the temples and supported the translation and publication of Buddhist texts.[21] During the Chosŏn period (1392–1897), the neo-Confucian oppression of Buddhism in addition to patriarchal social norms had a serious impact on women's public participation in temple rituals, but their devotion to the *buddhas* and *bodhisattvas* remained central to their religious identity and spiritual development.[22] During the twentieth century and since, women have contributed actively to temples, meditation halls, educational institutions, and diverse social welfare projects.[23] The meditation tradition known as Sŏn (Chinese: Chan; Japanese: Zen) is well preserved in South Korea, and nuns are strong practitioners.

In 1982, when I received full ordination as a *bhikṣuṇī* at Bŏmŏnsa Temple in Pusan, South Korea (see figure 3.2), a prominent Sŏn practitioner named Hye Chun Sunim was among the ten *bhikṣuṇīs* who officiated at this groundbreaking dual ordination ceremony, which included both ten *bhikṣu* and ten *bhikṣuṇī* ordination masters for the first time in many years. Born in northern Korea in 1918, to a family of privilege, Hye Chun Sunim had found her life turned upside down by the Korean War in the early 1950s. When she traveled south as a refugee, she found solace in a Buddhist monastery and decided to become a nun. Determined to reach enlightenment, she went through unimaginable hardships to be accepted as a disciple of the monk Seong Cheol Sunim (1912–93), one of the most renowned Sŏn masters of her day—something unheard of for nuns at the time.

When I met Hye Chun Sunim one afternoon in October 1982 in a sparse room with woven straw matting (*tatami*) at the monastery, she asked my name, in a very formal manner. I responded that my name

Figure 3.2. The ordination of *bhikṣuṇīs* held at Bŏmŏnsa Temple at Pusan, South Korea, in 1982. Credit: Photo courtesy of Bŏmŏnsa Temple.

was Hye Gong ("Wisdom of Emptiness"), a Korean name that had just been given to me by Pangjang Kusan Sunim (1908–83), another renowned Sŏn master. Suddenly, I heard my name ring out through the room: "Hye Gong!" Startled, I responded, "Yes?" She then asked, "Who responded when I called your name?" This popular Korean *huadu*, similar to a Japanese Zen *kōan*, is a question for contemplation designed to spark direct insight into one's own true nature. "What is it? (*i mwŏ kko*)" calls us to wake up and attend to the experience of the moment. Ultimately, this question awakens the wisdom of self and selflessness, and calls us to question the true nature of our identity. The selfless wisdom of Hye Chun Sunim exemplifies the embodied practice of Korean Buddhist women.[24]

Buddhist Women of Japan

The Buddhist teachings were officially received in Japan in the mid-sixth century CE and flourished during the reign of Prince Shōtoku (574–622), who personally received the *bodhisattva* precepts, built many temples and nunneries, and wrote commentaries on several Buddhist scriptures. It is said that the first Japanese monastics were three nuns who traveled to Korea and received the *bhikṣuṇī* precepts in 590.[25] They returned to Japan, but the lineage of full ordination for women did not continue because there were not enough nuns to perform the ordination. There are records of nunneries in Japan that became "divorce temples," safe havens for women escaping domestic violence and unhappiness.

A variety of Buddhist schools of thought and practice were transmitted to Japan, and most continue to be practiced up to today. Until the end of the eighth century, women were excluded from official monastic ordinations, but as East Asian religions scholar Lori Meeks has documented, during the Heian (794–1186) and Kamakura (1186–1336) periods, aristocratic women could receive "lay novice" ordinations instead of receiving the traditional *vinaya* precepts of a *bhikṣuṇī*.[26] For example, in the year 1026, the ordination of Empress Shōshi (988–1074) was conducted with great fanfare and attended by a cohort of eminent monks. Meeks argues that "elite women used their wealth and status to commission and maintain their own complex ordination traditions that allowed them to take the vows of lay, bodhisattva, or even novice ordinations in the comfort of their own quarters."[27] Multiple innovative interpretations of ordination (known as *jukai*, "receiving the precepts") allowed women the flexibility to live a religious life without having to shave their heads, wear monastic robes, or conform to the restrictions of monastic lifestyle.

Today, many Japanese women are devout Buddhists, and they have a range of paths to choose from. In 1872, the Meiji government passed an edict that discouraged Buddhist monastics from observing a celibate, vegetarian lifestyle;[28] most monks subsequently married, but most nuns continued to live celibate lives.[29] Although more women are serving as temple priests than before, the number of celibate nuns in Japan is currently declining. Still, there are more than a thousand nuns who maintain traditional temples, preserve ancient Buddhist rituals, and serve their communities. Nuns in the Sōtō Zen School train very strictly, practice meditation, and train in traditional contemplative arts such as tea ceremony and flower arrangement that have developed in Japanese Buddhist culture over many centuries.[30] Japanese nuns and many laywomen strive to observe the ten major precepts of a *bodhisat-*

tva as described in the *Brahmajāla Sūtra*: not to kill, steal, lie, become intoxicated, engage in sexual misconduct, talk ill of others, praise oneself, become angry, be stingy, or denigrate the Three Jewels (the Buddha, Dharma, and Saṅgha).[31] In Japan today, half of those registered as teachers of Buddhism (*kyōshi*) are women.[32] Among the remarkable Buddhist women in Japan today are Shundo Aoyama Roshi (b. 1933), a prolific writer and Zen master who leads Aichi Senmon Nisōdō, a nuns' training institute in Nagoya;[33] Seigyoku Takatsukasa (b. 1929),[34] the illustrious abbess of Zenkōji Temple in Nagano; and Jakucho Setouchi (b. 1922), a well-known writer who became a nun in the Tendai School.

Due to unique historical circumstances, most Buddhist priests in contemporary Japan are married with children and their temples have become hereditary.[35] In this religious environment, a woman may choose to practice as a nun, a priest, or a temple wife. Occasionally, the daughter of a priest takes charge of her family's temple, or she may marry a man who becomes the priest of the temple. Temple wives play many important roles: managing the temple, preparing offerings, scheduling temple activities, and interacting with parishioners, in addition to their domestic roles and their duty to raise children to become priests and temple wives. These days, they may also conduct religious ceremonies. There are many variations among the different sects, however. In the Rinzai Zen and Tendai sects, the term for the wife of a priest is *jiteifujin* (temple wife); in the Jōdo Shinshū (True Pure Land) sect, the term *bōmori* (lit., temple guardian) is more common. Since the time that Shinran (1173–1263), founder of the Jōdo Shinshū school of Buddhism in Japan, made the decision to marry, most Jōdo Shinshū priests have been married with children. In the 1990s, *bōmori* began to be officially recognized through participating in an initiation rite.[36] Today, there are several thousand women priests in this sect, including some in North America. Laywomen are active in Japanese temple life and are beginning to gain recognition for their contributions. The domestic Dharma practices that have sustained Japanese laywomen for centuries are also gaining increased attention.

East Asian Women in the Twenty-First Century

Buddhist women of East Asia are currently experiencing a revitalization of Buddhist traditions in a time of greater freedom and opportunity for women. In Taiwan, women are at the epicenter of a resurgence of interest in Buddhist culture and practice. Religious identities in Taiwan tend to be eclectic, with broad participation in ritual activities of multiple religious traditions, combining devotion to the *buddhas* and *bodhisattvas* with a pantheon of Chinese and local gods. In the 1950s, when a number of leading Buddhist scholars and accomplished practitioners from Mainland China relocated to the island, women were pivotal to their successful resettlement and have thrived in collaboration with them. In this vibrant religious landscape, countless devotees have taken the lay and *bodhisattva* precepts and thousands have ordained as monks and nuns. Today, the number of nuns surpasses the number of monks by more than three to one. As Buddhist institutions have grown stronger, the number of Buddhists has increased in Taiwan, as have opportunities for Buddhist education and meritorious activity. Buddhist women are leaders in this revitalization, and several nuns have become prominent figures in education and social engagement.[37] The early history of Buddhist women in Taiwan has not been well documented, but it is well known that many women who adhered to the "vegetarian religion" (*zaizhao*) prior to 1950 gradually became ordained as Buddhist nuns.[38] In recent years, Taiwan has become a model for communities of devout, well educated, and independent Buddhist women, with many highly respected Buddhist nuns as teachers. Luminary figures such as Bhikṣuṇī Cheng Yen (b. 1937),[39] Bhikṣuṇī Chao Hwei (b. 1957),[40] Bhikṣuṇī Shig Hiu Wan (1913–2004),[41] and Bhikṣuṇī Wuyin (b. 1940)[42] have made major contributions to ensure the flourishing of Buddhism in Taiwan in the future by educating and training successive generations of disciples and students.

In Mainland China in recent decades, like other religious traditions, Buddhism has seen successive waves of resurgence and repression. As sociologist Lizhu Fan and historian of religions James D. Whitehead notes, modern Chinese women may reject organized religion but acknowledge Buddhist concepts such as karmic connections (*yuanfen*) and the interdependence of cause and effect (translated as "fateful coincidences").[43] Many are suspicious of connections between religion and government, and many are also hesitant to evince any interest in religious matters at all, but in response to a perceived spiritual void following the Cultural Revolution, some are exploring religious

Figure 3.3. Nuns chanting at a temple on Mount Wutai, China. Credit: Photo by Wu Jin.

alternatives. Many Chinese women have grown up with the legend of Miaoshan, a young girl who chooses a life of renunciation over a distinguished suitor and, after being severely punished by her father, becomes a goddess. Most are also familiar with the gender transformation of the Dragon King's daughter, described in the *Lotus Sūtra*, who transformed her female body into that of a male *buddha*, illustrating the mutability and seeming irrelevance of gender distinctions in the awakened state. These legends have helped to keep the spiritual aspirations of Chinese women alive until the present day.

In the Buddhist traditions of East Asia, thousands of highly educated fully ordained nuns and millions of lay followers are genuinely committed to serving others.[44] Unlike monks and laymen, nuns are able to mix freely with the throngs of women who visit the temples and counsel them about any personal difficulties they are experiencing. They work tirelessly to uphold and preserve Buddhism by cleaning the temples, cooking vegetarian food, organizing *sūtra* recitations and other Dharma activities (such as the chanting ceremony at a temple on Mount Wutai pictured in figure 3.3), providing Buddhist education for children and adults, and promoting Buddhist arts and culture. In recent decades, many have received high levels of education and developed the confidence needed to engage in a wide range of hands-on efforts to assist the disadvantaged and transform society. Through their selfless practice, they set a high standard for those who strive to embody the Buddha's teachings.

4

Buddhist Women in Inner Asia

Buddhist texts and teachings were transmitted from India to Central Asian lands and Tibet. The process of transmission began as early as the second century CE, during the time of King Kaniṣka, who ruled over an area stretching from the Gangetic plain to Gandhāra (now part of Afghanistan and Pakistan) to Turfan (now in the People's Republic of China). Beginning in the seventh century, Buddhism traveled to Tibet over the Himalayas and, from the thirteenth century onward, moved north from Tibet to Mongolia and then to Siberia. These successive transmissions, based on orthodox Buddhist teachings derived from India, developed distinctive characteristics and traditions as they were introduced and became firmly rooted in far-flung Himalayan regions and beyond. Throughout this centuries-long process of transmission and adaptation, women devoutly practiced Buddhism and supported its cultural development. The Vajrayāna (adamantine vehicle) branch of Mahāyāna Buddhism incorporates advanced meditation practices that are described in the tantric texts that appeared in India as early as the sixth century. The Buddhist *tantras* were composed in Sanskrit in India through the twelfth century, and many texts were translated into Tibetan and Chinese after the tantric teachings were transmitted to those regions. The tantric texts are replete with numerous meditational deities (*yidam*), enlightened figures used as objects of visualization practice, including *ḍākinīs* (Tibetan: *khandroma*, lit. skygoer), female embodiments of wisdom, and *buddhas* and *bodhisattvas* in female as well as male form. For the practitioner, these *yidams* serve as ever-present reminders that sentient beings, regardless of gender, are capable of achieving the highest goal of perfect awakening. By tracing women's contributions to these unique cultural transformations, we will also discover many confluences.

Buddhist Women of Tibet

Images of Tibetan monks are a familiar sight in the media, but it is only recently that Tibetan nuns have come to popular attention. Tibetan nuns wear the same robes and live the same lifestyle as monks but have never been as numerous or visible. Today, a seismic shift is occurring, with significant changes for women everywhere, including Tibetan Buddhist cultures. As women gain new educational opportunities and confidence, they are entering monasteries in record numbers and taking their place in the world's religious imagination. In the last few decades, scholars have uncovered the stories of remarkable women in the Tibetan tradition, providing fresh insights into the practices, perspectives, and accomplishments of realized women practitioners over the centuries, up to today. Much has been lost, since women's practice has often been ignored or discounted, but the lives of a number of extraordinary women practitioners give us glimpses of the challenges women faced in gaining access to the teachings and shine light on their exceptional attainments. Women practicing Tibetan Buddhism today are the inheritors of an inspiring lineage of eminent women going back to Mahāprajāpatī[1] and Gelongma Palmo (eleventh to twelfth centuries) in India;[2] Mandāravā (eighth century) in India and Nepal;[3] Orgyan Chökyi (1675–1729) in Nepal;[4] and Yeshe Tsogyal (757–817),[5] Machig Labdrön (1055–1153),[6] Samding Dorje Palmo (1422–55),[7] Sera Khandro (1892–1940),[8] and Tāre Lhamo (1938–2003)[9] in Tibet. English readers owe a great debt of gratitude to the translators of their biographies.

The accomplishments of these extraordinary practitioners demonstrate that women are capable of achieving great spiritual heights and taking their places as teachers, translators, and spiritual mentors. Their biographies also reveal that women practitioners have encountered great challenges on the path to spiritual realization. Reading their stories reminds us of the multiple advantages that modern privileged women enjoy—literacy, leisure, confidence, independence, material resources, and access to teachers—and also reminds us of the many obstacles that hindered earlier generations of women in their quest for awakening. It is inspiring to learn about the resilience and determination that women throughout history demonstrated in their efforts to realize the fruits of Buddhist practice. While it is disheartening to learn about the many obstacles they faced, it is also encouraging that so many women were recognized for their spiritual achievements.

Prominent female figures emerge early in the history of Tibet. In its creation myth, the Tibetan people are described as being the descendants of a cave-dwelling ogress and the *bodhisattva* of compassion, Avalokiteśvara, manifest in the form of a monkey.[10] The land of Tibet itself is identified with a supine demoness who vehemently opposed the introduction of the Buddhist teachings. For Buddhism to take root in this wilderness so that the benevolent Dharma could thrive, the demoness had literally to be nailed down by the *mahāsiddha* (great adept) from India, Guru Padmāsambhāva, and dominated by the construction of thirteen Buddhist temples.[11] Once she was subdued and Buddhism began to take root in the eighth century, illustrious women practitioners began to appear. At least two of the six wives of the seventh-century Buddhist king Songtsen Gampo were earnest Buddhists: Bhṛkutī Devī from Nepal is identified with the female *bodhisattva* of health, longevity, and wisdom, White Tārā,[12] and Wencheng from China is identified with the female *bodhisattva* of virtuous activity, Green Tārā. In the eighth century, Yeshe Tsogyel became an acclaimed scholar-practitioner as well as the consort and biographer of Padmāsambhāva, the tantric master from the kingdom of Oddiyāna who is credited with establishing Buddhism in Tibet.[13] Many Vajrayāna practices focus on enlightened beings and *bodhisattvas* in female form, who are visualized, supplicated, and revered by women and men alike. Female protector deities, such as Palden Lhamo, have been continuously venerated up to the present day. In Tibetan cultures, there is also a strong tradition of female oracles who serve as mediums, often for female gods.[14]

Two women are the progenitors of unique practice lineages that are extremely popular in the Tibetan cultural sphere and beyond. The practice of *chöd* ("cutting") was developed by Machig Labdrön, a precocious female practitioner who lived in Tibet during the eleventh and twelfth centuries. After mastering the *prajñāpāramitā* (perfection of wisdom) teachings, she underwent many hardships but persevered in various tantric practices until she achieved realization. The practice of *chöd* entails visualizing oneself making offerings of one's severed body parts to meet the needs and appease the cravings of sentient beings and to cut through one's attachment and self-cherishing. Although *chöd* can be practiced by anyone, because the practice was developed by Machig Labdrön, a woman, some argue that it has special meaning for women.

The *nyung ne* fasting practice originated with an Indian princess who also lived during the eleventh and twelfth centuries. Rejecting marriage, Bhikṣuṇī Kamalā (Tibetan: Gelongma Palmo) became a nun and the abbess of a large monastery. After some years, she was afflicted by leprosy and exiled to the forest, where she had a vision of the thousand-armed Avalokiteśvara, *bodhisattva* of compassion, who gave her the *nyung ne* practice to cure her leprosy. The two-day practice entails observing eight vows, chanting, and prostrations, with fasting and silence on alternate days. Although *nyung ne* can also be practiced by anyone, women have become especially accomplished and enthusiastic participants. In towns and villages throughout the length and breadth of the Himalayas and the steppes of Mongolia and Russia, women gather devotedly for *nyung ne* practice on special days and months in the lunar calendar. *Chöd* and *nyung ne* have become mainstays of Buddhist practice wherever Tibetan Buddhist influence has reached, from the Indian Himalayas to Siberia and around the world. One reason for the popularity of these practices among women is that *chöd* and *nyung ne* can be practiced individually and in small groups, in homes and village temples, outside the male-dominated religious hierarchies and institutions that characterize the major Tibetan Buddhist lineages.

Even so, despite the existence of illustrious female practitioners, enlightened exemplars, protector deities, and oracles in Tibetan-speaking societies, gender inequalities are very obvious. Women are reminded of their alleged inferiority every time they hear the word "woman" (*skye dman*), meaning "lower birth." Women often internalize feelings of inadequacy that are reinforced in the social sphere, including religious hierarchies. Whether ignored or excluded, women are largely missing from the historical record after the eleventh and twelfth centuries.[15] Throughout history, they have also been systematically excluded from learning institutions and the upper echelons of power in all four extant schools of Tibetan Buddhism: Nyingma, Kagyu, Sakya, and Gelug. Women are allowed to attend large public Buddhist teachings, but until recently, few had access to formal Buddhist education, and consequently most understand only the broad outlines of the Buddha's teachings.

Women have not had easy access to Buddhist practice lineages or retreat opportunities. Unless a woman was born into or married into a family of scholars or skilled practitioners, opportunities to receive oral transmissions and in-depth instructions on Buddhist teachings and practices were few. Even being born into or marrying into a family of scholars or advanced practitioners did not guarantee that a woman would gain access to Buddhist learning or in-depth practice opportunities. As can be seen from the biographies of realized women practitioners, a woman who entered into an intimate relationship with a male tantric practitioner outside of marriage often faced obstacles, risks, and scorn. A female renunciant faced similar difficulties and discouragement from both her family and society, which preferred to see women in domestic roles. Monasteries for women were few, remote, and poorly supported. The Tibetan term *lama* was used only for males. This is still generally the case even today.

The good news is that women have proven their dedication to the Dharma through sheer determination. In the last few decades, more women in Tibet, Nepal, India, and elsewhere have completed intensive retreats than ever before. As educational opportunities have opened up, women have applied themselves diligently to mastering Buddhist philosophy and emerged triumphant. Female Buddhist scholars in the Nyingma and Kagyu traditions have earned *khenmo* degrees and are being recognized as fully qualified teachers, especially for other women. In December 2016, in a celebration held at Drepung Monastery in South India and attended by His Holiness the Fourteenth Dalai Lama, Tenzin Gyatso (b. 1935), a crowd of thousands applauded the first twenty women in Buddhist history to earn the *geshe* degree, the highest scholarly achievement in Buddhist philosophy in the Tibetan tradition, an accomplishment that was inconceivable just thirty years ago (see figure 4.1). Ten more nuns were awarded the *geshe* degree in 2018 at a ceremony held at Kopan Nunnery outside Kathmandu in conjunction with the annual intermonastic debate tournament attended by more than six hundred nuns from nine monasteries in India and Nepal. Women throughout the Buddhist world are becoming respected teachers, translators, counselors, and spiritual mentors. With the encouragement and generosity of kind teachers and benefactors around the world, women practicing in the Vajrayāna Buddhist tradition are beginning to take their place in the pantheon of Buddhist masters.

Figure 4.1. The first nuns in the Tibetan tradition to be awarded the *geshema* degree in Buddhist philosophy, at Loseling Monastery, Bylakuppe, India, in 2016. Credit: Photo by Karma Lekshe Tsomo.

In the Tibetan tradition, most nuns take the thirty-six precepts of a novice, just like novice monks. These precepts are the same as the ten novice precepts of the Theravāda tradition, except that some precepts have been subdivided. A lineage of fully ordained monks (*bhikṣus*) was established in Tibet during the eighth century and has flourished until today, but there is no equivalent lineage of fully ordained nuns (*bhikṣuṇīs*) and no historical evidence that one was ever established. In the absence of *bhikṣuṇīs* to conduct ordinations, monks conduct the novice ordinations of women but do not generally take an active role in the support or training of the nuns, nor do the monks perform *bhikṣuṇī* ordinations. Whether because of the nuns' novice status or their lack of education and training, until recently Tibetan nuns stayed quietly in the background, doing retreats, reciting prayers, performing rituals, and sharing the Dharma with those who come to them for counsel. In recent years, however, Tibetan nuns are taking new roles and seeking new opportunities that have begun to put them in the spotlight. Some nuns have taken active roles in political activities and in the resistance against Chinese Communist rule in Tibet.[16]

Luminary Figures

Much research remains to be done to uncover and translate biographies and fragments of information about women in all periods of Tibetan history. Meanwhile, selected narratives about eminent female figures in Tibetan Buddhist history provide background for understanding the lives of women in the Tibetan diaspora in the modern period, which began with the takeover of Tibet by the People's Republic of China in the second half of the twentieth century. Among the most well-known nuns of earlier centuries was Samding Dorje Phagmo, who was not just one individual but a lineage of teachers that extended from the fifteenth century until the present day. Unlike illustrious figures such as Machig Labdrön, Orgyan Chökyi, and Jetsun Lochen Rinpoche (1865–1951), who were singular figures, the lineage of Samding Dorje Phagmo extends over many lifetimes, as one woman after another has been recognized as the rebirth of her predecessor. The Dorje Phagmo lineage of luminary women masters, one of the very few documented lineages of female *tülkus*, began with Chökyi Dronma (1422–55/65). Looking closely at her life from a feminist perspective, we find many remarkable features. Born as a princess in the region of Nyemo in Central Tibet, she wanted to become a nun when she was young but encountered considerable opposition, from both her natal family and her prospective in-laws. Eventually, she was allowed to become a nun, albeit only after she had married and given birth to a daughter. She was supported in her decision to receive the novice precepts by her teacher, the renowned *lama* Bodong Chogle Namgyal (1376–1461), who was reportedly very sympathetic to women. It is said that "he established new rituals for nuns that revitalized Buddhist traditions from India" and "encouraged Chökyi Dronma to initiate performance of ritual dances at a time when female roles were usually performed by monks."[17] According to her biography and information culled from other texts, Chökyi Dronma traveled freely in Tibet throughout her short lifetime. Accompanied by a close female companion, she was revered by the local population everywhere she went. According to her biography, she faced certain "social and cultural challenges" but was skilled at overcoming them.[18] The biography mentions that she was fully ordained as a *bhikṣuṇī*, but there is no documentation to verify a living lineage of full ordination for women in Tibet at that time. She is said to have "devoted herself to the recruitment and training of nuns" and was especially concerned about the paucity of education available to nuns, which was due to the patriarchal nature of the male monastic establishment.

After the passing of her *lama*, Chökyi Dronma mediated disputes regarding the distribution of his relics.[19] She was responsible for editing and reproducing the entire corpus of his teachings, so we can surmise that she was highly literate—no mean feat, considering the difficulty of written Tibetan—which was quite unusual for a woman then or even now. In facilitating this project, she produced "some of the earliest examples of printing produced in Tibet."[20] Chökyi Dronma was very successful at raising funds to complete this project and also helped to raise funds for the accomplished master Chung Riwoche's famous project to build a *stūpa* (reliquary or burial mound that contains sacred objects) in northern Lato. She was keen to construct water channels in Palmo Chöding to support a learning center. Although this project was never fully realized, it indicates the expanse of her vision and her intense determination, which was remarkable for a woman of her era. In her spiritual practice and teaching style, Chökyi Dronma was reportedly "an adept of the tradition of the 'crazy saints,'" unconcerned about her physical comfort or appearance. It is said that she "used transgressive behavior to convey essential spiritual messages," teaching that "appearances and conventions" are unreliable indicators in "assessing spiritual value."[21] At a time when women, especially princesses, were expected to maintain elaborate, socially acceptable standards of beauty, this utter disregard for appearances was code for spiritual realization.

Another source of information about Chökyi Dronma is the biography of her teacher, Bodong Chogle Namgyal. The visibility of women in this biography suggests that women had a hand in writing it. Social anthropologist Hildegard Diemberger notes that women are "mentioned by name, whereas it is much more common in Tibetan sources to find nuns and nunneries mentioned generically, if at all."[22] The biography appears to be the collaborative work of multiple authors, in a time when single-authored works by monks were the norm, suggesting that Chökyi Dronma's transgressive tendencies extended to her scholarship. Her collaborative approach to writing may be a concrete example of the "soteriological inclusiveness" of Buddhist liberation, meaning that women were regarded as equally capable of achieving enlightenment. In the Tibetan cultural sphere, such a disinterest in personal acclaim is taken as a mark of greatness. After all, she was assumed to be no ordinary person, but rather a recognized embodiment of an awakened being, Dorje Palmo (Sanskrit: Vajrayoginī).

Freedom in Exile

In 1950, the Tibetan Buddhist world experienced a cataclysmic shift as the People's Liberation Army of the People's Republic of China invaded Tibet from the east. For the next nine years, His Holiness the Fourteenth Dalai Lama and his government attempted to dialogue with Chinese leaders to ensure the security of Tibet and its unique cultural heritage, but ultimately all attempts were unsuccessful. A Tibetan uprising ensued in 1959, after which His Holiness the Dalai Lama and an estimated one hundred thousand Tibetans fled to Nepal and India. In the widespread popular resistance to the Chinese Communist occupation of Tibet, some nuns emerged as respected leaders. Many were arrested and tortured, while many others fled to India and Nepal in search of religious freedom. Filmmaker Ellen Bruno's documentary, *Satya: A Prayer for the Enemy* (1992), depicts the hardships that Tibetan Buddhist nuns have endured under Chinese Communist rule, while filmmaker Paul Wagner's *Windhorse* (1998) dramatizes the aftermath of these tragic events. Because nuns have no families of their own to support and protect, they have courageously voiced their opposition to religious oppression by the People's Republic of China and have frequently been jailed and tortured for their efforts. As a result of political and religious restrictions, many nuns have attempted the long treacherous journey from Tibet to Nepal, frequently traveling from Nepal to India especially to see His Holiness the Dalai Lama in Dharamsala. The heartbreaking stories they tell are a testament to their heroism and their devotion to their Buddhist beliefs. Many suffer lingering posttraumatic stress disorders as a result of rape, imprisonment, harassment, torture, and surveillance in the People's Republic of China.

Since the 1980s, Tibetan women have made substantial progress toward gender equity in the field of education, both secular and religious, in Tibet and in the diaspora.[23] The increasing availability of general education for girls in Nepal and India parallels a global trend toward greater educational opportunities for nuns. These new opportunities have raised educational standards for girls and women across a broad spectrum of society. Coeducational institutions, such as the Tibetan Central Schools, the Tibetan Children's Village, and Tibetan Homes in India and Nepal, have made education available to tens of thousands of Tibetan girls and young women, but there have been hindrances along the way for laywomen as well as nuns. As recently as the 1980s, the highly regarded Central Institute for Higher Tibetan Studies, in Sarnath, near Varanasi, India, did not admit women students, and even now a quota is imposed to limit the number of female students admitted each year. Even so, because the Central Institute for Higher Tibetan Studies is an accredited institution of higher learning that prepares students to become teachers, it is significant that opportunities have opened up for more laywomen and nuns to study there. Many more female students, most of whom are not able to pass the entrance exam because they never received secondary schooling, live around the Central Institute and study privately.

Since 1976, despite circumstances of dire poverty and physical and psychological dislocation, a few monasteries for Tibetan and Himalayan women have been established in India and Nepal. The hardships of adjusting to a new climate and cultural environment have been offset by the opportunity to meet and receive teachings from His Holiness the Fourteenth Dalai Lama and other renowned Tibetan Buddhist teachers. In exile, Tibetan nuns not only have the opportunity to practice their faith freely and without fear but also have gained access to educational opportunities that were previously rare or nonexistent in Tibet. Since the 1980s, whenever security along the border between Tibet and Nepal has eased, Tibetan refugees have arrived in India on pilgrimage. Once there, they have sought out public teachings, such as the Kalachakra empowerment conferred by His Holiness, and teachings from other *lamas* as well.

In addition to those nuns who had received novice ordination in Tibet, many young women also became nuns after arriving in exile and meeting the Dalai Lama. For many of these young women, the choice to pursue a religious vocation is a natural response to their newly found freedom and the lessons learned through suffering and hardship. After gaining insight into the fleeting nature of human life, they come to see the Buddhist teachings as representing a profoundly meaningful way of life. Other young Tibetan and Himalayan women, growing up in India, come to the same realization through their encounters with modern secular life that promises happiness but does not always lead to fulfillment. For most of these women, the decision to enter monastic life is not the result of encouragement from their families or society. Instead, the decision to devote their lives to Dharma practice is a personal choice to make the most meaningful use of the human opportunity to achieve awakening. The decision to become a nun may also reflect a wish to avoid the potential problems of domestic life. Many nuns also feel a deep commitment to help sustain Tibetan Buddhist culture, now facing the threat of extinction in its homeland. Their commitment is spurred by the sad reality that Tibet's precious Buddhist cultural heritage may ultimately be best preserved outside of occupied Tibet.

More than 1,290 Tibetan nuns now live in exile in India and Nepal. Some nuns who have escaped from Tibet still suffer the long-term psychological and physical effects of the sexual abuse, rape, torture, imprisonment, and surveillance that they experienced under Chinese Communist rule.[24] Since 1987, with international assistance, the Tibetan Nun's Project, the Jamyang Foundation, and other organizations have worked to establish monasteries for women and provide medical services, food, housing, and education for the influx of refugee nuns from Tibet into Nepal and India. They have been joined by many young women from the Indian Himalayan border regions (Arunachal Pradesh, Kinnaur, Ladakh, Lahaul, Spiti, and Zangskar), Bhutan, Mongolia,

Figure 4.2. Buddhist laywomen from the Mon-Tawang region of Arunachal Pradesh, India. Credit: Photo by Olivier Adam.

Nepal, and elsewhere (see figure 4.2).[25] The documentary *Becoming a Woman in Zanskar* (2007), by director Jean-Michel Corillion, dramatizes the uncertainties entailed in the courageous choice to become a nun in the Himalayas. Although ethnographic studies about the lives of Himalayan nuns are rare, Kim Gutschow has published a book about nuns in Zangskar and Linda LaMacchia has written about nuns in Kinnaur.[26]

Buddhist Studies and Full Ordination for Women

In Himalayan cultures and societies, where monastics have primarily been monks, the road to ordination for women has been arduous. Many fundamental disparities remain between the circumstances of nuns and monks, especially regarding education, access, and financial support, and efforts to minimize these disparities are ongoing. While many young nuns born in Nepal and India have had the benefit of some public education, most nuns born in Tibet had little or no formal education prior to escaping their homeland and have had to struggle to make up for lost time. In the past thirty years, nuns in the Tibetan tradition have made significant strides academically, particularly in the study of philosophy, an area that was previously not open to them. Several nunneries in Nepal and India now offer intensive educational programs focused on philosophical studies. Other nunneries offer Buddhist studies programs that integrate basic Buddhist studies, ritual practices, and intensive meditation retreats. Nuns in India and Nepal now have the opportunity to hone their intellectual reasoning skills by competing in the intramural philosophical debate tournaments for nuns that have been held annually since 1990—tournaments modeled after the famous Jang Kunchö debate tournaments that were organized for monks at Tibet's most prestigious monastic universities every winter in Lhasa.

Having access to philosophical studies is a key factor to consider when assessing gender equity between nuns and monks in Tibetan culture. In Tibet, nuns were traditionally excluded from Buddhist studies programs at the key monastic universities of Deprung, Ganden, and Sera, which were the exclusive domain of monks. Since these were the institutions that provided the best Buddhist studies program and granted the prestigious *geshe* degree, it was a distinction that previously could be earned only by men. Since 1987, the situation has radically changed and new pathways for the systematic study of philosophy and debate have opened to women. Although facilities are limited, nuns in India and Nepal now have access to educational opportunities that allow them to progress toward the *geshe* degree. In December 2017, after decades of intensive studies, twenty nuns successfully passed their examinations and were awarded the *geshe* degree by His Holiness the Fourteenth Dalai Lama at Drepung Monastery in exile in Karnataka, India. This historical achievement marked a major step in achieving gender parity in the Tibetan Buddhist tradition. Women now have the chance to demonstrate that they are fully capable of excelling in Buddhist studies in an environment that has rarely recognized women as *lamas* (religious teachers) or *tülkus* (recognized rebirths of accomplished beings). A few women have been recognized as *lamas* and *tülkus*. Contemporary examples of recognized female *tülkus* are Khandro Tsering Chodrön (1929–2011), the wife of Jamyang Khyentse Chökyi Lodrö (1893–1959), and Khandro Rinpoche

(b. 1967), the daughter of Mindrolling Trichen Jurme Kunzang Wangyal (1930–2008), who teaches internationally.[27]

Buddhist education need not be a formal pursuit. Many Tibetan nuns devote themselves to ritual studies in small shrines, retreat centers, and monasteries throughout the Tibetan cultural sphere. Many nuns also pursue meditation and ritual practices in solitude, in caves and isolated locations throughout the Himalayan region. Although nuns who practice quietly in the mountains receive little attention, their religious practice is a significant contribution to women's empowerment and, they believe, to peace in the world. Greater attention is now being paid to the religious lives of women, and the biographies of exceptional women practitioners in the Tibetan tradition are increasingly being researched, translated, and published.[28]

Nuns are now able to participate in ceremonies and events previously reserved solely for monks, such as constructing sand *maṇḍalas*, performing sacred dances, debating philosophy, and participating in the Great Prayer Festival (Monlam). However, full ordination for women remains a controversial matter in Tibetan Buddhism. The controversy centers on questions about the transmission of the *bhikṣuṇī* (Tibetan: *gelongma*) lineage. There is no evidence that the *gelongma* lineage was ever transmitted to Tibet from India in an officially sanctioned way, and so at present there is no lineage of fully ordained nuns in the Tibetan tradition. Tibetan nuns receive the thirty-six precepts of a novice nun (Sanskrit: *śrāmaṇerika*; Tibetan: *getsulma*) and are considered part of the *saṅgha*, but their status is significantly lower than that of a fully ordained monk (Sanskrit: *bhikṣu*; Tibetan: *gelong*).

Strategies for introducing the *bhikṣuṇī* lineage are now being considered seriously. One possibility is for Tibetan nuns to receive full ordination through the unbroken lineages transmitted from India and Sri Lanka to China, Korea, and Vietnam. Many Tibetan scholars understand the *vinaya* texts to say that a quorum of ten *bhikṣus* and a quorum of twelve *bhikṣuṇīs*, including two additional witnesses, is required to confer the *bhikṣuṇī* precepts and that *bhikṣus* alone cannot administer a full ordination ceremony for nuns. If this is the case, it is possible that the first cohort of Tibetan nuns could receive the ordination from fully ordained nuns and monks from Korea, Taiwan, or Vietnam. Another possible solution is for Tibetan nuns to be ordained by Tibetan monks alone, a procedure that has been used in Korea, Taiwan, and Vietnam without much controversy. Yet a third solution is a combined approach in which nuns from Korea, Taiwan, Vietnam, or perhaps together, could conduct the *bhikṣuṇī* ordination alongside Tibetan monks. With the backing of His Holiness the Fourteenth Dalai Lama and senior *bhikṣus*, any of these solutions could be implemented. From recent enthusiastic discussions on this issue, it appears that support is growing for establishing a lineage of *bhikṣuṇīs* in the Tibetan Buddhist tradition.

The Central Tibetan Administration (Tibetan Government in Exile), based in Dharamsala, India, has yet to sanction officially any of these possible solutions. His Holiness the Fourteenth Dalai Lama has expressed his personal desire to see the *bhikṣuṇī* lineage established within the Tibetan tradition. However, he states that the issue must be put before a senior *saṅgha* council and that he lacks the authority to make the decision alone. To help resolve the issue, His Holiness the Dalai Lama has repeatedly called for an international conference with representatives of all the major Buddhist traditions to examine the fine points of Buddhist monastic law and work toward a consensus on the matter. He has also raised the issue at several meetings of high-ranking *lamas*. In-depth studies of the monastic texts have been undertaken to compare the *bhikṣuṇī* precepts and the procedures for receiving the *bhikṣuṇī* ordination in the Chinese and Tibetan Buddhist monastic traditions. Scholars are also investigating whether the existing *bhikṣuṇī* lineages have been transmitted in an unbroken lineage from the time of Buddha Śākyamuni until today, a daunting task. Meanwhile, opinion is divided. On one side, opponents assert that the full ordination of nuns in the Tibetan tradition cannot be conferred, because the requisite quorum of fully ordained Tibetan nuns is unavailable. This assertion ignores the fact that more than sufficient numbers of nuns practicing in the Tibetan tradition have already received full ordination in the Chinese, Korean, or Vietnamese traditions. On the other side, proponents assert that the *bhikṣuṇī* ordination can proceed on the grounds that Buddha Śākyamuni initially ordained nuns without a quorum of fully ordained nuns and he thus set a precedent for this procedure.

While the controversy awaits resolution, Tibetan and Himalayan nuns continue to establish new nunneries and retreat centers in India and Nepal. These nunneries function largely autonomously, with the nuns responsible for their own governance, maintenance, and support. Financial support, in the form of donations from the local community or from abroad, is critically important in helping nuns establish and maintain their nunneries and retreat centers. This is a tremendous challenge; even in the area of financial support, nuns generally experience discrimination, because the laypeople prefer to support monks. Despite these obstacles, nuns remain dedicated to Dharma practice and to the preservation of their precious Buddhist cultural heritage. As Tibetan nuns continue their practices and studies, they chip away at previous restrictions and outdated notions about the inferiority of women. They have become role models for women in Tibet and throughout the Himalayan region, actively promoting the Buddha's egalitarian philosophy through social engagement, such as counseling women according to the Dharma and helping develop their communities.

The intensive scholastic approach to textual study using the method of philosophical debate or dialectics is not the only way to study Buddhism in the Tibetan tradition. An alternative method, employed in many Kagyu and Nyingma study centers (Tibetan: *shedra*), requires students to reiterate the previous day's lesson in front of their teachers and peers. This approach to scriptural studies, in which students are selected at random to expound publicly the meaning of the text, has the advantage of encouraging students to study well and also gives them teaching experience. Other Buddhist teaching styles involve personal interactions between teachers and students. For example, the "direct transmission" teaching method of Dzogchen (Great Perfection), which is typical of tantric instruction in Tibetan Buddhism, entails an intimate relationship between master and disciple. Women may be disadvantaged in establishing such relationships because of their gender. Because the sexual symbolism that occurs in the tantric texts is liable to misinterpretation, these teachings are generally transmitted secretly. Consequently, women may encounter more obstacles in gaining access to great masters and advanced teachings. Training more women as teachers in the various Tibetan lineages is therefore an urgent concern.

Tracing the Footsteps of Women in Bhutan

Buddhism has been influential in Bhutan since the seventh century, when it was introduced to this remote mountainous region by the Tibetan king Songtsan Gampo (r. 627–649). Since its unification by *lama* Ngawang Namgyal (1594–1651) in the seventeenth century, Bhutan has been a Buddhist kingdom, officially belonging to the Drukpa Kagyu school, with strong Nyingma influence and pockets of pre-Buddhist Bön practice. Today, there are more than two thousand monasteries in the land, including twenty-six for nuns. Although the history of Bhutanese Buddhism is dominated by male figures, women draw inspiration from both female and male *buddhas*, *bodhisattvas*, meditational deities (*yidams*), realized beings, and dedicated practitioners. In spite of the Buddha's declaration that women have the potential to attain liberation, most women face limitations in the religious pursuit and many still pray to be reborn in a male body, which they believe will make it easier to achieve realization. Nuns frequently reference women acclaimed as great practitioners, including historical figures such as Gelongma Palmo and more recent figures such as the venerated nun Loponma Paldon (b. 1926), who served as the abbess of Jachung Karmo, a nunnery a few hours' walk from Punakha. Sadly, the stories of illustrious female practitioners in Bhutan have rarely been documented.

Some assert that spiritual awakening is beyond gender distinctions. Once beings have achieved realization, it matters little whether they are female or male. In the realm of everyday reality, however, conditions for religious learning and cultivation on the path are very different for women and men. Becoming a full-time monastic practitioner is still applauded for men, but often discouraged for women, who are assumed to be more suited to domestic life and ill equipped for the rigors of renunciation and retreat. If a woman perseveres in her quest for spiritual attainment, she will find it more difficult to acquire the material requisites she needs than if she were a man.

Education opportunities for women in Bhutan have certainly improved since the 1980s, but the improvements have largely been in secular education, supported by the government and conducted in English. Although there are more study programs for nuns than before, most are informal and weakened by the scarcity of qualified teachers, learning resources, and government support. It is said that no sincere practitioner in Bhutan will lack sufficient food, but still there is a lack of systematic education for nuns, and therefore many nuns have gone to India for Dharma studies. Recent decades have seen a marked change, however. Nuns in twenty-six monasteries in Bhutan are now getting more education and are much more likely than before to be invited to perform rituals, recite texts, and explain the Buddha's teachings for the benefit of the lay community. Nuns serve the laypeople humbly, without expecting recognition or remuneration, and are appreciated for their diligence and devotion.

Increasingly, nuns are taking more visible roles in Bhutanese society. In earlier years, it was common for nuns to simply keep their hair short, observe the five precepts of a layperson, and wear a yellow *kira*, the traditional dress of Bhutan. Since the 1980s, however, it has become more common for nuns to shave their heads, receive the novice precepts, and wear maroon monastic robes. In 2014, the Bhutan Nuns Foundation[29] organized the first large-scale novice ordination ceremony held in Bhutan. Conducted by some of the most high-ranking monks in the country and attended by 140 nuns from seven nunneries, the ordination was held at Sangchhen Dorji Lhendrup Nunnery in Punakha. Recognizing the need and encouraged by Her Majesty Tshering Yangdon Wangchuck (b. 1959), the Queen Mother, there are presently initiatives afoot to make Buddhist education more broadly available to Bhutanese Buddhist women, especially nuns.

Women in the Revival of Buddhism in Mongolia

There is little mention of women in the Buddhist histories of Mongolia. We do find occasional references to devout noblewomen who patronized Buddhist activities, such as Sain Uzesgelent, consort of Kubilai Khan (1215–94), who encouraged him to follow the Sakya *lama* Drogön Chögyal Phagpa (1235–80) as his spiritual teacher, and Tsogt Dari, who in the nineteenth century helped found a temple known as Duinkhor Datsan in what is today Ulaanbaatar. The powerful Mongolian Queen Jönggen (1551–1612) played key roles in returning the remains of the Third Dalai Lama to Tibet for cremation, selecting the Fourth Dalai Lama, and commissioning the translation of the Kangyur, the Tibetan Buddhist canon, into Mongolian.[30] Although all the major monasteries in Mongolia were reserved for male *lamas*, women have been faithful devotees and generous supporters of these monasteries for centuries.

Throughout decades of Soviet persecution and oppression of Buddhism, beginning in the 1930s, women practitioners in Mongolia privately maintained their spiritual values and many observed the five lay Buddhist precepts of not killing, stealing, engaging in sexual misconduct, lying, and using intoxicants. The political and economic liberalizations that followed the breakup of the U.S.S.R. in the early 1990s and Mongolian independence from the Soviet Union ushered in a cultural renaissance, including a revival of interest in Buddhism, but these greater freedoms have also opened the door to an influx of competing values and religious groups that pose challenges to traditional institutions.

A unique facet of Mongolian Buddhist women's history is the recognition of specific women as being emanations of Tārā, enlightenment in female form, known as the "savioress."[31] The blessings of these revered women are sought by devotees from near and far, who bring offerings and seek protection, healing, and advice on personal and spiritual matters. Later in life, after their husbands pass away, many Mongolian women shave their heads and focus on Buddhist devotional practices, such as the recitation of prayers and mantras. There are many stories of women with high spiritual attainments, including some who are skilled healers and exorcists, but there has been no trace of formally ordained nuns in Mongolia until recently.

Since 1990, when Mongolia reasserted its independence with a nonviolent democratic revolution, more than two hundred *datsans* (monasteries and temples) have been rebuilt or newly established. Among them, several were established by and for women, including Tugsbayasgalant Center of Mongolian Buddhist Women, Narkhajid Monastery, and Dulmaalin Monastery. During the daytime, dozens of laywomen and nuns diligently chant and perform Buddhist ritual services together, frequently joined by visitors. In the evening, the laywomen return to their families, while the nuns reside in the monastery full time. Donations from lay adherents support the functioning of the *datsans*.

Many Mongolian Buddhist women are dedicated practitioners of *chöd*, the ritual practice of generosity that entails offering one's vital organs and other body parts, in imagination, to relieve the sufferings of sentient beings. As we saw earlier, with roots in Indian tradition, the practice is generally traced to the accomplished Tibetan *yoginī*, Machig Labdrön. Although there has been little systematic analysis of Mongolian *chöd* traditions, two popular lineages of *chöd* are taught by Gelugpa teachers: the Ganden oral lineage and the Dākinī oral lineage. These *chöd* lineages have been passed from teacher to disciple and often practiced in relative secrecy outside formal monastic settings. The practice is lively, as each of the practitioners plays a hand drum (*ḍamaru*) in unison with the others. In recent years, an annual gathering of practitioners known as Chöd Monlam has been held at Ganden Monastery in Ulaanbaatar.

Women in the Buddhist Republics of Russia

The experiences of Buddhist women within the Soviet Union (1922–91) have been similar in many ways to those of women in Mongolia. Buddhism was repressed and nearly destroyed under Joseph Stalin (1878–1953), who ruled the U.S.S.R. from 1922 to 1953, and decades of Soviet control. Today, a struggling resurgence is underway in all three Buddhist republics of the Russian Federation: Buryatia, Kalmykia, and Tuva. The transmission of Buddhism to these regions began with Mongolian and Tibetan *lamas* who propagated the teachings among the Mongol tribes across the steppes as early as the fourteenth century. In time, Buddhism evolved its own unique character in these regions, often in dialogue and competition with indigenous shamanic traditions. During the past century, the competing ideologies of Communism and secularism have posed even greater challenges, yet Buddhist values and religious traditions have endured and are reemerging with unexpected vitality.

As in Mongolia, monastic training in Buryatia, Kalmykia, and Tuva was closed to women. Even a casual glance reveals that women held a subordinate status in religious contexts. No matter how free the nomadic women may have been, the subordinate status of women was mirrored in other spheres of society. Yet while the visible, male-dominated Buddhist institutions were readily crushed during the Soviet era, women managed to continue their devotions surreptitiously.[32] For all its injustices and restrictions, Communist ideology, and the social structures it produced, was a step forward for women in terms of opportunities for education, political representation, and economic independence. These egalitarian opportunities never applied to religious structures, however, and Buddhist monasteries have remained bastions of male privilege up to the present day. If gender is performative,[33] then male dominance in religious education, rituals, and power structures makes it clear that the stage is set for men's achievement of enlightenment, with women cast in supportive roles.

In recent years, attitudes have begun to shift as a new generation of well-educated, socially liberated women has begun to take an interest in the Buddhist teachings, particularly ethics and psychology.[34] Today, Buddhist women in the Russian Federation have access to popular Buddhist literature, academic Buddhist studies, and many public teachings and activities, so the future looks bright. As these women become more involved in Buddhism, however, they may begin to question the asymmetry of gender ratios in the religious status quo. Just as in other parts of the world, if the Buddhist teachings do not offer the same benefits to women as to men, modern-thinking women will naturally question their exclusion and subordination, and make a hasty retreat, losing interest in a seemingly arcane and rigged system. To date, there are only four Buddhist nuns in the whole of the Russian Federation; there are no monasteries where female seekers can live a monastic lifestyle and nowhere in the country where they can receive Buddhist education and training. Nevertheless, women in the Buddhist republics of the Russian Federation now have greater opportunities than ever before in secular life and are increasingly attracted to the philosophy and methods purveyed by their own spiritual heritage. Women from families and areas of the federation that are not traditionally Buddhist are also showing interest in Buddhist ideas and practices, fueling a need for qualified teachers and more materials for learning about Buddhism in Russia. Hopefully, with perseverance and insight, Russian Buddhists will be able to address these needs and begin to redress the gender imbalance in Buddhism by encouraging women to take teaching and leadership roles.

Enlightened Transformation

The diverse Buddhist traditions of the extensive sphere of Vajrayāna cultural influence emerged from common sources in India, spread through Tibet and beyond, and developed along unique cultural pathways, all beneficiaries of the Mahāyāna Buddhist path to spiritual awakening. The experiences of women in these Buddhist societies are a microcosm of this diversity, but the analogy is imperfect. The Buddhist goal of awakening is portrayed as a concrete eventuality for all sentient beings, not simply an abstraction, yet women in Vajrayāna Buddhist communities are not adequately represented in formal religious institutions. Vajrayāna theory tantalizes practitioners with the promise of awakening "in this very body, in this very life," yet this promise is difficult for women to realize without adequate resources for fulfilling that potential. Few Vajrayāna institutions sustain the Buddha's affirmation of women's potential for awakening; for example, no women have ever been admitted to either the Gyümé or Gyütö tantric colleges, now relocated from Tibet to India, which are exclusively male, and some tantric practices and consecrated spaces are off-limits to women. The contradiction is even more glaring in the modern context, when the obstacles of religious life for women stand side by side with the opportunities open to women in the secular world. Perhaps, it may be argued, Buddhist women are content with their lives of devotion and moral virtue, and do not require the same cumbersome organizational structures as male religious adepts. Perhaps women can practice just as well at home, without renouncing their families and the comforts of domestic life. Perhaps women can achieve the highest spiritual goal without launching a movement to overhaul the delicate monastic institutions that have been so painstakingly reconstructed after years of persecution by the People's Republic of China and the U.S.S.R.

These are questions for women in the Buddhist communities of the Vajrayāna Buddhist cultural sphere to consider among themselves. The researcher can only point out the obvious de facto exclusion of women from Buddhism's highest religious institutions in these countries. This exclusion is not random but rather part of a patriarchal fabric that has been in place in most societies for a very long time. What continues to surprise is the striking contradiction between the theoretical equality of women embedded in the Buddha's egalitarian teachings, on one hand, and the persistent exclusion and subordination of women at all levels of society, on the other. That contradiction is at the heart of much suffering and injustice, and women's theoretical equality is often used to mask very real social inequities and exploitation. Since women and men are equal in Buddhism, what is the problem?

The Buddha's social vision indisputably brought constructive changes for women in the religious communities he established. In addition to affirming women's equal potential for enlightenment, he is credited with providing women with alternatives to domesticity by establishing the order of nuns, the *bhikṣuṇī saṅgha*. In view of the gender inequalities prevalent in South Asian society at the time of the Buddha, these initiatives were significant departures from the status quo. Nonetheless, the *vinaya* texts that regulate Buddhist monastic communities were themselves shaped by patriarchal attitudes and reinforced women's subordination to monks. Successive generations of Buddhist women have been influenced and subordinated by the patriarchal assumptions embedded in these texts. Although Buddhism's history of male dominance has not prevented any number of women from achieving high levels of spiritual attainment, many Buddhist women throughout history had little or no access to education, ordination, or the resources to develop their potential, and few emerged as religious leaders. An understanding of the inequalities inherent in the codes that regulate monastic life is therefore critical for a feminist assessment of the traditions. In a world where traditional assumptions about women are being reassessed, such a study is long overdue. The relevant issue is not only the extent to which the texts support or hinder women but also the practical matter of how to transform Buddhist institutions along the lines of gender equity and social justice.

5

Buddhist Women in the West

As should be clear by now, Buddhism is not a singular tradition but a collection of traditions that reflect the evolution and adaptation of the Buddha's teachings as they spread for twenty-five hundred years across the countries of Asia. As these teachings were translated and integrated into the languages and cultures of each new land, they retained a core of key concepts while transforming others. As the imported ideas were assimilated, Buddhist art and architecture morphed as they were influenced by local aesthetics. Today in the West, the liturgies may be chanted in English and the altars sprinkled with chocolates, with authentically Buddhist sentiments expressed in the local idiom. As the traditions adapt, one notable change is the increasing prominence of women.

These days, women are playing significant roles in transmitting and transplanting Buddhism in countries outside of Asia—in North and South America, Europe, Australia, New Zealand, and elsewhere. Women have been active as teachers, translators, and counselors, and have also done networking and assumed other important responsibilities in the spread and integration of Buddhism in new lands. A number of articles, books, and videos have documented the lives and experiences of Western Buddhist women, and international conferences have served as places for them to speak about their own unique experiences of Buddhist practice.[1] Workshops, such as those held at the Sakyadhita conferences, give women opportunities for interactive, experiential learning (see figure 5.1). A multitude of books present their personal interpretations of Buddhist teachings.[2] Understanding women's involvement brings into focus some key issues in the complex process of adopting and adapting Buddhism in non-Asian cultures.

Buddhism is well known for its adaptability, which has enabled it to adjust to local beliefs and customs. The current transmission of Buddhism to Western countries is an ongoing process of assimilation similar to that of Buddhism's transmission to China in the fourth

Figure 5.1. Buddhist women at a workshop at the 14th Sakyadhita International Conference on Buddhist Women held in Yogyakarta, Indonesia, in 2015. Credit: Photo by Olivier Adam.

century. The challenge of introducing a highly developed intellectual tradition into cultures that already have their own intellectual traditions involves drawing connections between analogous or seemingly analogous concepts and making the appropriate adjustments. Sometimes the acculturation process requires so many accommodations in interpretation that one might question whether the resulting interpolations can legitimately be called Buddhism.

The transmission of Buddhist traditions to the West has created a complex terrain. Each variant tradition of Buddhist thought and practice transmits its own unique cultural values and mores together with rituals and iconography to new countries. Each phase of transmission is mediated through the translation of words and ideas by people whose levels of education and language abilities vary, as do their proficiency and experience in Buddhist practice. Each instance of transmission is received by equally varied students. The teachings and practices of these various traditions are evaluated and adapted by different people in individual ways. For example, meditation and practical Buddhist methods for managing anger, resolving disputes, achieving happiness, and developing peace of mind were among the first practices to gain currency in North America. Some other aspects of Buddhism, such as ritual and devotion, appeal to only a segment of the population and are flatly rejected by others. Egalitarian sensibilities are rankled by gender discrimination and hierarchical ideas that hold that lineage transmission, full ordination, and Buddhahood are exclusively male privileges. To be acceptable in ways that are authentic to liberal Western values, Buddhists are finding that they must address these discriminatory hierarchies, which include gender inequality and patriarchy, and also the authoritarianism and secrecy of Buddhist institutions regarding sexual exploitation. Many Western students are more interested in solving the problems of everyday life than in achieving enlightenment. Thus, the process of transmitting Buddhism to the West is both fascinating and fraught with challenges and contradictions.

Pioneering Buddhist Women

Some of the earliest pioneers of Buddhism in the West were immigrants from China and Japan who settled in California and Hawaiʻi toward the end of the nineteenth century. These émigrés are often missing from accounts of American Buddhism, which make little mention of Asian or Asian American contributions, especially from women. Many early Buddhist immigrants were followers of Pure Land Buddhism, who relied on the infinite wisdom and compassion of Amitābha Buddha and aspired to take rebirth in his Pure Land after death. As Rennyo (1415–99), a Japanese Pure Land master, assures us, "Women who remain in lay life should realize and never entertain the slightest doubt that those who, without any calculation, deeply rely on Amida [Japanese for Amitābha] Buddha single-mindedly and unwaveringly, entrusting themselves to the Buddha for their emancipation in the afterlife, will all be saved."[3] Today, women both lay and ordained are playing increasingly prominent roles in Pure Land temples in the West.[4] In 2018, Patricia Kanaya Usuki (b. 1953) was elected chair of the Buddhist Churches of America Ministers' Association, which provides leadership for Jōdo Shinshū temples in the United States. Since the association began at the turn of the twentieth century, the chair has always been held by a man. The election of Usuki heralds a breakthrough in gender boundaries.

Irene Eshin Matsumoto (b. 1929) is an example of a Japanese American woman who has devoted her life to Buddhist practice. Her mother-in-law, Kiyo Myosei Matsumoto (1884–1959), founded Palolo Kwannon Temple in Honolulu along with her husband in 1935. She was ordained as a Tendai priest in Japan in 1936 and, after her husband died, served as the second abbot of the temple from 1944 to 1958. After Irene married Myosei's son, Bishop Richard Chiko Tomoyoshi (1927–95), she served as a temple wife, in addition to teaching elementary school. When her husband died in 1986, she became the fourth abbot of the temple and has led her community since then in their devotion to Kannon (Chinese: Guanyin), the *bodhisattva* of compassion in female form. The many graceful images of Kannon on the temple grounds remind parishioners of the liberating power of compassion, while Irene Eshin Matsumoto herself continues to model compassion in action.

Another pioneering Buddhist woman was Ruth Fuller Sasaki (1892–1967), an American who studied in the Zen tradition with Nanshinken Roshi at Nanzen Temple in Kyoto, and later with Daisetsu Teitaro Suzuki (1870–1966) and Shigetsu Sasaki (1882–1945), two Japanese men deeply involved in the early transmission of Zen to North America.[5] In 1932, while pursuing *kōan* practice,[6] she experienced a sudden awakening (*satori*) and was then allowed to practice *zazen* (sitting meditation) with the monks.[7] In time, she became the first Westerner to be named a priest at the Daitoku-ji temple in Kyoto, the first woman ordained in the Rinzai Zen tradition in Japan, and the abbot of Ryōsen-an (Dragon Springs Hermitage). She established the First Zen Institute of America in New York City in 1951 and a similar institute in Japan, where she assembled a team of translators and devoted the rest of her life to translating and publishing classic Zen teaching texts, booklets, poems, and *kōans*.

From the 1960s on, many women began to practice *zazen* in North America and Europe, and a number of them became recognized Dharma heirs and teachers. The English nun Jiyu-Kennett Roshi (1924–96), the first Westerner to be ordained in the Sōtō Zen lineage, founded Shasta Abbey near Mount Shasta, California, in 1970.[8] She wrote numerous books on Zen training, developed a liturgy in the style of Gregorian chants, and established the Order of Buddhist Contemplatives, which has several branches internationally.

In the 1970s, Canadian-born Maureen Stuart Roshi (1922–90) established the Cambridge Buddhist Association in Massachusetts and became its guiding teacher.[9] Around the same time, in 1977, Zenkei Blanche Hartman (1926–2016) was ordained as a priest in the Sōtō Zen lineage of Shunryū Suzuki (1904–71), who helped popularize Zen in the United States, and served as co-abbess of the San Francisco Zen Center from 1996 to 2002. She also taught *nyohō-e*, the traditional art of sewing monastic robes, and was a strong advocate for women and children. Gesshin Prabhasa Dharma Roshi (1931–99), who was born in Germany, was ordained as a nun in 1968. Trained in the Rinzai Zen lineage, she founded the International Zen Institute in 1983 in Los Angeles and taught in both Europe and the United States. Roshi Joan Jiko Halifax (b. 1942), a medical anthropologist, became the founder and abbess of Upaya Institute and Zen Center in Santa Fe, New Mexico. She is particularly recognized for her work in the area of death and dying.[10] Some of the other Western women who have become well-known teachers of Zen in North America are Barbara Rhodes (Soeng Hyang Soen, b. 1948), Jan Chozen Bays (b. 1945), Charlotte Joko Beck (1917–2011), Yvonne Rand (b. 1936), Patricia Dai-En Bennage (b. 1939), Wendy Egyoku Nakao (b. 1949), Eijun Linda Cutts (b. 1947), Roshi Enkyo Pat O'Hara (b.1941), and Meian Elbert (b. 1947). Each has a unique story to tell about practicing Zen as a Western woman.[11]

Women have also been active in establishing Theravāda Buddhist traditions in the West. One of the earliest pioneers of *vipassanā* (insight) meditation was Ruth Denison (1922–2015), a German laywoman who settled in California and founded a *vipassanā* retreat center called Dhamma Dena in Joshua Tree in the Mojave Desert.[12] She became a student of the Burmese lay meditation teacher U Ba Khin (1899–1971), who authorized her, in 1969, to teach *vipassanā* in the West. Her innovative, informal teaching style highlighted sensory awareness and mindful movement. She also introduced retreats exclusively for women. Well known for her distinctive personality, Ruth inspired many students on the path of Dhamma, especially women. Her students appreciated her loving personality and her patience with neurosis.

Ayya Khema (1923–97) was born in a Jewish family in Berlin and, after fleeing Nazi persecution, spent two years in Scotland and then relocated to Shanghai, where the family was confined to the Shanghai Ghetto for stateless refugees in Hongkew (modern Hongkou District). She married and had a child but was forced to flee the Japanese occupation that started in 1932 and gave birth to a second child in California. She lived in many different countries before landing in Australia, where, in 1978, she founded the Thai-style Wat Buddha Dhamma outside of Sydney. In 1979, she became a nun in Sri Lanka, where she learned *jhāna* meditation, and in 1988, she received full *bhikṣuṇī* ordination at Hsi Lai Temple in Hacienda Heights, California (see figure 5.2). She founded the International Buddhist Women's Centre for training nuns and the Parappuduwa Nuns' Island for retreat in Sri Lanka. She also helped found the Sakyadhita International Association of Buddhist Women in 1987 in Bodhgaya, India, and in Germany, established Buddha Haus in Oy-Mittelberg in 1989 and Metta Vihara in 1997. She was the author of many books and the first Buddhist nun to address the United Nations in New York City.[13] Today, there are many Western women who have become respected Theravāda and *vipassanā* meditation teachers, among whom are Sharon Salzberg (b. 1952), one of the founders of the Insight Meditation Society in Barre, Massachusetts; Michele MacDonald of Vipassana Hawai'i; Marcia Rose, founder and guiding teacher at the Mountain Hermitage in Ranchos de Taos, New Mexico; Christina Feldman, cofounder of Gaia House in the United Kingdom; Ayya Medhanandi, the *bhikkhunī* founder and guiding teacher of Sati Saraniya Hermitage, a forest monastery for women in Canada; Ayya Tathaloka (b. 1968), the *bhikkhunī* founder of Dhammadharini Vihara in California; meditation and mindfulness teacher Sylvia Boorstein (b. 1936); and Kamala Masters, one of the founders and teachers of the Vipassana Metta Foundation on Maui.

In the Tibetan tradition, three Western women have followed remarkably similar paths and played influential roles in transmitting the Buddhist teachings. Khechok Palmo (Freda Bedi, 1911–77) was the earliest Western woman to become ordained as a Buddhist nun. Born in England and educated at Oxford University, she settled in India in 1934 with her Sikh husband and became active in the Indian independence movement. After His Holiness the Fourteenth Dalai Lama and an estimated one hundred thousand Tibetans fled to India and Nepal in 1959, she set

Figure 5.2. Nuns attending the *bhikṣuṇī* ordination held at Hsi Lai Temple in Hacienda Heights, California, in 1988. Credit: Photo by Karma Lekshe Tsomo.

up the Young Lamas' Home in Dalhousie and Karma Drubgyu Thargay Ling in Tilokpur, both in Himachal Pradesh, India, to educate a generation of refugee Tibetan monks and nuns in India.[14] She received novice ordination with the Sixteenth Gyalwa Karmapa (1924–81) in 1966 and *bhikṣuṇī* ordination in Hong Kong in 1972, and taught many Western students.

Jetsunma Tenzin Palmo (b. 1943), another practitioner born in England, as a librarian in London developed a strong interest in Buddhism. In 1964, she traveled to India and began teaching English at the Young Lamas' Home in Dalhousie, where she met and became the disciple of the Eighth Khamtrul Rinpoche (1931–80), a Drukpa Kagyu *lama*. Soon thereafter, she decided to become a nun. In 1967, she received novice ordination with the Sixteenth Gyalwa Karmapa in Rumtek, Sikkim, and in 1973 received *bhikṣuṇī* ordination in Hong Kong. After twelve years of solitary contemplative practice in a cave in the Himalayan region of Lahaul in Himachal Pradesh, India, from 1976 to 1988,[15] she decided to create an environment where nuns could train and continue the lineage of *togdenma* in the Drukpa Kagyu school and, in 2000, began establishing Dongyu Gatsal Ling Nunnery in Tashi Jong, northern India. She teaches internationally and has served as the president of Sakyadhita International Association of Buddhist Women since 2012.

Pema Chödrön (b. 1936) began by studying English at Sarah Lawrence College, then received a master's degree in education from the University of California, Berkeley, and raised a family before studying Buddhism with Chögyam Trungpa. In 1974, she received novice ordination with the Sixteenth Gyalwa Karmapa in Rumtek, Sikkim and, in 1981, received *bhikṣuṇī* ordination in Hong Kong. Since 1984, she has been the guiding teacher and acting director of Gampo Abbey in Nova Scotia, Canada. She is the author of numerous popular books on Buddhism.[16]

Some of the other female Western authors and teachers in the Tibetan tradition include Tsultrim Allione (b. 1947), teacher and cofounder of the Tara Mandala retreat center in Colorado; Janice Dean Willis (b. 1948), author and professor emerita of religion at Wesleyan University; Chagdud Khadro, spiritual director of Chagdud Gonpa in southern Brazil; Lama Tsering Everest (b. 1954), resident *lama* of Chagdud Gonpa Odsal Ling in São Paulo, Brazil; Anne Carolyn Klein (b. 1947), professor of religious studies at Rice University and cofounder and resident teacher at Dawn Mountain in Houston, Texas; Thubten Chodron (b. 1950), founder and resident teacher at Sravasti Abbey in Washington State; Sarah Harding, translator and teacher in the Shangpa Kagyu tradition; Rita Gross (1943–2015), author and American Buddhist feminist scholar of religions; and Elizabeth Mattis Namgyel, author and teacher at Longchen Jigme Samten Ling in Colorado. There are many more.

Other examples of pioneering Buddhist women teachers in the West are the environmental activist, author, and scholar Joanna Macy (b. 1929); Karuna Dharma (1940–2014), the first American-born woman to become a fully ordained Buddhist nun (in 1976); and Catriona Reed (b. 1949), a trans woman teacher of Thiên (Vietnamese Zen) Buddhism with a background in *vipassanā* meditation. All of these women have drawn from several Buddhist traditions. Western Buddhist women are prominent in virtually every field, including performers such as Tina Turner (b. 1939) and k. d. lang (b. 1961); writers Ruth Ozeki (b. 1956) and bell hooks (b. 1952); actors Uma Thurman (b. 1970) and Sharon

Stone (b. 1958); scholars Jan Nattier (b. 1949) and Janet Gyatso (b. 1949); activists Zenju Earthlyn Manuel (b. 1952) and angel Kyodo Williams (b. 1969); artists Mayumi Oda (b. 1941) and Tiffani Gyatso (b. 1981); and poets Jane Hirshfield (b. 1953) and Anne Waldman (b. 1945). Certainly, there are Buddhist women across every discipline who also deserve recognition, including many from diverse backgrounds.

In the United States, some noted performing artists identify as Buddhist and draw from Buddhist teachings in their art. Meredith Monk (b. 1942) is a vocal artist who draws explicit connections among Buddhism, breath, meditation, and the healing quality of sound. The Tara Dancers are an example of Buddhist feminist awareness expressed through movement. Prema Dasara, an American trained in Indian classical dance in India, discovered Buddhist dances that had been preserved for hundreds of years in Odisha, eastern India, and created a nonprofit organization called Tara Dhatu to help preserve them. She has composed a series of dances that honor and manifest the qualities of *buddhas* and *bodhisattvas*, especially those in female form. Since 1998, Tara Dhatu has organized workshops around the world to train women to dance and to teach the dances to convey important aspects of the Buddhist teachings. Her latest series of dances portray the twenty-one aspects of the female *bodhisattva* Tārā. Wearing masks specially crafted in Bali, the dancers seek to embody the qualities of these awakened manifestations for the benefit of all beings.[17]

Challenging Patriarchy, Building Alliances

One of the greatest contributions Western Buddhist women have made is to draw public attention to gender bias within the Buddhist traditions. This is not to say that Asian Buddhist women are unaware of the male dominance and gender discrimination in their traditions and communities. Buddhist women across Asia, from Korea to Sri Lanka, have been leaders in advocating for women and have initiated projects that question and seek to redress the gendered status quo. Gender inequalities that handicap women's achievements persist in Western countries too. Challenging patriarchy is a daunting task everywhere; as with all social justice movements, it requires considerable confidence, wisdom, and patience, and entails significant social risks. It is important to question why equal opportunities for women are limited and regarded as threatening in most cultures around the world, including Western countries.

Another major contribution of Western Buddhist women has been to encourage international networking and foster intra-Buddhist understanding in countries and communities around the world. The Sakyadhita International Conferences on Buddhist Women are good examples of egalitarian Buddhist transnational cooperation. By creating forums that give voice to women of all backgrounds, not simply educated elites, Sakyadhita has moved the feminist conversation forward in innovative, inclusive ways. Meanwhile, a healthy exchange of mutual influences continues to travel back and forth between Asia and the West, furthering both cultural literacy and deeper understandings of Buddhist teachings in a dynamic multidimensional process. The Buddhist ideal of enlightenment for all can be transformative for women and men alike, even if such a lofty ideal has yet to be translated into social reality.

As we have seen, many Asian and Western Buddhist practitioners, both female and male, contend that meditation practice is free of gender, that Dharma has no gender, and therefore there is no reason to focus on the question of women in Buddhism. Since the Buddhist teachings focus on cultivating awareness and purifying the mind, and since consciousness has no gender, this argument goes, all human beings are capable of reaching liberation, hence the question of women in Buddhism is irrelevant. Yet even though it is theoretically true that the Dharma is genderless, the social applications of Buddhist teachings and practices are profoundly gendered. Not offering women equal opportunities for ordination or education denies them full participation in the Buddhist heritage. It also stigmatizes women as incapable of achieving the highest goals of Buddhist philosophy and practice, which is in direct contradiction to the Buddha's own views. It is time for gender training to be offered alongside meditation training in Buddhist centers.

Buddhism and Sexuality

In recent years, Western scholars have made important contributions to research on Buddhism, sexuality, and gender.[18] Until recently, however, the topic of sexual exploitation has generally been avoided. A Buddhist analysis of sexual misconduct begins by explaining the ethical principles that are the foundation of all Dharma practice. Buddhist laypeople—male (*upāsaka*) or female (*upāsikā*)—voluntarily observe five precepts. One of these is a pledge to refrain from sexual misconduct, generally interpreted as adultery, rape, or otherwise harming anyone through one's sexual behavior. Buddhist monastics voluntarily observe many more precepts, including one to refrain from sexual intercourse altogether. A monk or nun is celibate by definition. Buddhist teachers may be laypeople, ordained monastics, or, as in some Japanese and Tibetan contexts, clergy who are neither lay nor celibate monastics. Not everyone who is a qualified teacher is celibate, and not all celibate monastics are qualified teachers. Nevertheless, Buddhist teachers, being in a position of authority, are expected to set a high standard of moral behavior for their followers and for society in general. Whether they choose to be celibate or not, Buddhist teachers are expected to avoid unwholesome sexual behavior. It is problematic when a teacher, whether wearing the robes or not, transgresses the precept of sexual restraint that he or she has personally vowed to observe, much less engages in sexual exploitation or sexual abuse.

According to legend, the Buddha was quite familiar with sexual desire, having indulged in the pleasures of an extensive harem when he was a pampered prince. In fact, the decision to renounce his life of luxury was triggered by the illusion-shattering experience of seeing his consorts sprawled in disarray around him.[19] After his spiritual awakening, he explained that the most attractive thing to a man is a woman and the most attractive thing to a woman is a man. Despite this heterosexist typology, the Buddha regarded desire as an affliction for all beings. Based on incidents that occurred during the Buddha's time, the first precept for monastics is a prohibition against sexual intercourse with a person of either the opposite sex or the same sex; renunciants were voluntarily celibate and were not supposed to engage in any sexual activity. The early Buddhist texts do not discuss homosexual behavior involving laypeople, who do not take precepts to avoid sex.[20]

The causes of sexual misconduct are not difficult to understand. Sexual desire is a potent emotion fed by habitual tendencies. Buddhism classifies it as a deluded state of mind, along with greed, lust, and attachment. Desire and attachment give rise to jealousy and disappointment, entangling beings in a perpetual cycle of dissatisfaction and suffering. Only through understanding these causes and connections can beings disentangle themselves from this cycle.

One potential source of confusion about sexuality is the male/female (Tibetan: *yab/yum*) imagery of male and female beings in union that is used in certain tantric meditation practices in Vajrayāna Buddhism, symbolizing the union of skillful means and wisdom.[21] Although sexual union is discussed as a spiritual practice in Buddhist *tantra*, it is reserved for highly advanced *yogis* who are not monastics, and it is doubtful that more than a few such beings, if any, exist in the world today. Using these practices as a pretext for sexual exploitation is said to have disastrous karmic consequences. When he was informed about instances of sexual abuse by Buddhist teachers, His Holiness the Fourteenth Dalai Lama clearly stated that when a teacher transgresses the precepts, the student must openly address the teacher's misconduct.[22]

The independence that many women have achieved today opens up new realms of experience as well as challenges. Women are becoming more confident as they acquire higher education and new avenues open up for them. However, happiness is not guaranteed. In Buddhist centers everywhere, women generally expect teachers to behave ethically and may naïvely dismiss sexual advances as a type of cross-cultural misunderstanding. Now, however, the issue can no longer be brushed aside, due to the disclosure of multiple serious incidents of sexual abuse at several Buddhist centers.[23] Consequently, there is certainly a new awareness that the topic of responsible sexual conduct in Buddhist communities needs to be addressed urgently.

Clashes and Acculturation, Cultural and Conceptual

The experiences and concerns of Western Buddhist women may be quite different from those of Asian Buddhist women. Western women are generally interested in practical everyday applications of Buddhist teachings in relationships, family life, and work. They find the teachings helpful for coping with the overwhelming complexity of modern life and use meditation as a tool for dealing with fear, stress, and confusion. Some Asian Buddhist women participate in chanting ceremonies, some in charitable

Figure 5.3. Laywomen practicing meditation at a Korean Buddhist temple. Credit: Photo by Lunah Kim.

activities, and others in meditation retreats (see figure 5.3). Those who are concerned with issues of gender equity, the environment, and justice try to apply Buddhist solutions to social crises such as racism and poverty. Some have found Buddhist teachings a lifeline to recovery from addictions.[24] Many find Dharma practice spiritually enriching, even liberating. The goal is not some transcendent *nirvāna* but a healthy way to work calmly with troubling emotions and free themselves from the complications of daily life by staying attentive to the present moment.

Although many Western women have only a passing interest in Buddhism, some are strongly committed to Buddhist scholarship and practice. Many are well educated, creative, and forward thinking. Some have completed extensive retreats of three years or longer, and some have become translators and interpreters. Some decide to become Buddhist monastics, even when their decision to renounce social freedoms and professional advancement to join an Asian monastic order may be inexplicable to others. In contemporary Western cultures, monasticism is often poorly understood, even denigrated, whereas in traditional Buddhist cultures, the monastic commitment to scholarship and practice has been highly prized, at least for men. In fact, the monasteries were often the only way to get an education. In an era of widespread revelations of sexual abuse, many people are questioning the value of celibacy and monastic life, but as history records, Buddhist monasteries were fountains of qualified teachers and spiritual guides. Without the support that monasticism provides for in-depth scholarship and intensive Dharma practice, other, egalitarian environments for educating and training qualified teachers will need to be created in the West.

Women in contemporary cultures question certain other concepts also when they encounter Buddhism. For one, they may wonder whether it is still possible to experience love and intimate relationships if they are strongly committed to Buddhist practice. One Buddhist response would be to examine the meaning of the terms. For example, if the word "love" denotes sexual attraction or attachment, then that is something quite different from the universal loving-kindness (Pāli: *mettā*; Sanskrit: *maitrī*) that is featured in the Buddhist texts. Sexual attraction, while seductive and sensually pleasurable, is only temporary and may ultimately become unfulfilling and problematic. Attachment to friends and family members, while an understandable human emotion, can also be a source of problems and pain as we are inevitably separated from them. From a Buddhist perspective, attachment to loved ones reveals a bias toward some sentient beings over others, perpetuating self-concern rather than the universal love that Buddhism teaches. An early Mahāyāna text counsels against "the thought of excessive affection toward [one's children], while not doing so toward other beings," because the mind of the *bodhisattva* is impartial and does not make these kinds of distinctions.[25]

In the West, women interested in Buddhism have typically received educations comparable to men. Nevertheless, gender inequalities persist in Western countries. When Western women encounter sexist elements in Buddhist texts or teachings, some run for the nearest exit, while others decide that the benefits may outweigh the defects and give it a try. After all, the Buddha exhorted his disciples not to react in anger to slights and abuse but rather to remain centered, calm, and undisturbed.[26] Buddhist methods of responding to harm with nonharm and to hatred with loving-kindness stand in contrast to many contemporary methods of addressing trauma and abuse. Tolerance of gender discrimination and oppression is not corrective; other means must be found.

Some contemporary interpreters of Buddhism argue against tradition and advocate for a "Buddhism without beliefs,"[27] in hopes that mindfulness and introspection will, on their own, be sufficient. For others, the current rationalistic adaptation of Buddhism is a distortion rather than an accurate representation of the teachings. In the eyes of these critics, Westerners tend to ignore core Buddhist teachings, such as karma, no self (Pāli: *anatta*; Sanskrit: *anātman*), and death, and shy away from the difficult work of inner transformation. They "cherry-pick" a venerable wisdom tradition and make it into "Buddhism Lite." While there is certainly scope for "demythologizing Buddhism" and for recognizing the malleability of the tradition, there is also a danger that, instead of waking up to the deeper truths of the human condition, the Buddha's teachings may simply become a kind of feel-good, self-help therapy, replacing one illusion with another.[28]

Meanwhile, many women are forging ahead, finding great value in Buddhist psychology, fashioning their own interpretations of the human situation, and valiantly tackling their "inner demons."[29] Many of these women are finding that Buddhist strategies can be deployed skillfully to confront issues of abuse, abandonment, and neglect. One powerful source of inspiration has been discovering the stories and spiritual achievements of Buddhist women that have been lost or hidden in the shoals of time. After all, there are records of the noble contributions and advanced attainments of Buddhist nuns and laywomen since the Buddha first gave teachings. Another powerful source of inspiration is for women to encourage others by writing their own stories about their experiences with Dharma practice. Buddhist women in the West today are not only helping reclaim Buddhist women's histories but also creating their own contemporary histories.

Obstacles as Opportunities

In a sense, the obstacles that women face today practicing Buddhism in the West are the same as for anyone attempting to practice Buddhism in the messiness of everyday life rife with distractions such as relationship issues, cultural clashes, conflicting priorities, and so on. Perhaps we can say that all the same mental afflictions with which the Buddha grappled and talked about so long ago—clinging, grasping, attachment, aversion, ignorance, confusion, pride, jealousy, and all the rest of it—are pretty much the same today as then. The Buddha's antidotes to these mental afflictions—generosity, ethical conduct, patience, joyful effort, mindfulness, wisdom, loving-kindness, compassion, and other wholesome mind states—are equally relevant today as before.

6

Women's Ordination across Cultures

According to texts transmitted by Buddhist monks, the Buddha admitted women to the *saṅgha* sometime during the fifth century BCE. These texts preserve stories about the women's travails and joys on the Buddha's path of liberation, and some are described in the words of liberated nuns (*arhatī*) themselves. These stories, found in the codes of monastic discipline (*vinaya*) and related texts, were transmitted to China, Korea, Tibet, and other countries as part of the centuries-long process of appropriation, adaptation, and reconfiguration of Indian Buddhist philosophy, practice, and institutional structures we have been tracing. This chapter examines the classical Indian *vinaya* texts for a fully ordained Buddhist nun (Pāli: *bhikkhunī*; Sanskrit: *bhikṣuṇī*) and the surviving accounts of renunciant women's lives as variegated lenses for understanding Buddhist nuns' experiences from early times up to the modern period.[1] It reviews the history of ordination for women in the Buddhist traditions, examines the reasons that opportunities for ordination are important for women, and reflects on the prospects for change in those traditions where women currently do not have opportunities for full ordination.

As we have seen, the gender imbalances that exist in Buddhist societies today are reinforced and perpetuated by the gender inequalities that exist in the early monastic texts as well as by social custom. Recent feminist studies of women in Buddhist cultures often include some analysis of the monastic codes and commentaries to assess how gender bias in these texts are reflected in societal attitudes and gendered expectations of women over the centuries until today. The attitudes and assumptions about women in these texts, both beneficial and potentially harmful, seem to correlate with opportunities and obstacles for women related to education, full ordination, and leadership opportunities in Buddhist institutions. Until recently, the ubiquitous claim that men and women are equal in Buddhism has obscured women's limited access to the pathways to liberation. As we have discussed, theoretical claims of equality are often deployed to mask gender inequities in Buddhist societies. Buddhist feminist thinkers are hopeful that further studies of the early texts and their subsequent interpretations will reveal the distorted thinking and logical inconsistency implicit in placing limitations on a path that promises equal access to awakening.

In the texts, the Buddha explains that a society complete with four pillars—consisting of monks (*bhikkhus*), nuns (*bhikkhunīs*), laymen (*upāsakas*), and laywomen (*upāsikās*)—will be stable and harmonious.[2] Unfortunately, today some Buddhist societies are missing *bhikkhunīs*, thus upsetting the balance of the four pillars, leading to gender injustices. Contemporary initiatives to restore access to full ordination for all women who wish to receive it are concerned with redressing this imbalance. These initiatives may be understood both as a reform movement to implement the Buddha's egalitarian social ideal and as a revolutionary movement to address gender inequities in Buddhist societies. The Buddha himself is credited with founding the *bhikkhunī saṅgha*, so to restore the fourfold community is seen by activists to fulfill the Buddha's own intention.

As we have seen, today women who choose to become nuns in the Theravāda traditions of Myanmar (Burma), Cambodia, Laos, Nepal, and Thailand generally take eight precepts, do not have access to full ordination, and are not regarded as members of the *saṅgha*. As a consequence, they receive less material and moral support from the lay community than do monks. In recent years, opportunities for ordination for Theravāda women have opened up, especially in Nepal and Sri Lanka, where Theravāda nuns may take ten precepts and live as a *sāmaṇerī* or *dasasilmātā*, or can choose to receive full ordination as a *bhikkhunī*. In the Mahāyāna Buddhist traditions of China, Korea, Taiwan, and Vietnam, women may receive the ten precepts of a novice nun and then later choose to receive full ordination. Fully ordained nuns are regarded as members of the *saṅgha* and receive good (if not equal) support from the lay community.

The Debate over Full Ordination for Women

In recent times, the ordination of women has become a hot-button issue for Buddhists around the world. Mahāpajāpatī's insistence that women be allowed to join the *saṅgha* and her determined persistence—one of the earliest historical instances of public feminist advocacy—are a tribute to her sense of social justice. The Buddha's reported hesitation to admit women to the *saṅgha* seems baffling, unless we take his sociohistorical context into consideration. After all, the incident dates to a time several hundred years before the Common Era when women were widely regarded as the property of men. The fact that the Buddha eventually acceded to Mahāpajāpatī's request, despite social disapproval and risks of abuse and assault that unprotected women were likely to face, can be considered evidence of his even-mindedness and compassion. However, as we have learned, his agreement was dependent on Mahāpajāpatī's willingness to observe eight weighty rules that ensured the dominant status of the monks.[3] As we have seen, however, there are inconsistencies in this story, as Buddhist studies scholar Liz Williams and others have pointed out.[4] In a chapter published in 2000, Sri Lankan scholar Bhikkhunī Kusuma Devendra cites evidence of inconsistencies and contradictions among the rules and in the legend that admitting women to the *saṅgha* would shorten the duration of the Buddha's teachings.[5]

Beginning during the fifth century BCE, the early Buddhist *vinaya* texts on monastic discipline were transmitted orally by monks for several centuries before being committed to writing. Many of these texts were subsequently translated from Pāli and Sanskrit into Chinese and Tibetan, but only a fraction of them have been translated into European languages. The *vinaya* texts are a rich source of information for understanding the interactions between the monastics and the surrounding community upon whom they relied for their practical needs. The texts describe the ideal lifestyle of women in monastic life in the same terms as for men, and the rules for nuns are very similar to those for the monks, with some additions. The precepts, organized into categories according to seriousness of transgression, number more than two hundred for monks and more than three hundred for nuns, depending on the *vinaya* lineage. Transgressing a rule in the first category, such as murder or sexual intercourse, is grounds for expulsion.

When the *bhikkhunī saṅgha* was founded, some years after the *bhikkhu saṅgha*, the *bhikkhunīs* inherited most of the two hundred-plus precepts said to have been set forth by the Buddha due to the misconduct of certain monks. After the *bhikkhunī saṅgha* began, about eighty more precepts were set forth either due to the misconduct of certain nuns or to protect the nuns from assault and exploitation. For example, nuns are not allowed to walk alone on a road, a rule that was promulgated to protect them from sexual assault and harassment. The additional precepts for nuns are often presumed to indicate that women have more delusions than men, when in fact more than twice as many precepts were created on the basis of certain monks' misconduct. For example, as the Korean Buddhist scholar Inyoung Chung (Sukhdam Sunim) explains, the four additional *pārājikas* ("defeats" resulting in expulsion from the *saṅgha*) for *bhikkhunīs* seem to be safeguards to protect the *bhikkhunīs* against sexual assault by men.[6] In all, the additional precepts specifically for *bhikkhunīs* are less than half the number of precepts created for monks. This disproves the allegation, frequently cited in East Asian Buddhist societies, that because nuns have twice as many precepts as monks, they must have twice as many delusions.

The Case for Celibacy

Perhaps the first question to consider is why any woman in her right mind would want to become a nun. Now that women in many parts of the world have won the freedom to direct their own lives and bodies, why would they want to relinquish that freedom? The Buddha realized the power and ramifications of sexuality for human beings. He candidly acknowledged the sexual attraction that women and men feel toward each other. Yet he also recognized sexuality as a potential source of emotional entanglement and attachment, both of which ultimately cause dissatisfaction and suffering. Sex is portrayed as a shackle, a source of bondage. Although sexual desire is a very basic human instinct, human instincts are not necessarily constructive. For example, sexual desire is useful for reproduction, but it can also be the source of conflict, obsession, jealousy, and other negative emotions. Because both men and women are prone to sexual temptation, the Buddha recommended celibacy and established rules restricting the interactions between women and men who entered the monastic order. After entering the monastery, nuns and monks eschewed all sexual activity, both heterosexual and homosexual.

The Buddha taught a path to awakening that was accessible to all, but he spoke especially to an audience of celibate practitioners, the *saṅgha.* Celibacy ("the pure life," *brahmācarya*) is exalted in the Buddhist texts and is considered a way of being in the world that is conducive to spiritual attainment. In a post–"sexual revolution" world, celibacy may seem anachronistic, irrelevant, repressive, or even worse, and therefore the topic requires clarification.[7] The Buddha recognized that human beings are prone to sexual desire and identified desire as a distraction and a hindrance to liberation. He gave useful advice on how to live a happy family life free from deluded actions that give rise to conflicts. For those keen on achieving awakening, he recommended a celibate lifestyle as the best working basis for transforming the mind. Even today, a consideration of the psychological foundations of the practice of celibacy may be relevant and helpful.

In the social environment of South Asia during the fifth century BCE, the Buddha encountered widespread criticism for recommending that women and men of all ages leave their families and follow the path to liberation. He was charged with making women widows by encouraging their husbands to enter the monastic life, and with destroying the family, the bedrock of society. This highlights a paradox that exists in Indian society even today between the renunciant ideal and the social stigma associated with opting out of family life, except for men who are approaching the end of their lives and encouraged to renounce household affairs and concentrate on spiritual goals. Women have also pursued spiritual goals, both during and toward the end of their lives, but generally at home, while tending to their families. The Buddha did not require celibacy for all since many people have other interests or obligations and are not suited for monastic life, but he certainly viewed it as a highly useful way to cut through desire and attachment. He distinguished carefully between loving-kindness, the pure wish that all beings be happy, and emotional entanglements that may be mistaken for love and are often mixed with attachment and expectations that inevitably lead to quarreling and disappointment. To be free of suffering, it is necessary to eliminate desire, since desire is a cause of dissatisfaction and disappointment. It is not realistic to glamorize desire and at the same time hope to be free of it. Following desire leads to further desires; to imagine that desire can be eliminated by indulging it is deluded thinking. For this reason, the Buddha prescribed a life of celibacy for those who are seriously interested in liberation. In two canonical texts that she studied, religious studies scholar Kate Blackstone found statements asserting that those who fail to appreciate the benefits of the monastic lifestyle are "fools."[8]

Some may say that renunciation is an orthodox, Theravāda Buddhist concept, but in the Mahāyāna Buddhist traditions, also, renunciation is one of the pillars of awakening, known as the three principles of the path: renunciation, the altruistic aspiration to awakening (*bodhicitta*), and direct insight into emptiness. In fact, renunciation is considered the most basic of the three and the foundation for the other two. Without renunciation, specifically renunciation of sexual desire, hopes for liberation from *saṃsāra* are mere fantasies. Sensual desire is never ultimately fulfilling, but simply leads to further desire. We torture ourselves with the notion of romantic love, which inevitably ends in separation. Worse yet, we find ourselves consigned to stale, dull, formulaic relationships. This tradeoff is the price we pay for sex. Even though sexual activity is necessary for procreation, it can also be life threatening. HIV/AIDS aside, every minute a woman dies of the complications of pregnancy and childbirth. A thoughtful, realistic assessment of the human sexual experience makes the idea of renunciation more comprehensible.

The attainment of perfect awakening (Sanskrit: *samyaksaṃbodhi*; Pāli: *sammāsaṃbodhi*) may sound too lofty and remote an achievement for ordinary people today, so it may be well to consider the ramifications of sexuality on a purely practical, realistic level. For example, one downside of sexual activity is that it ordinarily entails great concern for physical appearance. Although this may vary from culture to culture, the concepts of beauty and attractiveness factor into intimate relationships everywhere. The media plays to these concerns and needlessly creates many personal and social expectations and frustrations, disproportionately for women. Yet as one popular poster reminds us, "Three billion women in the world and only eight super models." The media incessantly broadcasts images of the sexually attractive woman as the prototype of happiness, often unrealistically thin and modeling a certain racially biased and ethnocentric standard of beauty. Measured by this unrealistic standard, consumers of the happiness myth, particularly young women, can hardly be blamed for feeling inadequate. The Buddha reminds us that the bodies of living beings, no matter how beautiful or desirable their appearance, are deteriorating all the time. Time and money spent on the pipe dream of reversing the aging process are but futile attempts ultimately misspent to avoid the inevitable. The more realistic human beings are about the realities of imperfection and impermanence, the more comfortable we will be about our physical appearance and, as a result, the more energy we will have to devote to more meaningful pursuits, such as relieving the sufferings of the world and spiritual cultivation. Awakening is not a place but a state of deep clarity that includes insight into emotions such as desire, greed, and attachment. A deep understanding of sexuality, for example, does not mean repressing it or even necessarily avoiding it. However, from a Buddhist perspective, understanding the emotions entailed in sexuality can help human beings avoid much suffering and nurture healthier, happier relationships.

In addition to the emotional and spiritual benefits of learning to restrain sexual desires, there are also social and personal advantages for nuns in patriarchal societies. By maintaining a celibate lifestyle, nuns are able to control their own sexual reproduction and are free from the constraints and obligations of women who are forced into the roles of wife and mother. If they have previously been wives and mothers, by becoming nuns they are able to escape from those constraints and obligations. As celebrated by the early Buddhist nuns in their verses of liberation in the *Therīgāthā*, nuns are free from having to serve their husbands and in-laws, who may be abusive. Released from childbearing, childrearing, and social entanglements, nuns have free time to devote to meditation and other contemplative practices. Nuns also have more leisure time to devote to social welfare activities for the benefit of others, beyond their family circle. In societies that reserve educational resources for boys and men, becoming a nun may be one of the few avenues to intellectual development for women and one of the only ways to gain deeper knowledge of the religious texts and practices. Today, in an age of widespread social freedom, it may be good to appreciate the simple pleasure of being able to personally control one's own coming and going.

Ordination for Women in the Theravāda Tradition

As we have seen, the lineage of *bhikkhunīs* was discontinued around the eleventh century CE in India and Sri Lanka, and may never have been established in other Theravāda traditions in Southeast Asia. Like monks in these traditions, nuns aspire to attain liberation and be free from the sufferings of cyclic existence. In these traditions, it is assumed that the more effective lifestyle for practicing toward this freedom is to renounce the household life. For some, this may mean choosing monastic life, while for others this may mean solitary retreat. In either case, women face special challenges. In traditional patriarchal cultures, from a young age, women are raised with the social expectation that they will marry and raise children, even though this option does not always bring them happiness or security. Many women in Buddhist societies understand this, but they are not usually encouraged to pursue the renunciant lifestyle, as are men. Women who aspire to lead the life of a nun find that there are fewer monasteries for women, fewer qualified teachers, fewer education opportunities, and less moral and material support. Those who persevere to live the spiritual life need to be determined and courageous. A survey of the circumstances of nuns in a variety of Theravāda traditions will be useful for understanding their commonalities and diversity.

Renunciation has great meaning in the Buddhist worldview, especially perhaps in the Theravāda tradition, so it is important to examine the significance of renunciation for Theravāda women. On one hand, as evidenced in the *Therīgāthā* (Verses of the Elder Nuns), renunciation may arise from waking up to the suffering and dissatisfaction (Pāli: *dukkha*; Sanskrit: *duḥkha*) of unhealthy relationships and lead instead to a focus on the liberative path. It may also lead to questions about the exploitative aspect of sex and the commodification of human beings as sex objects. The decision to leave household life behind can be both heartrending and liberating, especially for women who desire motherhood. However, there are other women who may view monastic life as an ideal way to escape marriage and maternity. For those who choose lay life, renunciation may mean renouncing attachment, and through insight into *duḥkha*, replacing it with pure love that is free from attachment.

As we have seen, the status of renunciant women in Buddhist societies is generally lower than renunciant men, and although nuns may be respected, they are poorly supported. A woman who decides to leave lay life behind and take up the path of renunciation is clearly motivated not by a desire for material benefits or high status but by a wish to make her life more meaningful and meritorious. However, as religious studies scholar Donald Swearer observes,

> the traditional role of women in Southeast Asian society reflects the values of a patriarchal society. Women's roles were defined primarily by men in relationship to men. The ideal woman was portrayed as a loyal wife and devoted mother. When this portrayal is translated into the Buddhist monastic context, women are seen as mothers who produce sons who become monks, and as homemakers who prepare the food donated to monks.[9]

The option for women to live a renunciant life exists in Theravāda societies nevertheless, as illustrated by nuns in Nepal, Sri Lanka, and Thailand.

Theravāda Nuns in Nepal

The Theravāda Buddhist tradition has survived in Nepal, the birthplace of the Buddha, and today is thriving among the Newar community of the Kathmandu Valley in large measure due to the dedicated efforts of nuns. Growing up in an era when girls were prohibited from learning to read and when Buddhism had been suppressed by the ruling Rana Dynasty (1846–1951), two exceptional young women braved public censure and innumerable obstacles to become Buddhist nuns.[10] Dhammachari Guruma (1898–1978) and Bhikkhunī Dhammawati (b. 1934) renounced family life, founded monastic communities for women, taught Dhamma, and worked actively to benefit the needy. Dhammachari Guruma accomplished her work while observing the eight precepts of an *anagārikā*.

In 1950, at the age of fourteen, Bhikkhunī Dhammawati ran away from home and found her way to Burma, where she studied the *vinaya*, *suttas*, and *abhidhamma* at Khemarama Nuns' Study Center, and eventually earned the coveted *dhammācariya* (teacher of Dhamma) degree. In 1963, she returned to the Kathmandu Valley where she began teaching Buddhism to large audiences and founded Dharmakirti Vihar, a Theravāda Buddhist nunnery. A prolific author, she has published dozens of books in Newari and Nepali, and set up Buddhist studies programs for children and adults alike. Bhikkhunī Dhammawati took the courageous step of traveling to Los Angeles to receive the 348 precepts of a *bhikkhunī* in a large ceremony at Hsi Lai Temple in 1988, despite the strenuous objections of the *bhikkhu saṅgha* in Nepal. Today, she has thousands of disciples, including more than four hundred well-educated nuns.[11] Of these, two hundred are *bhikkhunīs* who have been ordained in Bodhgaya, China, or Taiwan, and returned to teach and practice Buddhism in Nepal. Despite opposition from the Nepali *bhikkhu saṅgha*, these courageous nuns boldly declared that women were capable of achieving liberation and gained large numbers of followers. Their groundbreaking efforts are visible today in the vibrancy of Theravāda Buddhist identity and practice in the Newar community.

Theravāda Nuns in Sri Lanka

In Sri Lanka, nuns have quietly and persistently forged ahead in their efforts to become fully ordained, despite institutional biases and official foot-dragging and obstruction by conservative factions of the *bhikkhu saṅgha*. Since the early twentieth century, at least, women in Sri Lanka have observed the ten precepts of a *dasasilmātā*. However, *dasasilmātās* are not accorded the status of a novice nun (*sāmaṇerī*) and are not recognized as members of the *saṅgha*. The reason given is that, in the monastic texts and commentaries, novice nuns who are candidates for full ordination should be trained and ordained by *bhikkhunīs*, but since around the eleventh century in Sri Lanka, there have been no *bhikkhunīs* to ordain them. This started to change in the late 1990s, when nuns from Sri Lanka began requesting ordination from *bhikkhunīs* from outside their own tradition.

The momentum to restore the *bhikkhunī* ordination lineage began with discussions at the first Sakyadhita International Conference on Buddhist Nuns held in 1987 at Bodhgaya, India. In 1988, despite vocal opposition, five nuns from Sri Lanka, along with the German nun Ayya Khema (1923–97) and others, received *bhikkhunī* ordination at Hsi Lai Temple in Los Angeles. Although the event drew international attention, the Sri Lankan nuns were not recognized as *bhikkhunīs* when they returned to their country. In 1996, a group of ten Sri Lankan nuns headed by Bhikkhunī Kusuma Devendra, a former biology professor and well-known commentator on Buddhism, received *bhikkhunī* ordination from

Figure 6.1. The ordination of Sri Lankan *bhikṣuṇīs* held in 1996 near the Dhamek Stupa in Sarnath, India. Credit: Photo by Karma Lekshe Tsomo.

Korean *bhikkhus* and *bhikkhunīs* near the Dhamek Stupa in Sarnath, India (see figure 6.1). In 1998, an international ordination was held in Bodhgaya, attended by thirty-two Sri Lankan nuns, the majority being abbesses of their monasteries.[12] Since 1999, *bhikkhunī* ordinations have also been held in Sri Lanka itself, beginning in Dambulla with an ordination officiated by a prominent *bhikkhu* named Inamaluwe Sumangala Thera.

Until today, however, the *bhikkhunīs* of Sri Lanka have received no official government recognition or support. In fact, it appears that the government, under pressure from certain *bhikkhus* who oppose the higher ordination of nuns, is instead supporting the *dasasilmātās* and effectively blocking the advancement of *bhikkhunīs* in various areas, for example, in their efforts to get their *bhikkhunī* status entered on their passports. Although not everyone in Sri Lanka publicly supports the revival of higher ordination for women, and some still strongly oppose it, of late, opponents are now the minority. The general public seems to appreciate the sincerity, helpfulness, and pure conduct of the *bhikkhunīs*, in addition to their value as an accessible field of merit.[13]

Theravāda Nuns in Thailand

There are said to be some twenty thousand Theravāda nuns in Thailand, most of whom are *mae chees*, women who observe eight precepts and observe the discipline of a fully ordained *bhikkhunī* but are not accorded the respect or status of a *bhikkhunī*.[14] Most Theravāda nuns in Bangladesh, Burma, Cambodia, and Laos also observe eight precepts. Some speculate that *bhikkhunīs* may have existed in Thailand long ago—there is a *bhikkhunī sima* (a boundary drawn to demarcate the space for an ordination ritual) in Chiang Mai, for example—but others believe the *sima* was erected for when the next Buddha arrives and reestablishes the *bhikkhunī* order. In recent decades, dozens of Thai nuns have received *bhikkhunī* ordination in Sri Lanka and increasing numbers of women are being ordained as *sāmaṇerīs* in Thailand. Former Thammasat University philosophy professor Bhikkhunī Dhammananda (b. 1944) received *bhikkhunī* ordination in Sri Lanka in 2003 and has been ordaining *sāmaṇerīs* annually since then at her temple outside Bangkok. In 2014, she organized an ordination of *bhikkhunīs* in Songkhla, southern Thailand, which prompted immediate censure from the Sangha Supreme Council of Thailand, composed exclusively of *bhikkhus*. Instead of living in one corner of a monks' monastery, as was previously the case, today at least one hundred *sāmaṇerīs* live in six independent nuns' monasteries around the country. In addition to *mae chees* and *sāmaṇerīs*, there are also many Mahāyāna *bhikṣuṇīs*, mostly Thai of Chinese heritage, who are well supported by the Chinese Buddhist community in Thailand.

Although many *mae chees* follow the monastic discipline more strictly than some monks, they are officially regarded as laywomen with shaved heads. Efforts to secure government recognition for them have so far failed. The justification given for not allowing these women to receive full ordination is that there is currently no Theravāda lineage of *bhikkhunī* ordination in existence. This belief ignores the lineages of *bhikṣuṇī* ordination that exist in Mahāyāna countries and the more than two thousand *bhikkhunīs* who, although not recognized officially, exist now in Sri Lanka and Thailand. Such justification also fails to recognize the fact that the full ordination of women was inaugurated by the Buddha, who himself ordained Mahāpajāpatī, whereas *mae chee* ordination is not a traditional category of ordination for women.

Nevertheless, *mae chees* tend to be content with their religious identity, positioned far from the cares of family life, yet not bound by the strictures inherent to the status of *bhikkhunīs*. Observing eight precepts strictly, including celibacy, *mae chees* are allowed to handle money, which enables them to travel and interact freely with people in their communities. If *mae chees* face a health crisis, have a family emergency, or run short on funds, they can easily revert to lay status and then reordain later, if they wish. Today in Thailand, *mae chees* have access to Buddhist studies programs, and many of them study the Pāli language in order to read the scriptures, especially texts on *abhidhamma* philosophy and meditation. Some rely on their families for material support; however, their practice, devotion, sincerity, and contributions to their communities have not gone unnoticed, and *mae chees* are increasingly respected and supported by the Thai Buddhist lay community.

Most *mae chees* in Thailand live on the margins of the monks' temples. When the monks come back from their alms round (*binthabat*), they generally share what they receive with the nuns; the nuns warm it up, supplement it, and eat the monks' leftovers. In recent years, a greater awareness of gender equity has had a noticeably positive effect on support for nuns from the lay community. A few *mae chees*, such as those at the Mahapajapati Buddhist College for Women, go for alms. Usually on their alms round, especially in poor neighborhoods, they receive donations of sticky rice and simple dishes but report feeling peaceful and content.

There are also around forty independent nuns' communities that are the residences of *bhikkhunīs* and *sāmaṇerīs* in training to become *bhikkhunīs*. Nuns are becoming empowered through education and are also gaining both the traditional and contemporary knowledge they need to develop as teachers. Thai nuns work in cooperation with devoted laywomen to practice virtue and create merit. Increasingly, both nuns and laywomen are also pursuing meditation practice, joining retreats whenever possible.[15] Thai nuns' greater awareness of Buddhist women's history and of the existence of *bhikkhunīs* in other countries have empowered them to pursue education and establish communities for nuns that are independent from monasteries for monks, while maintaining mutually beneficial relationships with the *bhikkhu saṅgha*.

Today, an estimated 150 Theravāda *bhikkhunīs* live and practice in ten different monasteries across Thailand. In addition, there are more than one hundred *bhikṣuṇīs*, mostly of Chinese descent, who live and practice in Mahāyāna monasteries.

People with a democratic sensibility may feel a natural inclination to advocate for equal ordination opportunities for nuns, yet it is important to understand the perspectives of Thai nuns themselves. Although Thai nuns lack access to an officially recognized *bhikkhunī* ordination, most do not consider themselves oppressed. On the contrary, nuns in Thailand count themselves fortunate to have the opportunity to devote themselves to the pursuit of *nirvāna* to whatever extent possible.[16] Women in Theravāda countries frequently state that their goal is liberation from *saṃsāra* (the wheel of repeated birth, death, and rebirth), and many feel it is not necessary to be fully ordained to achieve this. Some nuns and monks even consider the aspiration for higher ordination to be a misguided quest for worldly status. Many nuns are dedicated meditation practitioners who take full advantage of the numerous Theravāda meditation courses and centers open to them, confident they are on a steady path to liberation. Some nuns have become highly respected meditation teachers. Educational opportunities are also improving for Thai nuns, who currently have access to Pāli studies up to an advanced level.[17] Some nuns, such as Mae chee Kritsana Raksachom (b. 1964) at Mahachulalongkorn University, have earned PhDs and teach classes to monks and laity alike. Higher ordination is not required for these achievements and may even impose certain limitations, such as being under the authority of the *bhikkhu saṅgha*. An eminent Pāli scholar at Abhidhamma Jotika College named Supaphan Na Bangehang, who became a nun known as Mae chee Vimuttiya (b. 1949), noted that she prefers living as a *mae chee* rather than becoming a *bhikkhunī* because it allows her greater freedom.

Despite the lack of official recognition for *bhikkhunīs* in the Theravāda traditions, Theravāda nuns quietly continue to receive full ordination in India, Indonesia, Sri Lanka, and elsewhere. The strongest advocate for the full ordination of Thai women has been Bhikkhunī Dhammananda, the former philosophy professor from Bangkok, who relentlessly challenges the Thai *bhikkhus*' rejection of *bhikkhunī* ordination.[18] Since her full ordination in Sri Lanka in 2003, she has conscientiously campaigned for equal religious rights for women, despite continuing opposition from conservative monks. In November 2014, eight Thai nuns received full ordination (*upasampadā*) in a Theravāda *bhikkhunī* ordination held in Songkhla, southern Thailand. Mahindavamsa Mahathero, the Mahanayaka of Amarapura in Sri Lanka, served as the senior *bhikkhu* preceptor, and Bhikkhunī Dhammananda served as the senior *bhikkhunī* preceptor. The newly ordained *bhikkhunīs* are from Koh Yoh Island in southern Thailand, where they train under Bhikkhunī Dhammadipa, a nun who began as a white-robed eight-precept nun (*mae chee*) and received higher ordination in Songkhla in 2014. The ordination, widely acclaimed by advocates of full ordination for Thai women, was criticized by the Supreme Sangha Council of Thailand. A spokesperson for the Council of the Elders stated that the ordination compromised the security of Thai Theravāda Buddhism, and henceforth any foreign monk wishing to conduct an ordination in Thailand must have permission from the council, in accordance with a law promulgated in 1928. In response, three members of the National Reform Council announced that the statement by the Council of the Elders was a violation of the human right to freedom of religion, and so the debate continues. Although *bhikkhunīs* are not officially recognized in Thailand, they are gaining ground among devout Thai Buddhists for keeping high standards of moral conduct at a time when numerous monks have been embroiled in scandals.

The debate about the ordination of women has spread from Asia to monasteries located in Western countries. Some senior Western Theravāda *bhikkhus* have defended the claim of their root lineages in Asia, asserting that *bhikkhunī* ordination is not possible in the Theravāda tradition, because the lineage died out centuries ago and cannot be retrieved. However, some of these same *bhikkhus* have served as preceptors at *bhikkhunī* ordinations at the City of Ten Thousand Buddhas, a Chinese Mahāyāna monastery in northern California. In addition, while holding tightly to tradition in other ways, certain Theravāda *bhikkhus* have introduced new categories of monastic ordination for nuns that have no foundation in the *vinaya*. For example, in 1990, Ajahn Sumedho (b. 1934), Ajahn Paññasaro, and the English Council of Elders issued a Five-Point Declaration regarding a category of ten-precept nuns called *siladhara* (upholder of the precepts) first established by Ajahn Sumedho at Chithurst Buddhist Monastery in England in 1983. This declaration required that *siladharas* in that community agree to accept the seniority of the *bhikkhus* and not to seek *bhikkhunī* ordination henceforth. Needless to say, not all the nuns agreed to these terms. Defenders of the status quo see the situation as a tension between sacred ancient traditions in confrontation with new worldly demands for equality and women's rights. Others see it as a retrenching of dominant male hierarchies that have held sway for roughly 2,500 years, consigning women to positions of subordination and service while holding out the hope of a better (male) rebirth in the future. Now, however, sexist norms are being challenged.

The first cohort of Theravāda *bhikkhunīs* to be ordained in Australia set off a maelstrom. The ordination of these four *bhikkhunīs*, conducted by an international *bhikkhunī saṅgha* in October 2009 in conjunction with monastics from Bodhinyana Monastery and Dhammasara Nun's Monastery in Perth (see figure 6.2), was the first Theravāda *bhikkhunī* ordination ever held in Australia. The international tempest ignited by the ordination turned on not so much the legitimacy of the ordination per se but the fact that the senior *bhikkhu* preceptor, a well-known British Australian teacher named Ajahn Brahm (b. 1951), was subsequently dismissed from his order, based at Wat Pah Pong in northern Thailand. When Ajahn Brahm consulted the acting Sangharaja of Thailand (Somdej Phra Pootajarn), well in advance of the Perth ordination, about conducting a *bhikkhunī* ordination outside of Thailand, he was told three times, "Thai *sangha* law does not extend outside of Thailand." He therefore felt that his role in confirming an ordination rite that had been properly conducted by a quorum of *bhikkhunīs* was legitimate. Some senior *bhikkhus* disagreed. When Ajahn Brahm refused to recant and state that the four nuns were not *bhikkhunīs*, Bodhinyana Monastery was delisted as a branch of Wat Pah Pong, effectively excommunicating it.[19] The thousands of messages that appeared on social media as a result of the ordeal almost unanimously supported Ajahn Brahm and the newly ordained *bhikkhunīs*.

Figure 6.2. The international ordination of *bhikkhunīs* held in 2009 with monastics from Bodhinyana Monastery and Dhammasara Nun's Monastery in Perth, Australia. Credit: Photo by Annie Marie Keating.

Bhikṣuṇī Ordination in East Asia

As we have seen, the claim that woman cannot become fully ordained because there is no lineage of *bhikṣuṇī* ordination today is contradicted by the existence of continuous and thriving lineages of *bhikṣuṇīs* in the People's Republic of China, Hong Kong, Malaysia, South Korea, Singapore, Taiwan, Vietnam, and elsewhere. The total number of *bhikṣuṇīs* in the world today is impossible to calculate but, taking the nuns of China into account, may be higher than eighty thousand. These nuns observe the 348 *bhikṣuṇī* precepts of the Dharmaguptaka *vinaya* translated into Chinese at the beginning of the fifth century CE. There is a widespread misconception among Theravāda adherents that the monastics of East Asia follow a Mahāyāna lineage of *vinaya*. To counter this misconception, it is useful to know that the Dharmaguptaka lineage derives from the Mahīśāsaka lineage, a branch of the Sthaviravāda lineage, now known as Theravāda.[20] The differences among the various schools of *vinaya* are relatively minor.

The earliest nuns in China settled into monastic communities during the early centuries of Dharma transmission without the benefit of the rules they were expected to live by, since the *bhikṣuṇī vinaya* texts had not yet been received or translated.[21] There is no conclusive evidence that any Indian nuns ever visited China or that any Chinese nuns traveled to India. When Jingjian and four companions became the first Buddhist nuns in China to receive the precepts in the middle of the fourth century, the rite of ordination was conducted according to the recently acquired *bhikṣuṇī vinaya* texts but was presided over by *bhikṣus* alone, since there were no *bhikṣuṇīs* in China at the time. Only during the fifth century, when the texts of four different *vinaya* schools become available in Chinese, was the first officially recognized higher ordination ceremony for nuns (*bhikṣuṇī upasampadā*) conducted by Bhikkhunī Tesarā and her group of courageous *bhikṣuṇīs* who traveled from Sri Lanka for this express purpose. Unfortunately, the *Biographies of Buddhist Nuns*, which records this historic event, does not mention which school of *vinaya* these *bhikṣuṇīs* followed. Later, due to the influence of the *vinaya* master Daoxuan (596–667), the Chinese Buddhist authorities decided to adopt the Dharmagupta lineage of *vinaya* for all monastics throughout China.[22]

Today, *bhikṣuṇī* ordination ceremonies are held with great fanfare in most East Asian countries, often lasting as long as one or two months in order to impart strict monastic training and sufficient knowledge of the precepts. Whether located in cities or in the countryside, monasteries for *bhikṣuṇīs* generally function independently and self-sufficiently. Each monastery provides training in Dharma, monastic discipline, ritual, and meditation, as well as the practical skills needed to run a monastery: chanting, vegetarian cooking, counseling, calligraphy, flower arrangement, and much more. Beginning with Buddhist services held very early each morning—3:00 a.m. in South Korea, 4:00 a.m. in Taiwan—the nuns execute their many duties mindfully and often quite joyfully throughout the day. A young woman interested in monastic life generally serves in the monastery for some years as a Buddhist laywoman (*upāsikā*), picking up knowledge and skills, and gradually divesting herself of worldly responsibilities, before requesting a teacher to shave her head and confer the novice (*śrāmaṇerika*) precepts. After successfully observing the *śrāmaṇerika* precepts for a period of some years, the novice nun will request her teacher to allow her to receive the *bhikṣuṇī* precepts, often at a grand ceremony with nuns from other monasteries. After ordination, most *bhikṣuṇīs* continue to study the Dharma at a Buddhist college, at a university, or at the monastery. A two-year intermediate stage as a probationary nun (*śikṣamāṇā*) before higher ordination is observed in certain monasteries.

In East Asian countries, the option to receive precepts—in sequence, the five precepts of a Buddhist laywoman, the ten precepts of a novice nun, the six precepts of a probationary nun, and eventually the 348 precepts of a fully ordained nun—is available to any woman who wishes to receive them and who demonstrates her determination to observe them purely. Ordinations are held regularly, qualified *bhikṣuṇī* teachers serve as mentors to large numbers of students and devotees, Buddhist education is easily available to nuns at every stage of their development, and material support is generously offered by the lay community. Discipline is strict. The high standards require thorough training, sincerity, and determination on the part of the nuns. Laywomen often live, work, and practice along with the nuns, sometimes receiving ordination once their family responsibilities have been fulfilled. The Buddhist monasteries of East Asia are structured much like families, even using kinship terms to designate their interrelationships and displaying many of the same patterns of mutual care, expectations, hard work, joys, and occasional disappointments. Overall, these monasteries provide a welcome refuge for women who are inclined to the spiritual life.

Ordination for Women in the Tibetan Tradition

Sometime during the eighth to tenth centuries CE, the Sanskrit texts of monastic discipline for women of the Mūlasarvāstivāda *vinaya* lineage were transmitted to Tibet and translated into Tibetan. However, due to the difficulties and dangers of traveling across the high Himalayas, it seems that the quorum of twelve *bhikṣuṇīs* that is required to conduct a *bhikṣuṇī* ordination in the Mūlasarvāstivāda tradition never reached Tibet. Very few materials about women in this early period of Tibetan history survive, and there are no records of Indian nuns attempting the journey from India to Tibet. As Buddhism spread north across the mountains, the precepts of monastic discipline were adapted in response to the very different climate, geography, and social norms in the Tibetan cultural sphere. Gradually, as the Buddhist teachings took root in Tibet, women who aspired to the spiritual life began to settle in small practice communities or to practice like nuns at home. Although the history of ordination for women in Tibet is unclear, most nuns in the Tibetan tradition today receive ordination as a novice nun (*śrāmaṇerika*), observe the same precepts as novice monks (*śrāmaṇera*), and are regarded as members of the *saṅgha*.[23] In the absence of a lineage of full ordination for nuns, monastic institutions became overwhelming dominated by males. Monasteries for women were often located in remote areas, loosely affiliated with monks' monasteries, but left to fend for themselves at a subsistence level. Tibetan women were not forced to marry, but neither were they strongly encouraged to pursue monastic life. Without much support for women's monastic communities, some women lived the life of a nun while staying in their family homes, where they were addressed as "*ani*," meaning "auntie." Even so, over the centuries, outstanding female religious figures, both lay and ordained, emerged and made important contributions to Tibetan religious history.

In recent discussions, it appears that support is growing for establishing a lineage of *bhikṣuṇīs* in the Tibetan tradition. According to the Mūlasarvāstivāda *vinaya*, a quorum of ten *bhikṣus* and a quorum of twelve *bhikṣuṇīs* are required to confer the *bhikṣuṇī* precepts at a full ordination rite for nuns.[24] After answering certain questions to verify their suitability for ordination, the candidates first receive the precepts in the presence of the *bhikṣuṇīs* and then go to the *bhikṣus* for confirmation. Of the three potential solutions now being considered for introducing the *bhikṣuṇī* lineage into the Tibetan tradition, the first possibility is for the nuns to receive the *bhikṣuṇī* precepts from Tibetan *bhikṣus* alone, without the presence of *bhikṣuṇīs*. For *bhikṣus* alone to administer the *bhikṣuṇī* precepts is technically irregular. Even though the presiding *bhikṣus* would incur a slight transgression by doing so, the *bhikṣuṇīs*' ordination would be valid. *Bhikṣus* alone have frequently ordained *bhikṣuṇīs* in Korea, Taiwan, and Vietnam without much controversy. This is the procedure used by Buddha Śākyamuni himself when he ordained Mahāprajāpatī as the first *bhikṣuṇī* ordination in India. A second possibility is for the nuns to receive ordination from *bhikṣuṇīs* who have been ordained in the Dharmaguptaka lineage that is currently followed in China, South Korea, Taiwan, and Vietnam. A third solution is a combined approach in which *bhikṣuṇīs* ordained in the Dharmaguptaka lineage confer the ordination alongside Tibetan *bhikṣus* ordained in the Mūlasarvāstivāda lineage. With the backing of His Holiness the Fourteenth Dalai Lama and senior *bhikṣus*, any of these solutions could be justified.

Opponents question the validity of such an ordination on two counts: first, the purported need for the existence of an unbroken *bhikṣuṇī* lineage to confer the ordination, and second, the validity of the *bhikṣuṇī* ordination procedures. To answer the first objection, some attempts have been made to investigate whether the extant *bhikṣuṇī* lineages of East Asia have been transmitted in an unbroken lineage from the time of Buddha Śākyamuni until today. This is a daunting and probably futile task, since records of monastic lineages generally record only the names of male precept masters. To answer the second objection, several studies have compared the *bhikṣuṇī* precepts and procedures for receiving *bhikṣuṇī* ordination in the Chinese Dharmaguptaka and Tibetan Mūlasarvāstivāda traditions and found them to be substantially the same.[25]

Discussions of the possible options for instituting the *bhikṣuṇī* ordination in the Tibetan tradition have been ongoing since the 1980s. A number of Western women who received ordination as novice nuns (*śrāmaṇerika*) in the Tibetan tradition have received permission to take full ordination as *bhikṣuṇīs* in the Chinese, Korean, or Vietnamese traditions. Those nuns who have done so have been publicly acknowledged by His Holiness the Fourteenth Dalai Lama as *bhikṣuṇīs* practicing in the Tibetan tradition. In 2012, ten monk scholars representing the four schools of Tibetan Buddhism were invited by the Department of Religion and Culture of the Central Tibetan Administration to gather in Dharamsala, India, to review possible ways to accomplish the goal of establishing a lineage of *bhikṣuṇīs* in the Tibetan tradition. This research committee has been charged with finding a way to make full ordination available to nuns following the Mūlasarvāstivāda tradition, but so far their recommendations are inconclusive.

Although the Tibetan Government in Exile has yet to officially sanction any of these solutions, His Holiness the Fourteenth Dalai Lama has expressed his personal desire to see the *bhikṣuṇī* lineage established within the Tibetan tradition, has given his blessing to nuns in the Tibetan tradition to receive *bhikṣuṇī* ordination in lineages in other countries, and has publicly recognized the ordinations of those who have done so. However, he still maintains that the decision must be decided by a senior *saṅgha* council, not unilaterally. To help resolve the issue, he called for an international conference with representatives of all the major Buddhist traditions to examine the fine points of Buddhist monastic law and work toward a consensus on the matter. In 2007, at the conference was held at Hamburg University in Germany,[26] expectations were high that a *bhikṣuṇī* ordination would be forthcoming, but thus far there has been no official announcement to that effect. In 2015, the Seventeenth Gyalwang Karmapa, Ogyen Trinley Dorje (b. 1985), announced his intention to initiate a process of ordination for nuns practicing in the Tibetan tradition. In 2017 in Bodhgaya, a *śrāmaṇerika* ordination for twenty-nine nuns was conducted by *bhikṣuṇīs* from Taiwan, which was to be followed by a *śikṣamāṇā* ordination, leading eventually to *bhikṣuṇī* ordination under the auspices of the Karmapa, but the project has yet to be realized.

Slow Steps Forward

The debate about ordination for Buddhist women is not new. Women's capabilities to achieve liberation are not in doubt; as attested in the *Therīgāthā*, at the time of the Buddha many women achieved liberation, and it is theoretically possible for women to achieve liberation even today. However, Buddha Śākyamuni's reported hesitation to admit women to the monastic order and contradictions in the texts raise many important questions. Why did the Buddha require urging before admitting women to the *saṅgha*, when elsewhere he declared that a stable society was comprised of four quarters: laymen, laywomen, fully ordained monks, and fully ordained nuns? Why did he require Mahāpajāpatī to observe the eight *gurudharmas*, establishing a pattern of female subordination that has influenced attitudes toward women ever since? Although the provenance of the rules is unclear, the structures of gender inequality embedded in them have helped to perpetuate inequities between nuns and monks for more than two thousand years. Monastic identities, including the rite of ordination, are constructed on this unequal gender footing, with ramifications for women in Buddhist societies, both lay and ordained.

Even among nuns in the Buddhist traditions, opinion about the higher ordination for nuns remain divided. Those who are opposed assert that the full ordination of nuns cannot be conferred because the requisite quorum of fully ordained *bhikṣuṇīs* is not available in their particular traditions, even though there are sufficient numbers of *bhikṣuṇīs* who have received full ordination in the Chinese, Korean, Taiwanese, and Vietnamese traditions. Some are satisfied with a renunciant status independent of the *bhikṣu saṅgha*, even if it is less highly regarded. Those who support full ordination for women assert that the ordination can proceed, on the grounds that Buddha Śākyamuni himself initiated the ordination of nuns without a full quorum of *bhikṣus* and *bhikṣuṇīs*, and thus set a precedent for the ordination of *bhikṣuṇīs* solely by *bhikṣus*.

As many observers of the ordination debate have noted, few contemporary monks seem keenly interested in the intricacies of *vinaya* for monks but may become exceedingly concerned with such matters when it comes to the full ordination of nuns. For example, the *vinaya* texts are very specific in describing the process by which novice nuns are required to be trained and ordained by *bhikṣuṇīs*, yet few if any critics of *bhikṣuṇī* ordination in the Tibetan tradition have objected to the practice of *bhikṣus* ordaining women as novices. Some critics have openly wondered whether recent debates over the legal intricacies of *bhikṣuṇī vinaya* are a stalling tactic, a way to defer *bhikṣuṇī* ordination indefinitely.[27]

Meanwhile, a stellar example of women demonstrating their potential to achieve the highest goals of their tradition was the awarding of the *geshema* degree in Buddhist philosophy to nuns in the Tibetan tradition. In December 2016, twenty Tibetan and Himalayan nuns were awarded this highest degree for the first time in Tibetan history. Achieving equal access for women to attain the culmination of this highly demanding systematic study program in Buddhist logic, psychology, and philosophy was a great breakthrough. This example of women achieving gender parity in scholarly achievement not only sets a historic precedent for women in the Tibetan tradition but also is validation that women in all traditions have the capacity to reach the highest goals. Now that this major goal has been achieved, the stage is set for achieving the next goal: women's access to full ordination.

If religious freedom and gender equality are human rights, then it stands to reason that women should have the same religious freedoms and opportunities as men do. The point is not that every woman should become a nun, but that women must have equal access to higher ordination and other religious opportunities before Buddhists can claim that there is no discrimination in Buddhism. At present, however, all Buddhist women do not have access to full ordination as a *bhikṣuṇī* and many do not even have the right to ordain as a novice nun (*śrāmaṇerika*). Achieving equitable opportunities for women to serve in leadership roles in the Buddhist traditions is a matter of social justice and is also a barometer of Buddhist claims to wisdom and compassion.

7

Grassroots Revolution

Buddhist Women and Social Activism

"Socially engaged Buddhism" has become the buzzword for a new approach that takes spiritual practice out of the cave or monastery and into the streets. Buddhist practice is no longer conceived as simply a solitary contemplative quest for realization or inner transformation. The new socially engaged approach is an intentional effort to apply Buddhist teachings to address contemporary social issues and effect a broader transformation. Although women who enter monastic life generally do so because they are interested in achieving liberation, not because they wish to do social work, increasing numbers of nuns are participating in contemporary efforts to address the sufferings of society in practical ways. The Buddha's core teaching on *duḥkha* (suffering and dissatisfaction) is clearly manifested in the global poverty, corruption, militarism, environmental degradation, incarceration, economic and sexual exploitation, natural disasters, epidemics, and countless dehumanizing miseries that confront humanity today. For many, cultivating loving-kindness for the sufferings of others has become an ethical injunction. Expanding loving-kindness beyond the meditation cushion to those who are suffering in the streets and neighborhoods around us is viewed as a natural and necessary corollary of spiritual practice.

This overtly activist approach to Buddhism has critics as well as proponents. What does social activism have to do with attaining enlightenment? Is it possible to achieve perfect awakening while working at a soup kitchen or a homeless shelter? If so, why did the Buddha bother to meditate? Even if we were able to feed the hungry today, won't they be hungry again tomorrow? Don't those who become involved with the dust of the world become tainted by it? This tension between spiritual cultivation and social activism, the world renouncer and the world redeemer, is not simply a Buddhist dilemma but an ongoing concern in many religious traditions. This ethical dilemma posits spiritual development and social engagement as two poles and is unlikely to be resolved anytime soon. Some Buddhists today argue that the choice between contemplation and social engagement is an artificial binary. For them, social activism is not just defensible but both urgently required and invigorated by Buddhist ideals. Ultimately, the choice of how to balance these dynamics is left to the individual practitioner. This chapter looks at the history of Buddhist social engagement in diverse contexts to understand how Buddhist ideals can be expressed in the social sphere and what roles Buddhist women have played.

Being Good or Doing Good?

Contemporary Buddhist social engagement is often traced to Taixu (1890–1947), a monk, educator, political activist, and innovative reformer of Buddhism in China. Taixu's ideas about implementing Buddhist values in society and creating a Pure Land in the human realm had a major influence on the work of the Vietnamese poet-monk Thich Nhat Hanh (b. 1926) and other contemporary Buddhist teachers who have in turn had a major influence on Buddhism internationally. At the same time, it can also be argued that Buddhists have been actively engaged in society from the very beginning. Monastic centers (*vihāras*) often served as the schools, clinics, orphanages, old folks' homes, cultural centers, community centers, and counseling centers in their localities. The Buddha's teachings on avoiding harm and relieving the sufferings of sentient beings have never been simply theoretical. Buddhist meditation and other practices can be understood as preparing practitioners to put the teachings on nonviolence, generosity, loving-kindness, and wisdom into practice in everyday life. King Aśoka (268–239 BCE) of the Mauryan Dynasty is a legendary example. After extending his empire across the vast expanse of northern India and beyond, he woke up one day to see the carnage his armies had wrought and felt deep remorse for the suffering his military conquests had caused. He subsequently became an exemplary Buddhist ruler and initiated public welfare projects such as roads, wells, medical clinics, rest houses, tree plantations, and veterinary clinics for the humane treatment of animals. Throughout history, Buddhist rulers in China, Japan, Korea, Vietnam, and other countries have also been lauded for their efforts to implement Buddhist values for the benefit of their people. For centuries, Buddhist women and men have conscientiously applied themselves to implementing Buddhist values of generosity, loving-kindness, and compassion in communities around the world. What is new today is the increased diversity and visibility of Buddhist social welfare activities, ranging from food distribution to animal liberation, prison chaplaincy, disaster relief, peace activism, addiction treatment, recycling efforts, hospice programs, and more.

The enormous benefits of these charitable organizations are widely recognized, with programs ranging from tsunami disaster relief to innovative education to the promotion of breastfeeding.[1] A weakness of Buddhist social welfare efforts is that they are often limited to charitable activities. As beneficial as generosity (*dāna*) certainly is in relieving the immediate sufferings of people, many Buddhists remain unaware of or confused by the distinction between charitable activities and social justice efforts—between relieving the sufferings of the disadvantaged and working to transform the unjust social, economic, and political structures that are responsible for their sufferings. Some Buddhists consciously steer away from social activism, believing it may become political and that politics is somehow divorced from or in conflict with Buddhist priorities. Yet some Buddhists today, especially in Western countries, recognize that charitable giving alone does not change the unjust social, economic, and political structures that enable the injustices of poverty, exploitation, discrimination, and violence to persist. In some cases, for example, when Buddhists live under repressive governments, their lack of active, critical engagement in social justice issues is understandable, because expressions of dissent may be met with retaliation, imprisonment, torture, or execution. As both the Saffron Revolution in 2007 in Myanmar, which involved monks and nuns as well as laypeople, and Tibetan efforts to speak truth to power in the People's Republic of China have shown, voicing social concerns under oppressive regimes can have all these terrifying consequences, including the greatest torment of all: the silencing of conscience. In other countries where Buddhists constitute a religious minority, such as Bangladesh, Indonesia, Malaysia, Russia, and Singapore, the risks of engaging in social activism and speaking one's mind on political issues may be more subtle but still stifle free expression. Under the circumstances, Buddhist contemplative practice offers one of the few allowable avenues of expression. For example, in Myanmar and occupied Tibet, political oppression has resulted in a striking increase of interest in Buddhist identity and religious practice. Recent incidents of ethnonationalist and interreligious violence in Myanmar, Sri Lanka, and Thailand present serious challenges to narratives of Buddhist nonviolence.[2] Urgent questions remain as to how Buddhist ideals may be mobilized and implemented to correct and prevent all these social injustices.

Buddhism and Gender Justice

Buddhist women have made great contributions to the social good. First, a strong case can be made that giving birth and caring for children is a valid and laudable form of social engagement, one that is essential for the well-being of humanity. Second, one can also point to the many courageous Buddhist women who have raised their voices to support worthy social causes. As we have learned, Mahāpajāpatī was the first Buddhist feminist activist, having led a procession of five hundred women across northern India in the sixth century BCE to advocate for women's right to join the *saṅgha*, thus opening the door to liberation for countless women in India and around the world. The legacy of her contribution to social justice can be seen in Buddhist women's many meritorious activities throughout history, up to today. During the Edo period (1603–1868) in Japan, for example, the nuns and lay residents of Mantokuji Temple in Gunma Prefecture provided shelter and reconciliation counseling for women seeking to divorce their husbands.[3] In addition to offering sanctuary and spiritual solace through the practice of chanting the name of Amitābha Buddha, this "divorce temple" provided medical services, counseling, and other social services to the local community. Extrapolating from many such examples, it may be argued that social activism is sanctioned in Buddhism as a commendable application of the Buddha's teachings and his injunction to relieve the sufferings of sentient beings.

The core Buddhist values of loving-kindness, compassion, and peace act both as contemplative practices and as guidelines for active social transformation. The importance accorded to these values seems to sanction social and political activism as a natural expression of the Buddha's teachings. The initial emphasis is on cultivating wholesome mental states and avoiding all unwholesome actions of body, speech, and mind. As traditionally conceived, a person practices to purify all mental defilements and accumulate all virtues. In the process, one's self-cherishing and self-grasping attitude becomes transformed from a limited awareness to a universal awareness, from self-centered concern to concern for the welfare of all living beings. Buddhist practices of mental cultivation may make one a better activist, less apt to become enraged and obstinate. Activism informed by loving-kindness and compassion is more likely to be nonviolent and ultimately more effective.

In recent decades, more and more Buddhist women have been recognized publicly as exemplars of active compassion. In Thailand, Mae chee Khunying Kanitha (1920–2002) began the first women's shelter and the first home for women and children infected by HIV/AIDS.[4] In Taiwan, Bhikṣuṇī Chao Hwei (b. 1965) has campaigned for social justice, human rights, and animal rights. In remote, impoverished villages in Vietnam, nuns work on food security, flood relief, and compassionate care for the disabled. In Thailand, Mae chee Sansanee Sathirasuta works with women with HIV/AIDS and educates their children through Sathira Dhammasthan Center in Bangkok. In India, the Australian nun Ayya Yeshe Bodhicitta (b. 1978) works through Bodhicitta Foundation to relieve the sufferings of slum dwellers in India, especially women and children. Achieving greater equity and representation as well as greater access to knowledge, wisdom, and resources have been major steps forward for Buddhist women, enabling them to work effectively toward realizing the ideal of an enlightened society.

In the United States, women have often been on the front lines of social activism.[5] Joanna Macy (b. 1929), an environmental activist, prescribes collaborative methods of dealing with the despair that arises from seemingly insurmountable social and ecological crises. Susan Moon (b. 1942) is a writer who edited *Turning Wheel*, the journal of the Buddhist Peace Fellowship, for many years. Paula Green (b. 1937) founded Karuna Center for Peacebuilding, which offers peace training and dialogue to create a global network of peace activists. Zenju Earthlyn Manuel (b. 1952), former director of the Buddhist Peace Fellowship, writes about and applies Buddhist approaches to homelessness and other forms of social dysfunction.[6] Melody Ermachild Chavis (b. 1943) promotes social justice by legal means, especially mobilizing opposition to the death penalty.[7] In Buddhist temples throughout North America, Taiwanese nuns devote themselves to serving the needs of immigrant communities struggling to adapt to new social and economic realities.[8] Belying stereotypical images of reclusive meditators, Buddhist women today are actively engaged in a wide range of projects for the social good. Their Buddhist practice is what sustains them and enables them to work wholeheartedly, compassionately, and effectively for social change.

In countries with high educational standards, women have become increasingly active in social welfare work. Charitable activities take many forms, usually starting on a grassroots level and sometimes growing into vast institutions. A prominent example is Bhikṣuṇī Cheng Yen (b. 1937), a Taiwanese Buddhist nun who captured world attention by encouraging housewives to donate pennies from their grocery money each week to support charitable projects and hospitals in Taiwan. In 1966, she founded Buddhist Compassion Relief Tzu Chi Foundation, which has become the largest charitable organization in Taiwan and one of the largest in the world, with more than ten million members and programs in sixty-eight countries.[9] Tzu Chi Foundation is renowned for its global relief work, recycling programs, and free medical clinics, including one in downtown Honolulu. Other examples of the numerous Buddhist charitable organizations that are active today, both locally and globally, include Buddhist Global Relief, Lotus Outreach, Nonviolent Peaceforce, Jamyang Foundation, and Compassionate Hands Foundation.

In countries with poor educational standards, women are socially and economically disadvantaged. Illiteracy and a lack of educational opportunities are still common in many rural Buddhist communities, resulting in poverty, sex trafficking, and exploitation; therefore, correcting gender disparities in education has become a key social justice issue for women in recent decades. Buddhism has strongly emphasized education from earliest times, when the Buddha taught the path to liberation to large public audiences of women and men of diverse backgrounds. With his encouragement, the Buddha's disciples, female and male, learned and then transmitted these teachings to public audiences near and far. As Buddhism became institutionalized, however, educational structures became decidedly patriarchal and the vast majority of scholars and teach-

Figure 7.1. Young nuns reciting Buddhist texts at Yangchen Chöling Monastery in Spiti, Himachal Pradesh, India. Credit: Photo by Olivier Adam.

ers have been male. In recent years, Buddhist scholars, practitioners, and activists have promoted educational reforms to create a more equitable system.

In 1987, at the first Sakyadhita International Association of Buddhist Women conference held in Bodhgaya, India, when the subordinate status of women in Buddhist societies finally came to public attention, the importance of education was keenly recognized as *the* key to women's advancement. At that historic gathering, gender equity in education, especially Buddhist education, was extolled. More and better education was seen as essential not only for women's personal and spiritual growth but also for preserving Buddhist culture and working to benefit all living things. Since that initial gathering, the momentum to improve opportunities for girls and women, lay and ordained, has generated many new education projects, such as Yangchen Chöling Monastery in Himachal Pradesh, that have completely transformed perceptions of women's potential, both in society and in the minds of women themselves (see figure 7.1).[10]

Sakyadhita is a transnational movement that links Buddhist women together across boundaries of ethnicity, tradition, language, and socio-economic status. It integrates scholarship, social engagement, activism, contemplation, and the arts, to educate, empower, and advocate for change in the social structures that perpetuate conflicts, environmental degradation, gender inequities, and other ills. This movement has helped to link social action networks, especially for the benefit of women and children. Though much work remains, especially in areas such as sex trafficking, grassroots approaches to social transformation action are having far-reaching, liberating effects. Drawing attention to the spiritual achievements of Buddhist women that have heretofore mostly gone unnoticed has inspired women in many countries to greater social engagement.

Transnational Sisterhood: Women Transforming Buddhism

After centuries of patriarchal domination, it is understandable that a major focus of social justice awareness for Buddhist women is gender equity. For years in Buddhist communities around the world, socially constructed gender stereotypes that dictate expected behaviors for men and women have gone unchallenged and uncontested. The expectation that men should be assertive and dominant and that women should be gentle and compliant have operated alongside Buddhist ideals of gentleness and independent thinking, grounded on the Buddhist principle that women and men, despite certain biological differences, all have the capacity for mental cultivation, wholesome conduct, and spiritual liberation. Although it is recognized that no two individuals will ever be exactly the same, all sentient beings, including animals, have the potential to eventually liberate themselves from suffering, even if it takes many lifetimes to achieve. The most fortunate state in which to actualize this potential is as a human being. In this context, from a Buddhist feminist perspective, obstacles that impede women's spiritual liberation are both unjust and unwholesome. For this reason, the contemporary Buddhist women's movement spearheaded by Sakyadhita has worked to raise awareness of social and institutional injustices in Buddhist communities, especially drawing attention to the inequities Buddhist women face in education and ordination.

Traditionally, it has been acknowledged that women can achieve liberation from cyclic existence (*saṃsāra*), whether in this lifetime or future lifetimes, although it is also asserted that women face hindrances, both social and biological. Still, in most Buddhist traditions, women are regarded as incapable of achieving the state of a perfectly awakened being (*samyaksaṃbuddha*) because they do not have a "male sign" (in other words, a penis), which is one of the thirty-two major marks of a Buddha. A few lines of scripture and the fact that all known *buddhas* thus far have been male seem to be the only stumbling blocks that prevent women from achieving enlightenment. Ironically, even though Buddha Śākyamuni himself affirmed women's equal capacity to achieve liberation, the physical marker of the Buddha's masculine identity has been used to justify gender discrimination for millennia. At the same time, the Buddha is quoted as saying he would not pass away until there were laymen, laywomen, monks, and nuns who could teach the Dharma. The Buddha also made a point of teaching women, and he promulgated precepts to protect them from assault and exploitation. Based on the Buddha's egalitarian affirmation and the fact that he went to such lengths to include women in his newly founded religious community, it is clear that he recognized the same potential in women as he did in men. Despite this affirmation of spiritual equality, it is only in the past few decades that Buddhist women have begun to recognize and articulate their disadvantaged social and institutional status and to express a more gender-balanced vision.

In the past few decades globally, due to a confluence of socially liberating ideologies, women's studies research, and new communications networks, gender awareness has advanced remarkably. In the Buddhist world, women have gained greater access to education, information, and confirmation of their intrinsic value and potential in both the secular and religious spheres. New forums for discussion and learning about Buddhist women's history and contributions, such as the Sakyadhita conferences, publications, and social media channels, have been created. Whether they choose to practice as laywomen, nuns, or in roles beyond those traditional categories, Buddhist women are receiving validation and encouragement to expand their knowledge, think critically, express themselves creatively, and accept leadership opportunities in greater numbers than ever before. For those who choose monastic life, there are more opportunities to achieve the status of a nun. For those who choose household life, there are more practice opportunities. Women are increasingly visible as teachers and are gaining the skills to apply Buddhist solutions to address the problems of the world.

The grassroots revolution for women's rights in Buddhism has benefited from the backing of highly placed male allies. One of the most visible has been His Holiness the Fourteenth Dalai Lama, who has supported the fledgling Buddhist women's movement even in the face of opposition from conservative forces in the Tibetan monastic world. The 1989 Nobel Peace Prize winner has broken with patriarchal tradition in countless ways, including by addressing the first Sakyadhita conference in Bodhgaya, visiting many nunneries in the Tibetan diaspora, encouraging nuns to wear the formal yellow robe of an ordained *saṅgha* member, welcoming nuns to attend the Great Prayer Festival, establishing a commission to examine the issue of women's full ordination, and engaging in dialogue with influential female trendsetters such as Oprah Winfrey. In numerous press interviews, the Fourteenth Dalai Lama, who identifies as a feminist, has mentioned the possibility that the next Dalai Lama could be a woman.[11] Some observers question his characterization of women as "more compassionate, more caring," but he has backed up his support for women's rights with many innovations, such as enabling nuns in the Tibetan tradition to earn the *geshe* degree for the first time in history. He has repeatedly affirmed that women have great potential as leaders, has strongly encouraged women's education and active social engagement, and has cleared the path for women to assume positions of leadership in his own Tibetan tradition.

Buddhist Women and Social Justice: Intersections of Awakening

Buddhist women have been active agents of social change from the beginnings of the tradition through the modern period. Although they have received little attention for their efforts, their activities for the social good are regarded as a natural extension of loving-kindness and compassion. Buddhist women's steady, beneficent contributions throughout centuries belie the notion that they are merely passive supporters of men. Although they do work hard to care for their families and are not always recognized for their contributions, Buddhist women freely engage in projects to benefit their communities, including the monastics and the needy, placing others' welfare above their own.

One of the most radical decisions a woman may make in traditional Buddhist societies is to opt out of marriage and family to become a nun. The reactions of lay society are not always appreciative; by rejecting domestic life and reproduction, nuns signal that they place a higher value on social and spiritual independence. As sociologist Monica Lindberg Falk puts it,

> For Thai men, ordination and the life of a monk are ways to realise their masculine identity. . . . For Thai women, female identity is not realised by celibacy. In the contrary, women achieve maturity and female identity through marriage and motherhood, which are firmly tied to the secular realm. When a woman decides to reject the female reproductive identity, abandon her home life by assuming a religious identity and become a *mae chii*, she violates social norms of gender.[12]

The depreciation of female renunciation leaves women few alternatives for social and economic independence. Entering the sex trade is hardly a viable alternative, since it is notoriously exploitative of women. Changing attitudes toward education and monastic life for girls and women is therefore a valid social justice concern. To do so entails breaking the cultural code that devalues women's potential and learning to navigate social environments that are hierarchically structured by gender. Some recommend dismantling these structures altogether.

Since 1987, Buddhist women affiliated with Sakyadhita have been gathering every two years from around the world to discuss the status of women in Buddhism. Thus far, all the conferences have been held in Asia, where 99 percent of Buddhist women live. This represents a paradigm shift—an inversion of the presumption that the Buddhist feminist movement is a Western concoction, a women's rights "agenda," as it has been labeled by its opponents. The leadership teams of these conferences are predominantly Asian women, though men and Western women have played significant roles.

The twenty-first century is a time of tremendous changes and challenges for Buddhist women in countries as far-flung as Myanmar, Indonesia, Nepal, Taiwan, China, and Tibet. A survey of these changes and challenges not only provides background for understanding women's experiences in Asian Buddhist cultures but also serves as a barometer of changes that are sweeping Asian Buddhist societies in general. The question that guides this exploration is whether, and in what ways, Buddhism is liberating for women, and in what ways it is oppressive. To what extent are contemporary changes for women in Buddhist societies influenced by Western ideologies such as democracy and feminism, and to what extent are they shaped by traditional Buddhist concepts and values, such as karma, compassion, wisdom, and generosity?

Although Buddhist ethics provides a clear standard for ethical conduct, it has proven insufficient to protect disadvantaged sectors of society, to challenge exploitation, or to address the structural inequalities that allow exploitation to occur. Specifically, Buddhist ethical ideals, as valuable as they are, have proven to be inadequate in protecting the interests of the world's Buddhist women, many of whom live with poverty, illiteracy, and oppression, without adequate education, health care, or protection against abuse and exploitation. Women have been invisible in much of Buddhist history, which has been written from an androcentric, male-focused, perspective.

Historically, women have not been adequately represented in Buddhist institutional structures. All the category distinctions that we make when we consider Buddhism through a feminist lens—gender, woman, feminism, and justice—are distinctions that most women, especially Buddhist women in developing countries, have had little or no role in creating. Moreover, how relevant are Buddhist institutional structures for women if they have been created, operated, and dominated for two and a half millennia without reference to the experiences of women? Assuming an active voice, how can women challenge the stereotypes (the ubiquitous statement "Women have bad karma" comes to mind) and religious restrictions (such as the eight *gurudharmas*) that relegate women to a controlled, subordinate position? These questions have different meanings for women, depending on their social location, education, and awareness.

Queen Mahāmāyā is the archetype of maternal sacrifice in giving birth to the future Buddha and passing away just seven days later. Mahāprajāpatī models selfless devotion as she nurtures the young prince, and courageous leadership as she becomes the first woman to press for admission to the monastic order (*saṅgha*). Yaśodharā exemplifies the perfect conjugal companion in giving birth to Rāhula, the son who is testament to the prince's manhood and the depth of his renunciation. Sujātā appears as the archetypal nurturer who offers sustenance to the incipient Buddha just as he approaches the nadir of his ascetic spiritual quest. After the Buddha's awakening, countless women became his disciples and exemplified the effectiveness of his teachings by achieving liberation and becoming teachers themselves. Taken together, the dramatic appearance of powerful women at key junctures in the Buddha's spiritual career is a clear and enduring reminder of a woman's potential for awakening. However, even during the Buddha's lifetime, powerful women seemed to pose a challenge to some. Over time, women have become virtually invisible in the histories scribed by men. Without access to literacy, women's voices became muted or silent.

For Buddhist women today, therefore, the first essential step remains education. The expectation that people can advocate for structural change when they are poor and illiterate is unrealistic. As girls receive more education, they become more confident. As they grow into women, they begin to assume more visible roles: they run primary and secondary schools in Nepal,[13] teach in monasteries and primary schools in Bangladesh, and organize Buddhist institutes in Thailand and the Indian Himalayas. A few have established institutions of higher learning; in 1986, Bhikṣuṇī Shig Hiu Wan (1913–2004) established Huafan University, the first Buddhist university in Taiwan.[14] Bhikkhunī Dhammawati (b. 1934) has been a pioneer in Buddhist education in the Kathmandu Valley of Nepal and has trained hundreds of laywomen and nuns as teachers.[15] Cynthia Maung (b. 1959) is a Karen medical doctor who has received many awards for her charitable work with Burmese refugees and orphans at Mae Sot Clinic, on the Thai-Burmese border, since 1989. Vietnamese nuns initiate and oversee flood relief, health care, disability services, and elder care in many remote, impoverished villages in Vietnam.

Buddhist women have also been active in political and environmental activism with the intent to redress unjust social and political structures. Examples of social justice activists include Ani Pachen (1933–2002), who was a noted leader in the Tibetan resistance movement against People's Republic of China domination;[16] Aung San Suu Kyi (b. 1945), who led the movement for democracy and justice in Myanmar;[17] Bhikṣuṇī Jiyul Sunim (b. 1957), who fasted for a hundred days to protest the destruction of salamander habitat by a new high-speed railway in South Korea; and Bhikṣuṇī Chao Hwei in Taiwan, who has organized protests against gambling, nuclear proliferation, political oppression in Myanmar, the use of inappropriate language for nuns, and the subordination of women in the *saṅgha*.[18] Although there are few such outspoken Asian advocates of gender equity in Buddhist institutions, the signs of change are auspicious.

Social Justice, Inclusion, and Integrity

One option for Buddhist social justice is to work consciously to subvert the whole system. As feminist theory and colonial theory make clear, domination is successful when the oppressed remain silent. As proponents of civil disobedience can attest, the process of radical social and political change entails risks, and many Buddhists remain silent about injustices. Many even disavow the term "feminist," playing into the hands of patriarchal economic hegemonies and their media minions. The typical tactics of defamation, marginalization, and rejection to alienate, exclude, and dominate are tiresomely familiar. Even without articulating their subordinate status in the religious landscape, many Buddhist women work beneath the radar, independent of established institutions and bypassing all authorities, to create new Buddhist structures in which women have a fair place.

As we have discussed, although the Buddha himself forged a progressive path for women, Buddhist traditions still reflect the patriarchal structures of the societies in which they develop, and the Buddhist texts themselves are liable to patriarchal interpretations. Still, although Buddhist women still face many problems, they have become far more active and visible as agents of social change in the years since the first Sakyadhita conference in 1987. Given the current trajectory, there is little doubt that they will become an increasingly powerful force in years to come. Buddhist feminist activism has been effective because it is nonviolent, and the skillful means (*upāya*) used to challenge institutional gender discrimination have been nonconfrontational and therefore perceived as less threatening to the powers that be.

From a Buddhist perspective, the future will be the outcome of the actions we create now, so we seriously need to consider our collective future. As the Buddha taught, purifying our minds of greed, hate, ignorance, and other destructive emotions is the best way to improve our future. With sincere mental cultivation, it is within our power to live with integrity and alter the course of future events. In the case of humanity today, that is reassuring, since the alternative is planetary destruction. Even now, when systems analysts predict the worst possible outcome for our beautiful planet, and when greed, hatred, and ignorance seem to be raging out of control, Buddhism teaches that it is still possible for people of goodwill and for humanity as a whole to change our collective future by choosing to alter our actions. All the wisdom traditions teach the benefit of setting aside one's own self-interest and instead acting to protect and care for all creatures. This compassionate concern for all creatures requires a shift away from concern for "myself" and "my tribe," while replacing it with a genuine concern for the suffering and well-being of all living things. The law of karma functions not only for individuals but also collectively for all sentient beings. According to the Buddhist principle of dependent arising, wholesome and unwholesome thoughts, words, and deeds arise interdependently and therefore have interrelated consequences for all of life. This emphasis on the consequences of actions leaves Buddhists to grapple with questions like, What are the consequences of not acting to change injustices in the world? Ordinarily, actions that we do not create will not have consequences. A seed that is not sown does not grow into a plant. On the other hand, in a time when the world is full of unimaginable misery for millions of sentient beings, especially girls and women, what is the karma of doing nothing to alleviate their sufferings? UNICEF reports one billion suffering children in the world. The suffering of these children affects women disproportionately. Buddhists who take a more activist stance believe they cannot justify standing by and doing nothing to correct these injustices. Because loving-kindness and compassion are hallmarks of the Buddhist tradition, many women strongly feel that, as Buddhists, they have an obligation to work for social justice to help relieve the miseries of the world.

In the *Kālāma Sutta* in the Pāli canon, the Buddha counsels seekers of truth to examine his teachings with critical self-reflection. The *sutta* offers good advice about thinking for oneself, without relying on hearsay, tradition, rumors, scriptures, supposition, inference, appearances, preconceived notions, what is acceptable, or what is spoken by a respected ascetic. In this view, human beings are individually responsible for assessing what is wholesome and unwholesome, praiseworthy or blameworthy, wise or unwise, and conducive to happiness or to sorrow, and acting accordingly.[19]

After twenty-five hundred years of inequality, conditions are ripe for Buddhist women to work actively for change. There may be a preconception that the engaged Buddhist platform is a creation of the West, a human rights' "agenda" that is being imposed on Buddhists by activists from outside. In my view, this sentiment is unwarranted and uninformed. Although the Buddha may not have been a social activist in the contemporary sense of the word, the ideals of inclusion are not simply a modern Western concoction. Buddha Śākyamuni himself was a pioneer in social justice, opening up his community to women and to people of all caste backgrounds. His foster mother Mahāprajāpatī was certainly a social justice activist, leading a demonstration for women's right to be full participants in the *saṅgha*, as affirmed in the Buddhist texts. Socially engaged Buddhists are not starting something new in working for justice. These principles are already embedded in the Buddha's egalitarian message.

We live in times that demand action. Every day, the media report major atrocities and scandals. If senseless conflicts and dangerous toxins are threatening children's lives, that is something Buddhists should be concerned about. Of course, taking an active role in protesting injustices involves taking risks. One's social justice activism may become known to the authorities, to colleagues, and to prospective employers. We might even get arrested, raped, or tortured. But that is a risk we should be ready to shoulder. In fact, contemplating the sufferings of sentient beings may help spur our social conscience, inspiring us to speak out and work for social justice. Complacency is not an option for Buddhists with hearts of compassion. To be free to gather to discuss Buddhist insights on social justice and sustainable world peace is a privilege to be used wisely, to speak openly about critical issues and how to transform our troubled world.

The heart of the matter is that sustainable world peace is only possible in a just society where the basic needs of human beings, animals, and the environment are protected. Buddhists have an obligation to get behind the imperative work that is needed to implement social justice. Working from the core principles of compassion and loving-kindness, Buddhists can become examples of just and sustainable peace. Buddhist women have energetically rallied to the cause of social justice in all its many forms and have played major roles in taking Buddhist practice beyond the monastery and into the streets. The challenge is to provide women with the tools and encouragement to do what they know is right.

Conclusion

In the contemporary revitalization of Buddhism and its transmission to non-Buddhist societies, one of the most intriguing developments has been the emergence of a global Buddhist women's movement.[1] The conjunction of Buddhism and feminism is fertile ground for philosophical analysis and also has enormous social relevance. As a focus of both critical scholarship and cross-cultural exchange, Buddhists of all traditions are currently reassessing age-old assumptions about gender in light of current research and new attitudes toward gender in the modern world. In particular, the current awakening of awareness about the relationships among gender, authority, and violence against women has generated questions about gender justice in Buddhist societies and institutions that deserve scholarly attention and reflection. Elements of transnational feminist discourse and poststructuralist theory may be useful for understanding the contemporary Buddhist feminist movement.[2]

The chapters of this book have examined the lives and interactions of contemporary Buddhist women both as the legacy of a historical continuity and as a new transnational awakening of awareness. A generation of contemporary scholars—female and male—has begun to focus attention on Buddhist women through the lenses of anthropology, history, literature, psychology, sociology, and religious studies, using all the skills and resources of modern technology and communications. Many conclude that gender hierarchies and discrimination in Buddhism are remnants of a patriarchal social order that are incompatible with both the teachings of the Buddha and contemporary democratic values. The Buddha expounded fundamental insight into the nature of the human condition that transcends distinctions of gender, caste, ethnicity, culture, and other factors. Early Buddhist texts attest that the Buddha challenged caste and gender discrimination by admitting people of low social status and women to the *saṅgha*. He taught a doctrine of self-reliance and self-transformation that defies boundaries and conventions. South

Asian studies scholar Gail Omvedt convincingly argues that Buddhism represents an alternative to caste hierarchies,[3] and many believe it is also an alternative to gender hierarchies.

Buddhist Feminism in Asia: Intersections of Awareness

The transnational Buddhist women's movement that has emerged since the first Sakyadhita conference in Bodhgaya in 1987 has far surpassed the dreams and expectations of its founders. What began as a group of friends comparing notes about their experiences of exclusion and gender bias led to the creation of Sakyadhita International Association of Buddhist Women, an organization that has grown steadily and today represents the concerns, aspirations, and accomplishments of millions of women around the world. With little support from mainstream Buddhist groups and meager funding, women from a wide variety of Buddhist groups and traditions have joined forces to encourage each other to achieve goals that even recently would have been considered impossible. A steady stream of scholarly publications has uncovered the history of women in Buddhist societies from Siberia to Nepal to Indonesia. These publications have, in turn, inspired ethnographic research to document the lives of Buddhist women in diverse societies around the world. Although in some Buddhist countries the numbers of monastic women are quite low relative to the number of monks, a high percentage of studies focus on the ordination issue because it serves as a barometer of the status of women in that society overall. Shining a spotlight on gender inequalities has generated changes for women, particularly regarding education, but also in terms of support and respect for female practitioners, lay and monastic alike. The increased participation of women in Buddhist conferences and inspiration conveyed through improved communications technologies have motivated women to implement changes in their own communities. Landmark events in other Buddhist communities, such as nuns of the Tibetan tradition earning scholarly degrees that were previously available only to monks, send a signal to Buddhists everywhere that women are capable of mastering even the highest achievements.

At the same time, especially amidst the debate about full ordination for women, non-Asian women stand accused of attempting to talk Asian nuns into seeking higher status due to their "women's rights agenda." This critique seems to assume that feminism is an invention of the West and a contrivance to manipulate hapless Asian women to feminist ways of thinking against their will. While this "critique of the feminist perspective"[4] presumably aims to encourage indigenous voices, it also seems to imply that Asian voices have been missing from the conversation, when in fact Asian women have constituted the majority of participants at the biennial Sakyadhita International Conferences on Buddhist Women from the beginning. This critique also implies that Asian women have failed to recognize gender inequities or to resist oppression on their own, when in fact signs of resistance to patriarchy were apparent from the very beginning of Buddhism in the women's liberation movement spearheaded by Mahāprajāpatī and in the verses of realization recorded in the *Therīgāthā*.

Today, the richly complex cross-cultural feminist conversation is a panoply of perspectives, including those of Western-educated Asian women, Asian-educated Western women, monks, nuns, laywomen and laymen, feminist, and otherwise.[5] A close reading of Buddhist women's history and the burgeoning Buddhist feminist movement exposes many ironies. Confounding notions that Asian women are averse to social activism and public attention, Bhikṣuṇī Chao Hwei Shih in Taiwan is a very public social activist, organizing demonstrations in support of animal rights, women's rights, nuclear nonproliferation, respectful language for nuns, and many other noble causes.[6] In a nationally televised press conference in 2001, she rejected the eight weighty rules as not having been stipulated by the Buddha, and in 2012 she presided over the first same-sex Buddhist wedding ever held in Taiwan.[7] Bhikṣuṇī Jiyul Sunim in South Korea has launched a number of fasts, one lasting a hundred days in 2005 to protest the government's planned construction of a bullet-train tunnel at Mount Chunsung that would damage the habitat of endangered salamanders.

Mahāprajāpatī, the primogenitor of the Buddhist lineage of nuns, and Saṅghamittā, King Aśoka's daughter who took the *bhikkhunī* lineage from India to Lanka, were feminists who predate the contemporary feminist movement by more than two thousand years. Devasārā, the nun who led an expedition of nuns from Sri Lanka to China in the fifth century, is another prominent example of Buddhist feminist activism on a transnational scale. The first Buddhist monastics to become ordained in

Japan were three nuns who brought the ordination from Korea across the sea to Japan in the sixth century.[8] Nuns in Japan forged paths for renunciant women for centuries on their own initiative. As East Asian religions scholar Lori Meeks has documented, in Japan nuns of aristocratic background created links with monks of humble background who recognized the validity and value of supporting the female monastic *saṅgha*.[9]

These women were all highly significant transmitters of Buddhist tradition, initiating movements by and for women that were at once countercultural and liberating, at historical junctures when the words "women's rights" had yet to be uttered. Yet these innovators, who acted with great courage and determination, are missing not only from mainstream histories but also from feminist chronicles and women's history books. It is only in recent years that scholars have begun the rewarding task of uncovering numerous examples of illustrious Buddhist women who, often quietly and unsung, fomented monumental changes for women and society. It is vital both to commemorate these exceptional women and also to challenge the assumptions that feminism is a creation of Western society and that Buddhist feminism is a Western imposition.

Further sociological research will be needed to determine the extent to which the presence or absence of a *bhikkhunī saṅgha* correlates with the status of women in Buddhist societies, but presently quiet and consistent efforts to establish full ordination for women are moving the issue forward in countries including India, Nepal, Thailand, and Sri Lanka that previously lacked a *bhikkhunī saṅgha*. In these efforts, it has become apparent that the support of highly placed monks can be a powerful force for change in Buddhist societies, offsetting and sometimes overcoming the passive or overtly hostile attitudes of opponents. Events in one part of the Buddhist world increasingly generate responses in other traditions, as in the 2009 case of the charismatic Australian monk Ajahn Brahm, who risked censure from the forest tradition of the Thai Theravāda *saṅgha* to facilitate the ordination of the four *bhikkhunīs* in Australia. His resultant expulsion from his lineage, instigated by Western monks within that order, set off an international outpouring of support for him and for the nuns, kindling further support for full ordination for women internationally. In 2010, the Gyalwang Karmapa, Ogyen Trinley Dorje, the seventeenth lineage holder of the Karma Kagyu tradition who fled Tibet for India, spoke out strongly and publicly in support of *bhikṣuṇī* ordination despite foot dragging on the issue by conservative *lamas* in the Tibetan tradition. As a prominent Buddhist periodical reported, "The Seventeenth Gyalwang Karmapa stunned an international audience in Bodhgaya by making an unprecedented declaration of commitment to ordaining women as bhikshunis in the Tibetan Buddhist tradition."[10]

Not only have highly visible monk practitioners come out in support of restoring the lineage of *bhikkhunī* ordination, but so have academics. For example, the German scholar and Theravāda monk Anālayo has written a number of carefully researched articles on the *bhikkhunī* issue from a Theravāda perspective.[11] In a 2013 study titled "The Legality of *Bhikkhunī* Ordination," he concluded that the procedures followed during the historic *bhikkhunī* ordination in 1998 in Bodhgaya were legitimate according to the *vinaya* and that the resultant revival of the Theravāda *bhikkhunī saṅgha* was therefore valid.[12] Many of the 134 nuns at that ordination were from India and Sri Lanka, and belonged to the Theravāda tradition.[13] The efforts of such monks and scholars to support the revival of the *bhikkhunī saṅgha* demonstrate that the notion of equality for women is not a uniquely Western idea, despite disinformation efforts to portray the ordination issue as a "superimposition of Western colonization" or "merely a women's rights agenda." The fact that these monks are affiliated with conservative Buddhist traditions makes their support all the more powerful.

Gender Equity as a Transnational Buddhist Ideal

In the global transmission of Buddhism, one of the most significant transformations that has occurred is a trend toward egalitarianism. Influenced by ideals of social equality in the secular world, Buddhist centers in both Asian and Western countries are increasingly questioning traditional hierarchical, patriarchal models of organization. Indeed, many have begun implementing more democratic structures and procedures of shared decision-making to give a more equitable voice and representation to a wider constituency. If it is true that the Buddhist *saṅgha* was the earliest example of democratic governance, then a move toward more equitable representation would be not an innovation but a return to the early Buddhist ideals of shared governance set forth in the *vinaya.* One formula that occurs repeatedly in the *Bhikṣu* and *Bhikṣuṇī Prātimokṣa Sūtras* indicates that the organizational model for the *saṅgha* was consensus: "Is the *saṅgha* assembled? The *saṅgha* is assembled. Is it in harmony? It is in harmony."[14] Every fortnight, the *Prātimokṣa Sūtra* containing this formula is routinely recited by both monks and nuns in monasteries throughout the Buddhist world. The prescriptions in the *vinaya* allowed everyone in the assembly an opportunity to speak up. If everyone in the assembly was in agreement, they conveyed their assent by remaining silent.

The global trend toward shared governance and more equitable decision-making and responsibility seems to be having an effect on Buddhist communities and institutions in both Asia and the West. Evidence of this more egalitarian model is a greater valuing of the roles of women and the laity in Buddhist practice, scholarship, and leadership. Although the leadership of most international Buddhist organizations is still almost exclusive male, lay elected officers are not uncommon. Increasingly, lay Buddhists see themselves not simply as donors to the monastic *saṅgha*, contributing material goods in hopes of achieving a higher rebirth next time around, but also as Buddhist practitioners worthy of receiving teachings and practicing the teachings on an equal footing with those who choose a monastic lifestyle. Rather than simply commissioning rituals to ensure the protection and prosperity of their families and future lives, lay Buddhists are beginning to regard themselves as fully capable of practicing meditation and studying Buddhist texts on a par with monastics. Women are also assuming more visible leadership roles and responsibilities. Buddhist nuns of the younger generation see themselves no longer as simply reciters of mantras and supporters of monks, contributing their energies to support monastic institutions in hopes of achieving a male rebirth the next time around, but as practitioners worthy of studying texts and practicing the teachings on an equal footing with monks. Rather than simply living in a corner compound or adjacent to monks' monasteries, more nuns are establishing monasteries and practice centers that function autonomously under female leadership. More and more Buddhists are convinced that serious Dharma practitioners are worthy of respect, regardless of whether they are lay or ordained, and regardless of their gender or sexual orientation.

New attitudes toward women are perhaps the most visible aspect of the trend toward egalitarianism in contemporary Buddhist practice, especially among Western practitioners. This trend manifests in valuing women's practice and in welcoming women's full participation in Buddhist temples and organizations. A new global ethic of human dignity and equality is opening pathways to more visible roles for women in Buddhist institutions, including teaching and leadership. This is particularly evident in Western Buddhist centers, where women such as Pema Chödrön, Tenzin Palmo, Sharon Salzberg, Khandro Rinpoche, Sylvia Boorstein, Thubten Chodron, Joan Halifax, and Tsultrim Allione have become recognized as leaders, writers, and teachers on a par with men.[15]

Full gender equality may appear idealistic from a traditional perspective, but it is not unrealistic to expect gender equity in the twenty-first century. Today, with greater access to opportunities, women are beginning to outperform men in many fields.[16] According to reports, two-thirds of incoming college students in the United States are women and 52 percent of medical students and law students are women. These statistics indicate that, if admissions policies are gender blind and male and female students have equal access to education, highly motivated women will excel. The same trend could manifest in Buddhist societies and in the field of Buddhist studies if women have equal access and encouragement. Given equal opportunities, women could then contribute equally to preserving and revitalizing Buddhism in countries around the world. Considering the millions of Buddhist lives that have been lost to wars and social upheaval in the past few decades—in Cambodia, China, Laos, Mongolia, Russia, Tibet, and Vietnam, for example—Buddhist women's potential contributions cannot be ignored.

Gradually Buddhists are becoming aware that the equal religious rights of women are a universal value enshrined in the United Nations Declaration of Human Rights (1948).[17] The exclusion of women from Buddhist institutions of learning and from Buddhist monastic practice contravenes the principles of compassion and equal opportunity for liberation that are emblematic of the Buddhist traditions. From a Buddhist human rights perspective, gender discrimination and human suffering are closely related through cause and effect.

Due to a swell of interest in Buddhism, an unaccustomed spotlight is now shining on Buddhist women and especially Buddhist nuns.

Media outlets such as the *Huffington Post* have published a number of articles on Buddhist women with titles such as "10 Tibetan Buddhist Women You Need to Know," "The F Word in Buddhism: 'Daughters of the Buddha' Discuss How Buddhist Women Can Achieve Equality," and "Sravasti Abbey: A Dream Fulfilled for U.S. Buddhist Nuns."[18] A number of videos about Buddhist nuns have also appeared, including *The Buddhist Nun of Emei Mountain* (1995),[19] *Blessings: The Tsoknyi Nangchen Nuns of Tibet* (2009),[20] *In the Shadow of Buddha* (2010),[21] and *Mother Sela: Artist and Buddhist Nun* (2012).[22] The Yogini Project supports a website and a Facebook page that provides profiles of women practitioners in the Vajrayāna tradition.[23] Transnational efforts in support of Buddhist women and for the full ordination for nuns are steadily growing, providing validation for the aspirations of Buddhist women in communities around the world.

In the contemporary Buddhist women's movement, class, gender, education, and privilege combine in significant ways. As women gain greater access to education, especially Buddhist education, they are making significant advances socially, psychologically, and spiritually. A case in point is Mahapajapati Buddhist College in Thailand, where nuns who received higher education just twenty years ago are now qualified to teach and administer education programs for a new generation of nuns and laywomen.[24] These advances are not accessible to all Buddhist women equally, however, because of their vastly different economic, social, and political circumstances.

In assessing the conditions of Buddhist nuns in general, there seems to be a direct correlation between education, full ordination, and lay support; overall, nuns who have access to full ordination in South Korea, Taiwan, and Vietnam receive better education and better support from the lay community than those in countries where nuns, by no fault of their own, observe only eight precepts. According to ethnographic studies and my own observations, Buddhist monks typically have access to free education and are encouraged to receive full ordination, whereas nuns in many countries lack access to the same level of encouragement and support.[25] The lifestyle and perspective of a young poverty-stricken village woman in Myanmar or Nepal who has been sold or deceived into sexual slavery bears no comparison with the comfortable urbane lifestyle and perspective of an educated working woman in South Korea or the United States.

Figure C.1. Novice nuns interacting on the occasion of the 8th Sakyadhita International Conference on Buddhist Women held at Joong Ang Sangha University, Seoul, Korea, in 2008. Credit: Photo by Mike Barber.

Creating connections and understanding among women of such different backgrounds is precisely the purpose of the current transnational Buddhist women's movement. Interactions among nuns from different Buddhist cultures at gatherings such as the Sakyadhita conferences have sparked creative ideas, nurtured friendships, and created solidarity among women across the globe (see figure C.1). What is unique about this movement is that it links women of insight in diverse cultures and creates conversations about how to benefit all Buddhist women, their families, and their societies. Buddhist women's networks—international, national, and local—have held conferences, collaborated on projects, published books and articles, and exchanged views on topics as diverse as social activism, sexual ethics, and Dharma for children.

It is said that history repeats itself, and indeed the current activism aimed at improving the status of Buddhist nuns transnationally seems to mirror the activism of Buddhist nuns at the time of the Buddha as they struggled for inclusion in the *saṅgha*. The stories of renunciant and lay women practitioners through the ages, such as Yeshe Tsogyal in eighth- and ninth-century Tibet[26] and Orgyan Chökyi in seventeenth- and eighteenth-century Nepal,[27] chronicle the obstacles female practitioners have encountered when they defy social expectations and set their minds on following the Dharma. Although the tide of history now seems to be turning, nuns in the Theravāda and Tibetan traditions still face resistance from certain segments of society, particularly segments of male monastic society, similar to what nuns experienced in India centuries ago. The dedication and enthusiasm of Buddhist nuns today, expressed in their work and their writings, also seems to parallel those of the earliest Buddhist nuns. The International Congress on Women's Role in the Sangha: Bhikshuni Vinaya and Ordination Lineages held at Hamburg University in 2007, which featured talks both by scholars of *bhikkhunī vinaya* and by nuns currently practicing in Buddhist monastic traditions, demonstrated the vibrancy of contemporary Buddhist nuns' communities.[28] Current efforts to discover the missing histories of Buddhist women will surely reveal more parallels between the lives and strategies of resistance employed by nuns and lay women practitioners from earliest times to the present.

The example of the Buddha, who taught men and women equally and championed women's liberation by admitting women to the monastic order in the fifth century BCE, is a powerful motivating force for Buddhist women. Although, as we have seen, Buddha Śākyamuni is said to have hesitated before allowing Mahāprajāpatī to join the *saṅgha*, his progressive thinking on equity was certainly far ahead of the times in Indian society of that era. Sadly, many Buddhists are unaware of the positive images of women's enlightenment that are exemplified in the Buddhist texts, because they lack basic literacy and therefore have no access to the texts that could inspire them and awaken them to their own potential for enlightenment. The dire impact that a lack of female role models has on women practitioners cannot be underestimated.

In economically advanced countries where women have equal educational opportunities, Buddhist women are now becoming leaders in many fields. Taiwan, for example, has proved to be an especially conducive environment for Buddhist women's development. In 1966, Bhikṣuṇī Cheng Yen founded the Buddhist Compassion Relief Tzu-Chi Association, said to be the world's largest nonprofit organization; in 1990,

Bhikṣuṇī Shig Hiu Wan founded Huafan University, the country's first Buddhist university; and in 2000, Annette Liu (b. 1944), a feminist, Buddhist, and democracy activist, was elected vice president of the country, serving until 2008.

In many Buddhist societies, however, women still lag behind, especially in the spheres of religion and government. Not only are women in these societies educationally and economically disadvantaged, but also many lack confidence in their own capabilities, which prevents them from finding their voices and advocating for their own advancement. Hindered as much by self-deprecating attitudes as by overt oppression, many endure circumstances that impede their own development and their potential for community development. Transforming patriarchal attitudes is therefore as important for women as it is for men.[29]

Cross-cultural dialogue that examines such concepts as selflessness and compassion, power and powerlessness, from both Buddhist and feminist perspectives offers a rich opportunity for mutual understanding. These themes are addressed in the life stories of women compiled by author Michaela Haas in *Dakini Power* and in the philosophical analysis of Buddhist scholar Anne Carolyn Klein in *Meeting the Great Bliss Queen: Buddhists, Feminists, and the Art of the Self.*[30] Building on the successes of women's social activism in recent decades, Buddhist women are working to identify and eliminate whatever obstacles stand in the way of women's enormous potential for personal and social transformation. Validated by the Buddha's own unorthodox stance on social equality, a new generation is motivated to work for gender equity in Buddhist societies, beginning with a radical transformation of Buddhist institutions and a reexamination of Buddhist texts.

Buddhist Constructions of Gender

As we have seen, although the Buddha's liberating teachings are theoretically applicable to women and men equally, there is ample evidence of gender discrimination in the Buddhist canon. One example from the early texts is the notion that a woman cannot become a perfectly awakened Buddha.[31] Female *bodhisattvas* (beings working to become fully awakened *buddhas*) appear in certain Mahāyāna texts, but fully enlightened *buddhas* are male. Among the thirty-two major marks of a great person (*mahāpuruṣa*) that are ascribed to a *buddha*, one is explicitly a male organ.[32] On the one hand, the Buddha's teachings are regarded as liberating for women and men equally; on the other hand, the ultimate achievement, the perfect awakening of a *buddha*, is out of reach for women, at least in a woman's body. Two things strike one as curious about this disparity. First, it is odd that a state of realization, which pertains to consciousness, should be described in gendered terms, since states of consciousness do not have genitalia. Second, it is mystifying that women's alleged inability to attain the ultimate awakening of a *buddha* has been extrapolated to imply that women are handicapped in attaining other states of realization on the path, such as the state of a *bodhisattva*. The assumption that women are somehow handicapped in attaining the ultimate goal of Buddhahood has no doubt influenced attitudes toward women's intellectual and spiritual capabilities in general.

A major feminist critique of Buddhist patriarchy is that if women do not have the potential to become *buddhas*, then women cannot be said to have equal potential to achieve the ultimate goal of the path. In the soteriology of early Buddhist texts, and as demonstrated in the spiritual achievements of the first generations of female practitioners, it is clear that women can achieve liberation from *saṃsāra* as *arhats*, which is the goal for most Theravāda adherents. This is also attested in the poetic verses of liberated women in the *Therīgāthā*.[33] In the soteriology of later Buddhist texts, however, the goal is to become a perfectly awakened *buddha*, and women are said to be incapable of this because of their sex, the absence of a "male sign." The allegation that women are incapable of becoming *buddhas* sends a signal that women are somehow inherently inadequate and incapable of achieving the ultimate state of perfection that is deemed most beneficial for liberating beings from suffering. The idea that women are unable to achieve human perfection implies that women are inferior to men and gives rise to the widespread presumption that a female rebirth is the result of bad karma, that "the thoughts of a woman" are somehow less wholesome than "the thoughts of a man," and so on. Contentions such as these, in turn, clearly contribute to the persistence of gender inequalities in Buddhist societies. To extol women's equal potential continually while thwarting their equal participation in social and religious institutions is inconsistent.

To get at the root of the disparity between theoretical equality and social inequality, it is necessary to examine the notion of gender identity from both philosophical and sociological perspectives. If human perfection manifests only in male form, we must investigate what it means to be male or female from a Buddhist perspective in order to understand why being male is significant or special. Early Buddhist texts such as the *Therī-apadāna*[34] are replete with images of strong and virtuous women such as Mahāpajāpatī, Khemā, and Dhammadinnā who achieved liberation, so how did the tradition become male dominated? In his groundbreaking book, *A Bull of a Man*, Buddhist studies scholar John Powers contends that the Buddha's appeal was largely physical.[35] The ultimate human being was characterized not only by virtue but also with a powerful and beautiful masculine physique. The emphasis given to physical beauty is surprising, given that physical attractiveness can be a source of delusion and desire that can distract and derail the practitioner on the spiritual path. Sexual desire, arising naturally from physical attraction, is regarded as a major hindrance to renunciation and the achievement of liberation, so one would expect gender differences and physical beauty to be downplayed rather than stressed. The fact that the Buddha was admired specifically for his virility and masculine beauty creates a conundrum in Buddhist gender analysis.

The Buddhist project of achieving human perfection turns on transforming ordinary beings' deluded states of consciousness into awakened awareness, or enlightenment. In their ordinary unawakened state, human beings are beset by destructive emotions (*kleśas*) such as greed, hatred, ignorance, desire, anger, attachment, pride, jealousy, and confusion that give rise to dissatisfaction, frustration, and a host of problems. The shared premise of the Buddhist philosophical systems is that it is possible for sentient beings—beings who possess consciousness or awareness and the capacity to feel pain—to achieve liberation by eradicating the destructive emotions, achieving insight into the true nature of things, and becoming free from these hindrances. Nowhere in the texts is this goal stated in gender-specific terms. If the liberated state of consciousness achieved by an *arhat* is not different for women and men, then there is no reason to assume that the perfectly awakened awareness of a *buddha* should be different. And if the awakened awareness of a *buddha* is not different for women and men, there is no reason that the physical body of a *buddha* should necessarily be male or that the state of perfect Buddhahood should be restricted to men. On the contrary, as the embodiment of compassion and wisdom, a perfectly awakened *buddha* should be beyond such distinctions and therefore be free from all gender bias.

Based on the premise that ignorance is the root cause of all destructive emotions, in order to achieve awakening it is necessary to understand the true nature of things, especially the true nature of persons and the nature of consciousness. The physical nature of persons has a component of sexual identity, but consciousness, defined as "knowing and awareness," is unrelated to concepts of sex; Buddhist philosophical schools agree that consciousness and matter are two different categories, and sex distinctions are corporeal, or material, and impermanent. The root cause of all suffering is ignorance, namely, ignorance of the true nature of the self, the self being a conventional designation for the aggregates that comprise a person and ultimately are devoid of independent existence. Human beings are born with sex-specific characteristics, whereas gender identities are learned or constructed based on signals received from one's social and cultural environment. Those who are born with female biological characteristics are rewarded for behaving as society expects girls to behave; those born with male biological characteristics are rewarded for behaving as society expects boys to behave. Gender identity and gendered behavior are therefore social constructs that differ from culture to culture and change over time, not characteristics inherent to persons.

As with all compounded phenomena, gender identities are transitory, and clinging to gender identifications, like grasping at other transitory phenomena, can be a source of dissatisfaction and suffering. Impermanent identifications based on culture, gender, caste, and other conditioned factors or behaviors are not intrinsic to personal identities, which shift over time. From a Buddhist perspective, gender identities are also influenced by predispositions from previous lives. A person who is born as a male in one lifetime may have been born as a woman many times in past lives, and these past-life affinities may affect the person's current self-understanding and construction of gender identity. Although conventional identities and circumstances certainly influence human beings' personal development, they are not fixed and cannot be used to judge a person's potential to achieve liberation or enlightenment. The fact that the Buddha admitted women to the *saṅgha* and that many of these women became *arhats* defies essentialist notions of gender.

Transnational Pathways to Gender Equity

According to tradition, Buddha Śākyamuni declared women to be fully capable of achieving the fruits of Buddhist practice, including liberation. In the classic story of women's admission to the *saṅgha*, when Ānanda asked whether women are capable of attaining the fruits of the path, the Buddha did not hesitate to confirm that they are. Over the years, however, the Buddha's affirmation of women's equal potential for liberation and awakening has often been neglected. Throughout Buddhist history, males have dominated Buddhist institutions, education, ritual functions, and even contemplative practices, consigning women to supportive roles. Since 1987, however, patterns of male domination have slowly begun to change in the Buddhist world, reflecting a new global ethic of gender equality. Numerous conferences and seminars on Buddhist women, especially the international conferences organized by Sakyadhita, have provided forums for discussing and challenging the patriarchal status quo that persists in Buddhist societies and strategizing about how to transform it. These discussions and strategies have had a wide-ranging ripple effect, stimulating the creation of new schools, Buddhist studies institutes, retreat centers, translation teams, children's centers, research projects, women's shelters, and ordination training programs.

Some of the changes that have occurred as a result of the contemporary Buddhist women's movement, such as the revival of the *bhikkhunī saṅgha* in Nepal and Sri Lanka, have been totally unexpected historical landmarks.[36] Even in the face of widespread opposition to women's full and equal participation in Buddhism, a fundamental rethinking of normative traditions regarding gender has begun—one that makes sense in a new global culture that values all human beings equally. Without serious reassessment and critical reflection on the pernicious effects of gender inequality, Buddhism risks becoming irrelevant in the modern world—a quaint artifact from earlier times. For Buddhist egalitarian ideals to move beyond the realm of ideas into social reality, however, will require a total recasting of gender relationships in Buddhist institutions and Buddhist social relationships more broadly. Rethinking tradition may mean returning to an earlier, ideally egalitarian vision of Buddhist tradition, but to implement this vision will require a transnational effort that gives proportionate weight to tradition and modernity—a new vision of liberation that emerges from listening respectfully to the voices of women and men at all levels of society, especially the oppressed and marginalized.

One of the most striking outcomes of the Buddhist women's movement has been a surge of research on Buddhist women by a new generation of scholars and practitioners connected through mutual intellectual interests, friendship, and a common dedication to social transformation. Sharing information and working collaboratively across many disciplines, scholars have initiated projects that examine the roles of Buddhist nuns and laywomen in a range of countries and traditions, taking seriously the perspectives of practitioners on the ground. All these scholars owe a debt to the pioneering work of I. B. Horner, who published *Women under Primitive Buddhism: Laywomen and Almswomen* in 1930, and more recently to Rita M. Gross, who published *Buddhism after Patriarchy: A Feminist History, Analysis, and Reconstruction of Buddhism* in 1993. The work of a new generation of researchers has transformed scholarly understandings of nuns: Cristina Bonnet-Acosta and Hiroko Kawanami writing on Burma;[37] Beata Grant and Yuan Yuan, on China;[38] Paula Arai and Lori Meeks, on Japan;[39] Eun-su Cho and Jin Y. Park, on Korea;[40] Sarah LeVine and Joanne Watkins, on Nepal;[41] Susanne Mrozik and Nirmala S. Salgado, on Sri Lanka;[42] Elise DeVido and Yu-Chen Li, on Taiwan;[43] Bhikkhunī Dhammananda and Monica Lindberg Falk, on Thailand;[44] Janet Gyatso, Hanna Havnevik, and Charlene Makley, on Tibet;[45] Kim Gutschow, on Zangskar;[46] and many others. All of these scholars have dramatically changed the field of Buddhist studies by focusing their research on issues pertaining to women and have contributed substantially to the transnational character of feminist studies in the world's religions. The attention given to renunciant women in this book alerts us that there is still much to be learned about the lives of female householders and about women who identify as neither lay nor ordained.

Several aspects of these new Buddhist feminist scholarly endeavors are unique. One is that the field is not exclusively academic but incorporates practical, personal, and affective dimensions with accounts of hands-on social activism. Contemporary scholars in the field of women and Buddhism demonstrate genuine respect for those who devote themselves to traditional scholarship, for those who explore innovative alternatives to academic formulae and categorizations, as well as for those who eschew the scholarly approach to Buddhism. An intriguing dimension of this research is discovering connections among the Buddhist traditions by discussing them in comparative perspective, based on specific issues of relevance to women. The initial impetus for this approach arose from a practical problem: How could the validity of the extant lineages of *bhikkhunī* ordination be documented and presented to Buddhists of different traditions in effective and relevant ways? Making a case for these lineages entailed bridging the *vinaya* traditions and sorting out the preconceptions about monastic ordination and the diverse interpretations of the *prātimokṣa* precepts held by monastic adherents of Buddhist traditions that historically and philosophically diverged more than a thousand years ago. Among the first initiatives was the translation and comparative study of the *bhikkhunī vinaya* texts of extant lineages.[47] Other initiatives were cross-cultural dialogues focused on such questions as vegetarianism, which originally was not prescribed in the *vinaya* but has traditionally been practiced in East Asian Buddhist traditions. Others focused on the requirement of celibacy, which was traditionally prescribed in the *vinaya* but is no longer required in most Japanese Buddhist schools. These initiatives have not only been valuable exercises in cross-cultural awareness but also generated continuing cross-cultural, interdisciplinary research projects.[48]

In 1987, when the first international Buddhist women's conference was held in Bodhgaya, Theravāda, Mahāyāna, and Vajrayāna practitioners held many misconceptions about each other's beliefs and practices. The task of identifying and clarifying these misconceptions has been a central achievement of the Buddhist women's movement initiated by Sakyadhita. Buddhists practicing in diverse traditions have also come to recognize their commonalities and their common concerns, such as the disadvantaged status of women in their own temples and traditions. Fostering ecumenical dialogue, solidarity, and a concern for social justice in the global transmission of Buddhism are among the many achievements of this movement. Although an in-depth feminist analysis of gender in

Buddhism is currently underway, Buddhist studies institutes for women in developing countries and full ordination for nuns in certain traditions are yet to be accomplished. However, the momentum generated by the Buddhist feminist movement so far bodes well for the future of women in Buddhism.

A more thorough analysis of the unique gendered realities of both Asian and non-Asian Buddhist women will go a long way toward redressing the Eurocentric bias that is evident in many feminist writings, inspiring new paradigms for assessing gender identities and gender relationships. The category "women" is not a monolith, nor is the category "Asian women"; in truth, women are not categories but are living, breathing, feeling beings who aspire to realize their full potential just like other living beings. Each Buddhist culture, locality, and social setting has something to contribute to our understanding of women's experiences. Expanding transnational dialogue on these themes will enrich the fields of women and gender studies and Buddhist studies as well as human history.

ACKNOWLEDGMENTS

Every Buddhist woman I have ever met and every woman throughout history has, in one way or another, contributed to this book. The story of Buddhist women is a collective story, borne of all our experiences, joyful and tragic, mundane and illuminating. To the countless friends and mentors who have given freely of their time, wisdom, hospitality, and guidance, I express my heartfelt appreciation. Without your contributions, humanity would be diminished. To all those who have taught, corrected, and encouraged me, many thanks for your immense compassion. I am deeply grateful to the University of San Diego for numerous international travel grants and faculty research grants, which have made it possible for me to collect the information, witness the historic events, and meet the phenomenal people documented in these pages. Similarly, I am thankful for several Fulbright awards that made it possible for me to live among and learn from Buddhist women in Bangladesh, Indonesia, Nepal, and Sri Lanka. I humbly acknowledge my friends Margaret Coberly and Rebecca Paxton for their immense kindness, dedication, selflessness, and patience in editing this work. Words are insufficient to convey my affection and gratitude. May the merit of all these efforts give rise to peace, happiness, and liberation, for the benefit of all living beings.

QUESTIONS FOR DISCUSSION

INTRODUCTION: WHY STUDY WOMEN IN THE BUDDHIST TRADITIONS?

Why is it important to study about women in the Buddhist traditions?

How do the various traditions within Buddhism define "liberation" and "the full awakening of a Buddha" differently? Are these goals defined in terms of gender? If so, in what way does this affect women?

Is gender relevant to awakening? Why or why not?

CHAPTER 1: WOMEN IN EARLY INDIAN BUDDHISM

What are some possible reasons the Buddha is said to have hesitated in admitting women to the *saṅgha*? Why did he eventually agree?

Who are the major female figures, and what roles do they play?

What are some of the ways women are portrayed in the texts of various Buddhist traditions?

What patterns of representation of women seem to be common in these texts, and how do they play out in the lives of Buddhist women in the past and today?

Do you think that women's historical exclusion from Buddhist institutions has led women to primarily focus on contemplative practices, or are women naturally more inclined to contemplative practices?

What can be learned from Bhikkhu Anālayo's analysis of the various narratives of the founding of the *bhikkhunī saṅgha* and the report that the Buddha required nuns to adhere to the eight weighty rules (*gurudharmas*)?

How do notions of gender affect the practice, participation, and achievements of Buddhist women?

How is the notion of gender fluidity understood and represented in Buddhist scriptures?

CHAPTER 2: BUDDHIST WOMEN IN SOUTH AND SOUTHEAST ASIA

What are some distinctive features and common themes about Buddhist women's practice in South and Southeast Asian societies?

In what ways are women neglected or subordinated in the particular Buddhist traditions they practice? In what ways do women consider themselves fortunate?

What are some of the major challenges that face women in South and Southeast Asian Buddhist societies?

How have conditions changed for Buddhist women in Sri Lanka? What factors may help explain these changes? What obstacles remain?

CHAPTER 3: BUDDHIST WOMEN IN EAST ASIA

How did full ordination for women develop in China?

What are some unifying features of Buddhist women's experience in East Asia?

In what ways are the experiences of women distinct in China, Japan, Korea, and Taiwan? What social and cultural factors help explain these distinctions?

CHAPTER 4: BUDDHIST WOMEN IN INNER ASIA

What is the function of the images of awakened women in the Vajrayāna Buddhist tradition?

How can idealized images of enlightened female figures be reconciled with the social reality of gender bias in Buddhist societies?

What historical and political developments distinguish the lives of Buddhist women in Tibet and Mongolia from the lives of Buddhist women in Bhutan and the Indian Himalayas?

What is the status of women in the Buddhist republics of Russia?

CHAPTER 5: BUDDHIST WOMEN IN THE WEST

How are Western women participating in and contributing to the global transmission and transformation of Buddhism?

How are Western women interpreting and practicing Buddhism differently than women in Asian societies?

Can current concerns about the subordinate status of women in Buddhism be interpreted as a colonialist project, a "women's rights agenda," or a "Western imposition"? Why or why not?

What efforts are being made to create global solidarity among Buddhist women?

CHAPTER 6: WOMEN'S ORDINATION ACROSS CULTURES

Why is a life of renunciation attractive to some women in Buddhist societies? What are the advantages and disadvantages of monastic life from different Asian women's perspectives? Does the same logic apply to women in Western societies?

Why is access to full ordination for women considered important for Buddhist women? Why do some Buddhists, including some nuns, regard full ordination as unimportant?

Why is full ordination as a *bhikkhunī* available in some Buddhist traditions and not available in others? What are some reasons opponents of the full ordination of women give for opposing it? What are some of the arguments proposed in support of full ordination of women?

How was full ordination brought to Buddhist nuns in Nepal? Who were the major figures?

How was full ordination brought to Buddhist nuns in Sri Lanka? Who were the major figures?

What important work is being done by *mae chees* in Thailand, and who are some prominent *mae chees*?

Why was Australian monk Ajahn Brahm dismissed from his Thai order for giving full ordination to four nuns in Australia?

What is the ordination situation of Mahāyāna Buddhist nuns in China, Hong Kong, Malaysia, South Korea, Singapore, Taiwan, and Vietnam? What are the advantages of women's access to full ordination in these traditions?

What has been the situation of nuns in the Tibetan Buddhist traditions, and how is it changing?

CHAPTER 7: GRASSROOTS REVOLUTION: BUDDHIST WOMEN AND SOCIAL ACTIVISM

Why do some Buddhists feel that social activism is incompatible with the Buddhist goal of awakening whereas others believe it is compatible?

Who are some of the most famous social activists among Buddhist women?

To what extent is the movement for more active social engagement of women in the Buddhist world helping raise their profile?

What role does education play in improving conditions for Buddhist women? What kinds of education would be most helpful for transforming women's roles in society?

CONCLUSION

In what ways can Buddhism be socially or spiritually liberating for women, and in what ways could it be limiting or potentially oppressive?

Are women and men equal in Buddhism? Considering the rhetoric of equality in Buddhist discourse, are women equitably represented?

Compare and contrast the roles and potential of women in the Theravāda and Mahāyāna Buddhist traditions today. In what ways are women's experiences similar in these traditions, and in what ways are they different?

FOR FURTHER READING

Blackstone, Kathryn R. *Women in the Footsteps of the Buddha*. New York: Routledge, 2013.

Caplow, Zenshin Florence, and Reigetsu Susan Moon, eds. *The Hidden Lamp: Stories from Twenty-Five Centuries of Awakened Women*. Boston: Wisdom Publications, 2013.

Dresser, Marianne, ed. *Buddhist Women on the Edge: Contemporary Perspectives from the Western Frontier*. Berkeley, CA: North Atlantic Books, 1996.

Findly, Ellison Banks, ed. *Women's Buddhism, Buddhism's Women: Tradition, Revision, Renewal*. Boston: Wisdom Publications, 2000.

Gross, Rita M. *Buddhism after Patriarchy: A Feminist History, Analysis, and Reconstruction of Buddhism*. Albany: State University of New York Press, 1992.

Klein, Anne Carolyn. *Meeting the Great Bliss Queen: Buddhists, Feminists, and the Art of the Self*. Ithaca, NY: Snow Lion, 2008.

Murcott, Susan. *First Buddhist Women: Poems and Stories of Awakening*. Berkeley, CA: Parallax Press, 2006.

Paul, Diana Y. *Women in Buddhism: Images of the Feminine in the Mahāyāna Tradition*. 2nd ed. Berkeley: University of California Press, 1985.

Shaw, Miranda. *Buddhist Goddesses of India*. Princeton, NJ: Princeton University Press, 2015.

———. *Passionate Enlightenment: Women in Tantric Buddhism*. Princeton, NJ: Princeton University Press, 1994.

Tsomo, Karma Lekshe, ed. *Buddhist Feminisms and Femininities*. Albany: State University of New York Press, 2019.

NOTES

INTRODUCTION

1 In English, the word *brāhmaṇa* appears in its corrupted form, "Brahmin," to be distinguished from the Sanskrit word *brahman*, which refers to the unchanging and unseen ultimate reality.

2 See Thapar, "Householder and the Renouncer."

3 Young, "Hinduism," 74.

4 The *Sigālovāda Sutta* in the Dīgha Nikāya in the Pāli canon contains the Buddha's advice for harmonious family life, but this discourse does not include regulations similar to the Pāṭimokkha (Sanskrit: Prātimokṣa) codes of monastic discipline. The Pāli canon is the collection of Buddhist teachings that serves as the textual foundation of the Theravāda tradition. The Pāli recension of the teachings was transmitted to Sri Lanka during the third century BCE and was first written down during the first century BCE. The texts consist of four collections, arranged by length, that are known as *nikāyas* in Pāli and by the Sanskrit term *āgama* in the Chinese Buddhist tradition. Most of the original texts written in these and other languages have been lost to history, but fortunately a large number of texts were translated and have been preserved in Chinese and Tibetan.

5 Exceptions are found in Japan and Central Asia (Mongolia, Nepal, and Russia, for example) where religious specialists may be married with children.

6 In modern times, some religious specialists perform wedding ceremonies, especially in the Japanese diaspora in the Americas.

7 According to Dalai Lama XIV Bstan-dzin-rgya-mtsho, "Buddhism, Asian Values, and Democracy,"

> As for democracy as a procedure of decision making, we find again in the Buddhist tradition a certain recognition of the need for consensus. For example, the Buddhist monastic order has a long history of basing major decisions affecting the lives of individual monks on collective discourse. In fact, strictly speaking, every rite concerning the maintenance of monastic practice must be performed with a congregation of at least four monks. Thus one could say that the Vinaya rules of discipline that govern the behavior and life of the Buddhist monastic community are in keeping with democratic traditions. In theory at least, even the teachings of the Buddha can be altered under certain circumstances by a congregation of a certain number of ordained monks. (4)

8 Collins, "The Body in Theravāda Buddhist Monasticism."
9 On female rebirth and related ideas in early Buddhism, see Anālayo, "Karma and Female Birth."
10 Hüsken, "Eight Garudhammas."
11 Nattier, *Once upon a Future Time*, 128–33.
12 For example, see Young, "Female Mutability and Male Anxiety"; and Young, *Courtesans and Tantric Consorts.*
13 Bernard Faure takes up the question of purity and pollution in *The Power of Denial: Buddhism, Purity, and Gender.*
14 Her story is told in Shaw, *Buddhist Goddesses of India*, 306–55.
15 Prebish, *Buddhism*, 39.

1. WOMEN IN EARLY INDIAN BUDDHISM

1 Blackstone, *Women in the Footsteps of the Buddha*, 127–35.
2 Kloppenborg, "Female Stereotypes in Early Buddhism."
3 Young, "Hinduism," 60–72.
4 Bode, "Women Leaders of the Buddhist Reformation," 793–94.
5 Collett, "The Female Past in Early Indian Buddhism."
6 Digha Nikaya 16. Cited in Anālayo, "Women's Renunciation in Early Buddhism," 66.
7 For example, see Obeyesekere, *Portraits of Buddhist Women*; and Wijeyaratna, *Buddhist Nuns.*
8 These narratives can be found in Bode, "Women Leaders of the Buddhist Reformation," 763–98.
9 Collett notes, however, that women are almost entirely absent from the two major Pāli accounts of past *buddhas*. See Collett, "The Female Past in Early Indian Buddhism," 210–11.
10 Young, "Female Mutability and Male Anxiety."
11 Anālayo mentions that both the *Saṃyutta-nikāya* and Chinese translations of the *Saṃyukta-āgama* include an "explicit endorsement of women's abilities to reach awakening" whereby both women and men are capable of boarding the vehicle of wholesome qualities that leads to liberation. "The *Bahudhātuka-sutta* and Its Parallels," 137.
12 Walshe, *Long Discourses of the Buddha*, 200–201.
13 The major marks include a cranial lump, an extremely long tongue, shoulders like a lion, webbed fingers and toes, arms that extend to the knees, and other extraordinary physical features. See Powers, *Bull of a Man*, 172–74.
14 This extraordinary endowment is discussed in José Ignacio Cabezón, *Sexuality in Classical South Asian Buddhism*, 320–26; and Powers, *Bull of a Man*, 13–14.
15 Cabezón, *Sexuality in Classical South Asian Buddhism*, 521.
16 Cabezón, *Sexuality in Classical South Asian Buddhism*, 521. To some, the sheathed, retracted, or concealed nature of a *buddha*'s genitals suggests that they are ambiguous, whether intersex, supernormal, or possibly even clitoral, implying that he had transcended the gender binary.

17 Collett, "Buddhism and Gender," 57.

18 The texts of monastic discipline (*vinaya*) include ethical precepts, rules for harmonious monastic living, and rules of deportment.

19 See Anālayo, "Beautiful Eyes Seen with Insight"; and Trainor, "In the Eye of the Beholder."

20 Rajapakse, "Therīgāthā."

21 Battaglia, "Only Skin Deep?"

22 Young, "Female Mutability and Male Anxiety," 34–35.

23 Mrozik, *Virtuous Bodies*, 56–58.

24 Appleton, "In the Footsteps of the Buddha?"

25 Young, "Female Mutability and Male Anxiety."

26 Young mentions that stories about Uppalavaṇṇā can be found in the *Manorathapūrani*, the *Therīgāthā*, and a commentary on the *Dhammapada*, texts that were written down in Pāli in Sri Lanka sometime between the third and sixth centuries CE but were apparently based on orally transmitted stories dating back to the time of Buddha Śākyamuni, circa 563–483 BCE. Young, "Female Mutability and Male Anxiety."

27 Young, "Female Mutability and Male Anxiety," 20.

28 Grünhagen, "Female Body in Early Buddhist Literature."

29 Her story is told in Anālayo, "Chos sbyin gyi mdo."

30 In the Cullavagga, Mahāpajāpatī is portrayed as the first Buddhist nun, but other texts, such as the *Mahāparinibbāna Sutta*, *Dakkhiṇāvibhaga Sutta*, and the *Therīgāthā*, suggest another scenario. See Williams, "A Whisper in the Silence"; and Krey, "Some Remarks on the Status of Nuns."

31 Anālayo, "Mahāpajāpatī's Going Forth," 273.

32 Anālayo, "Mahāpajāpatī's Going Forth," 274.

33 Anālayo, "Mahāpajāpatī's Going Forth," 275. There may have been some reluctance in society at large to the idea of women leaving the household life, due to their vital role in reproduction. Although there is no direct evidence in the texts, such attitudes are evident today in culturally endangered Buddhist communities, for example, in Ladakh and Tibet.

34 Anālayo, "Mahāpajāpatī's Going Forth," 278–81.

35 In the traditional understanding, ultimately the term *saṅgha* means an *arya* (noble) being, one who has achieved realization or great insight. Conventionally, the term *saṅgha* means four or more fully ordained members of the monastic community. Today in Western countries, the term is being used to refer to a community of people who are learning and practicing Buddhism.

36 Anālayo, "Mahāpajāpatī's Going Forth," 294.

37 Young, "Female Mutability and Male Anxiety."

38 Gregory Schopen explains the rationale behind "the urban Buddhist nun" in *Buddhist Nuns, Monks, and Other Worldly Matters*, 3–6.

39 Anālayo, "Mahāpajāpatī's Going Forth," 287–88, 296–300.

40 Anālayo, "The *Cullavagga* on *Bhikkhunī* Ordination."

41 Anālayo, "Mahāpajāpatī's Going Forth," 289. The four Buddhist traditions whose *vinaya* texts depict the women as shaving their heads and putting on ochre robes before being admitted to the *saṅgha* are listed in 289n49 as the Dharmaguptaka, Haimavata, Mahāsāṃghika, and Theravāda. For the Theravāda *vinaya*'s account of Mahāpajāpatī's request, see *Cullavagga X* in *The Book of the Discipline*, vol. 5 (Cullavagga), trans. I. B. Horner (1952; repr., Oxford, UK: Pali Text Society, 2001), 352–56.

42 Anālayo, "Mahāpajāpatī's Going Forth," 290–93.

43 Anālayo, "Attitudes towards Nuns," 352–76.

44 Anālayo, "Mahāpajāpatī's Going Forth," 307.

45 Anālayo, "Mahāpajāpatī's Going Forth," 285.

46 In *Once upon a Future Time*, Jan Nattier documents that the predicted disappearance of the teachings in the texts gets moved back as the teachings survive their predicted demise.

47 Anālayo, "Attitudes towards Nuns."

48 Anālayo, "Attitudes towards Nuns," 363.

49 Anālayo, "Attitudes towards Nuns," 370.

50 Anālayo cites texts from the Mahīśāsaka *vinaya*, Mūlasarvāstivāda *vinaya*, *Madhyama-āgama*, and Theravāda *vinaya* as evidence that "in spite of having happily accepted the gurudharmas, Mahāprajāpatī Gautamī attempted to get the Buddha to approve that junior monks should respect senior nuns." "Women's Renunciation in Early Buddhism," 85.

51 Anālayo, "Mahāpajāpatī's Going Forth," 306.

52 According to Buddhaghosa's *Samantapāsādikā*, a *vinaya* commentary, Aśoka encouraged both his son Mahinda and his daughter Saṅghamittā to enter the monastic order so that he would qualify as "an heir of the Dispensation." Mahinda became a monk at the age of twenty after witnessing the supernatural feats of an accomplished elder monk, and a thousand other young men joined him. His sister Saṅghamittā became a nun at the age of eighteen after marrying and giving birth to a son, Sumana, who later became a novice monk. Saṅghamittā's husband, Aggibrahmā, a nephew of Aśoka, left her to become a monk. Strong, "Aśoka's Wives."

53 The *vinaya* requires that a woman be trained as a novice (*sāmaṇerī*/*śrāmaṇerika*) and as a probationary nun (*sikkhamāṇā*/*śikṣamāṇā*) by a fully ordained nun (*bhikkhunī*/*bhikṣuṇī*).

54 Jayawickrama, *Inception of Discipline*, 80–86.

55 According to the *Samantapāsādikā*, these women included "500 maidens and 500 ladies of the court." See Jayawickrama, *Inception of Discipline*, 89. The word "maiden" typically denotes a virgin.

56 As Lorna Dewaraja notes, Saṅghamittā "was the first woman ambassador mentioned in recorded history, sent from one Head of State at the express invitation of another Head of State." "Sanghamitta Theri."

57 Pao-ch'ang Shih, *Lives of the Nuns*, 54, 63, 70.

58 See Grant, "Female Holder of the Lineage."
59 See Lee and Han, "Mothers and Moral Activists."
60 Hallisey, *Therigatha*, vii.
61 Norman, *Pāli Literature*, cited in Anālayo, "Beautiful Eyes Seen with Insight," 44.

2. BUDDHIST WOMEN IN SOUTH AND SOUTHEAST ASIA

1 Seeger, "(Dis)appearance of an Author."
2 Recent research includes Seeger, "Changing Roles of Thai Buddhist Women"; Seeger, "Against the Stream"; and Seeger, "Reversal of Female Power."
3 Mrozik, "We Love Our Nuns"; Mrozik, "A Robed Revolution."
4 For a case study in Buddhist cultural survival, see Tsomo, "Factions and Fortitude."
5 For example, see Collins and McDaniel, "Buddhist 'Nuns.'"
6 Seeger, "Orality, Memory, and Spiritual Practice."
7 Harris, *Buddhism in a Dark Age*.
8 Carbonnel, "On the Ambivalence of Female Monasticism," 280.
9 For a full treatment of the subject with reference to Burmese Buddhist society, see Carbonnel, "On the Ambivalence of Female Monasticism."
10 For example, see Gutschow, *Being a Buddhist Nun*, 77–122.
11 See Jacobsen, "In Search of the Khmer *Bhikkhunī*"; and Tsomo, "Lao Buddhist Women."
12 Norsworthy and Khuankaew, "A New View from Women of Thailand"; Norsworthy and Khuankaew, "Women of Burma Speak Out"; and Norsworthy and Khuankaew, "Bringing Social Justice to International Practices."
13 Crookston et al., "Buddhist Nuns on the Move."
14 Jordt, *Burma's Mass Lay Meditation Movement*.
15 The term can also be used for monks. Kawanami, *Renunciation and Empowerment of Buddhist Nuns*, 43–36.
16 Kawanami, *Renunciation and Empowerment of Buddhist Nuns*, 16.
17 Kawanami, *Renunciation and Empowerment of Buddhist Nuns*, 114–16.
18 Bonnet-Acosta, "Brave Daughters of the Buddha," 42.
19 Carbonnel, "On the Ambivalence of Female Monasticism," 269.
20 Symes, *An Account of an Embassy*, 249. Cited in Andaya, "Localising the Universal," 5.
21 Toomey, *In Search of Buddha's Daughters*, 145–54.
22 Bonnet-Acosta, "Brave Daughters of the Buddha," 44–45.
23 Kawanami, *Renunciation and Empowerment of Buddhist Nuns*, 181–91.
24 Kawanami, *Renunciation and Empowerment of Buddhist Nuns*, 106.

3. BUDDHIST WOMEN IN EAST ASIA

1 Heirman, "Can We Trace the Early Dharmaguptakas?" 412–16.
2 Heirman, "Vinaya," 172–74.
3 Heirman, "Chinese Nuns," 275.

4 Considerable disparity exists among the questions posed to female candidates in the various *vinaya* traditions and sometimes also among various redactions of texts in the same tradition, for example, among the different Kangyur editions of the Mūlasarvāstivāda *vinaya* texts preserved in Tibetan. In the Mahāsāṃghika lineages, the questions are as follows: whether the candidate has permission from her parents or husband; has sought out a preceptor; has robes and bowl in hand; has completed two years as a probationer (Pāli: *sikkhamāṇā*; Sanskrit: *śikṣamāṇā*); has been accepted as a disciple by a preceptor; has killed her father, mother, or an *arhat*; has drawn blood from a Buddha; has caused a schism in the *saṅgha*; has caused a *bhikṣu* to break his precepts; is a thief; is a heretic; has self-ordained; is a slave; is in debt; is in the military; has committed treason; is a woman; is barren; has injured genitalia; has anus and vagina conjoined; has damaged her genitalia; has lost both breasts; has lost one breast; has continual menstruation; has no menstruation; has irregular menstruation; is impotent; or has any serious disease. See Hirakawa, *Monastic Discipline*, 60–62.

5 Cheng, "Tracing Tesarā."

6 The text was compiled during the early sixth century and is attributed to Baochang (Pao-ch'ang). English translations include Pao Chang, *Biographies of Buddhist Nuns*, trans. Jung-hsi Li (Osaka, Japan: Tohokai, 1981); and Shih, *Lives of the Nuns*.

7 Shih, *Lives of the Nuns*, 15–16.

8 For a fuller understanding of the practice of auto-cremation, see Benn, *Burning for the Buddha*.

9 Heirman, "Buddhist Nuns."

10 Heirman, "Buddhist Nuns," 36–37. For more on this prediction, see Nattier, *Once upon a Future Time*.

11 Hinsch, "Confucian Filial Piety," 49.

12 Shih, *Lives of the Nuns*, 20.

13 Adamek, "A Niche of Their Own."

14 Balkwill, "The Sūtra on Transforming the Female Form."

15 Harrison, "Women in the Pure Land."

16 Schopen, "Sukhavātī as a Generalized Religious Goal"; Harrison, "Women in the Pure Land."

17 Young, *Courtesans and Tantric Consorts*, 199–21.

18 Young, "Female Mutability and Male Anxiety," 38, citing Beyer, *Buddhist Experience*, 46.

19 Dobbins, "Women's Birth in Pure Land."

20 Yü, *Kuan-yin*.

21 Numerous examples are noted in various chapters of Eun-su Cho's edited volume, *Korean Buddhist Nuns and Laywomen*.

22 Cho, "Religious Life of Buddhist Women in Chosŏn Korea."

23 Narratives of the monastic lives of Martine Batchelor and Son'gyong Sunim are included in Batchelor, *Women in Korean Zen*. The story of Myoom Sunim's

contributions to the preservation of Korean monasticism is recorded in Chung, "Crossing Over the Gender Boundary."

24 Her story is told in Cho, "A Resolute Vision of the Future."

25 The names of these nuns were Zenshi-ni, Zenzo-ni, and Kenzen-ni. Hirakawa, "History of Buddhist Nuns in Japan."

26 Meeks, "Reconfiguring Ritual Authenticity."

27 Meeks, "Reconfiguring Ritual Authenticity," 53.

28 According to religious studies scholar Richard Jaffe in "Seeking Sakyamuni," 70, at the start of the Meiji Era (1868–72), "government leaders subjected Buddhist institutions to a series of harsh measures that led to the widespread laicization of the clergy and the closure or destruction of numerous temples." See also Jaffe, *Neither Monk nor Layman*, 4–6.

29 Arai, *Women Living Zen*, 47.

30 See Arai, "Japanese Buddhist Nuns"; and Arai, *Women Living Zen*.

31 The *Brahmajāla Sūtra*, translated into Chinese by Kumārajīva around 400 CE, lists ten major and forty-eight minor *bodhisattva* precepts. These precepts derive from a lineage different from the eighteen major and forty-six minor *bodhisattva* precepts cited by Asaṅga in the *Yogācārabhūmi Śāstra* and observed by practitioners in the Tibetan Buddhist tradition.

32 Borup, "Contemporary Buddhist Priests and Clergy," 108.

33 See Aoyama, *Zen Seeds*; and Arai, *Women Living Zen*, 74–80.

34 Mitchell, "Going with the Flow."

35 See Noble, "Monastic Experience"; and Noble, "Eastern Traditions."

36 Starling, "Rights, Centers, and Peripheries."

37 See Cheng, "Luminary Buddhist Nuns in Contemporary Taiwan"; and DeVido, *Taiwan's Buddhist Nuns*.

38 Li, "From 'Vegetarian Women.'"

39 Huang, *Charisma and Compassion*.

40 Lee and Han, "Mothers and Moral Activists."

41 Tsomo, "Illustrating the Way."

42 For a contemporary perspective on the monastic lifestyle of nuns, see Wu Yin, *Choosing Simplicity*.

43 Fan and Whitehead, "Spirituality in a Modern Chinese Metropolis."

44 The social welfare activities of nuns from Taiwan who work with Chinese-speaking immigrants are discussed in Tsomo, "Socially Engaged Buddhist Nuns."

4. BUDDHIST WOMEN IN INNER ASIA

1 Anālayo, "Mahāpajāpatī's Going Forth."

2 Vargas-O'Brian, "The Life of dGe slong ma dPal mo."

3 Chönam and Khandro, *Lives and Liberation of Princess Mandarava*.

4 Schaeffer, "Autobiography of a Medieval Hermitess"; and Schaeffer, *Himalayan Hermitess*.

5 Changchub and Nyingpo, *Lady of the Lotus-Born.*
6 Harding, *Machik's Complete Explanation.*
7 Diemberger, *When a Woman Becomes a Religious Dynasty.*
8 Jacoby, *Love and Liberation.*
9 Gayley, *Love Letters from Golok.*
10 Gyaltsen, *Clear Mirror.*
11 Gyatso, "Down with the Demoness."
12 Shakya, *Life and Contribution of the Nepalese Princess.*
13 For the life of Yeshe Tsogyal, see Dowman, *Sky Dancer*; and Kunga and Tsogyal, *Life and Visions of Yeshe Tsogyal.*
14 See Diemberger, "Female Oracles in Modern Tibet." In the 1990s, a woman named Namsel Donma from Kham, Tibet, was officially recognized as a medium by His Holiness the Fourteenth Dalai Lama, as was a woman known as Youdonma (Kelsang Dolma). See Sidky, "State Oracle of Tibet," 86–87.
15 Martin, "Woman Illusion?"
16 For example, see Pachen and Donnelley, *Sorrow Mountain.*
17 Diemberger, *When a Woman Becomes a Religious Dynasty*, 62.
18 Diemberger, *When a Woman Becomes a Religious Dynasty*, 62.
19 Diemberger, *When a Woman Becomes a Religious Dynasty*, 63.
20 Diemberger, *When a Woman Becomes a Religious Dynasty*, 63.
21 Diemberger, *When a Woman Becomes a Religious Dynasty*, 63.
22 Diemberger, *When a Woman Becomes a Religious Dynasty*, 83.
23 Tsomo, "Buddhist Nuns."
24 For example, Ani Pachen's story is told in Pachen and Donnelley, *Sorrow Mountain.*
25 See Tsomo, "Change in Consciousness." These nuns' communities include Dolma Ling Nunnery and Institute, Geden Choeling Nunnery, Jamyang Chöling Institute, Jangchub Choeling Nunnery, Tsogyal Shedrub Dargyeling Nunnery, Ngagyur Nyingma Nunnery, Karma Drubgyu Thargay Ling, Dongyu Gatsel Ling Nunnery, Drikung Kargyu Samtenling Nunnery, and Tsechen Shed-Dub Samten Phuntsok Ling in India; Khacho Ghakhil Ling Nunnery, Keydong Thukche Choeling, and Tek Chok Ling Nunnery in Nepal; and monasteries for nuns in Bhutan: Paro Kila Gompa, Siloka, Wang Sisina, and Jachung Karmo.
26 Gutschow, *Being a Buddhist Nun*; and LaMacchia, *Songs and Lives of the Jomo.*
27 Haas, *Dakini Power*, 15–38, 271–93.
28 Examples include Diemberger, *When a Woman Becomes a Religious Dynasty*; Harding, *Machik's Complete Explanation*; and Schaeffer, *Himalayan Hermitess.*
29 Bhutan Nuns Foundation, accessed February 17, 2019, https://www.bhutannuns.org.
30 Elverskog, "Whatever Happened to Queen Jönggen?".
31 Tsomo, "Nuns, *Dakinis*, and Ordinary Women: Buddhist Women of Mongolia," in Tsomo, *Eminent Buddhist Women*, 201–2, 207–9.
32 Tsomo, "Prayers of Resistance."

33 Butler, "Performative Acts."
34 Tsomo, "Transition and Transformation."

5. BUDDHIST WOMEN IN THE WEST

1 Some of the earliest anthologies to appear were Boucher, *Turning the Wheel*; Dresser, *Buddhist Women on the Edge*; Friedman, *Meetings with Remarkable Women*; and Gregory and Mrozik, *Women Practicing Buddhism*. More recent ones include Tsomo, *Buddhism through American Women's Eyes*; Haas, *Dakini Power*; Miller and the editors of the *Shambhala Sun*, *Buddha's Daughters*; and McGinnity, *Lotus Petals in the Snow*.
2 A recent example is Caplow and Moon, *Hidden Lamp*.
3 Nagao, *Letters of Rennyo*, 79.
4 Usuki, "American Women in Jōdo Shin Buddhism Today"; and Usuki, *Currents of Change*.
5 For example, see Kirchner, *Record of Linji*; and Miura and Sasaki, *Zen Dust*.
6 Chinese, Korean, and Japanese schools of what is called Zen Buddhism use contemplation of *kōans*, questions or short dialogues that demonstrate the limits of conventional logic and intellectual understanding, encouraging practitioners to step out of their conditioned ways of viewing the world and sparking direct insight into the true nature of things. Examples include "Who is it who now repeats the Buddha's name?" and "What was my original face before my parents were born?"
7 Sterling, *Zen Pioneer*; and Anderson and Schwartz, *Zen Odyssey*.
8 Jiyu-Kennett and MacPhillamy, *Roar of the Tigress*.
9 See Chayat, *Subtle Sound*; and Tworkov, *Zen in America*.
10 See Halifax, *Being with Dying*; and Halifax, *Standing at the Edge*.
11 See Bennage and Carney, *Zen Teachings*.
12 Her story is told in Boucher, *Dancing in the Dharma*.
13 Ayya Khema's books include *Being Nobody, Going Nowhere: Meditations on the Buddhist Path*; *When the Iron Eagle Flies: Buddhism for the West*; and *I Give You My Life: The Autobiography of a Western Buddhist Nun*.
14 MacKenzie, *Revolutionary Life of Freda Bedi*.
15 MacKenzie, *Cave in the Snow*.
16 Pema Chödrön's books include *When Things Fall Apart: Heart Advice for Difficult Times*; *Start Where You Are: A Guide to Compassionate Living*; *The Wisdom of No Escape*; *The Places That Scare You: A Guide to Fearlessness in Difficult Times*; *No Time to Lose: A Timely Guide to the Way of the Bodhisattva*; *Practicing Peace in Times of War*; *Comfortable with Uncertainty: 108 Teachings on Cultivating Fearlessness and Compassion*; and more.
17 Tara Dhatu: Dance for the Goddess, accessed September 17, 2018, www.taradhatu.net.
18 See, especially, Cabezón's comprehensive work, *Sexuality in Classical South Asian Buddhism*.

19 Lawergren, "Buddha as a Musician," 226–28.

20 Harvey, *Introduction to Buddhist Ethics*, 420–23.

21 Gayley, "Revisiting the 'Secret Consort.'"

22 In "Ethics in the Teacher-Student Relationship: The Responsibilities of Teachers and Students," His Holiness the Fourteenth Dalai Lama said:

> If one presents the teachings clearly, others benefit. But if someone is supposed to propagate the Dharma and their behavior is harmful, it is our responsibility to criticize this with a good motivation. . . . Buddhist teachers who abuse sex, power, money, alcohol, or drugs, and who, when faced with legitimate complaints from their own students, do not correct their behavior, should be criticized openly and by name.

See "Ethics in the Teacher-Student Relationship: The Responsibilities of Teachers and Students; From Notes Taken during the Meeting of H. H. the Dalai Lama and Western Buddhist Teachers in Dharamsala, 1993," Tibetan Buddhism in the West: Problems of Adoption and Cross-Cultural Confusion, accessed April 8, 2020, https://info-buddhism.com.

23 Bell, "Scandals in Emerging Western Buddhism"; Downing, *Shoes Outside the Door*; Andrea M. Winn, Buddhist Project Sunshine, accessed August 14, 2018, http://andreamwinn.com; and numerous news reports.

24 Available resources include Griffin, *One Breath at a Time*; Jacobs-Stewart, *Mindfulness and the 12 Steps*; and Littlejohn, *12-Step Buddhist*.

25 Nattier, *A Few Good Men*, 255.

26 In *Majjima Nikāya* 21 and 28, the Buddha counsels monks who are physically attacked to respond persistently with mindfulness and calm.

27 Batchelor, *Buddhism without Beliefs*.

28 See Wallis, *Critique of Western Buddhism*; and Wilson, "Mindfully Feminine?"

29 Allione, *Feeding Your Demons*.

6. WOMEN'S ORDINATION ACROSS CULTURES

1 As yet, there is no comprehensive study of *bhikkhunī vinaya*, but useful studies of specific traditions exist. For a survey of the literature, see Heirman, "Vinaya." For a comparison of the rules for *bhikkhus* and *bhikkhunīs*, see Chung, "Buddhist View of Women." For a translation of the rules for *bhikṣuṇīs* in Chinese and Tibetan, see Tsomo, *Sisters in Solitude*.

2 Charles S. Prebish takes up the question of the *cāturdisa-saṅgha* or "*saṅgha* of the four quarters" and its varied interpretations in "Varying the Vinaya," 46–49.

3 Schopen, "Suppression of Nuns."

4 See Williams, "A Whisper in the Silence"; Kusuma, "Inaccuracies in Buddhist Women's History"; and Krey, "Some Remarks on the Status of Nuns."

5 Kusuma, "Inaccuracies in Buddhist Women's History."

6 In Chung, "Buddhist View of Women," 34–37.

7 For an in-depth analysis of gender, sexuality, and monasticism in early Buddhist texts, see Cabezón, *Sexuality in Classical South Asian Buddhism*.

8 Blackstone, *Women in the Footsteps of the Buddha*, 40.
9 Swearer, *Buddhist World of Southeast Asia*, 191.
10 Guruma, "Two Generations of Eminent Nepalese Nuns."
11 LeVine, "At the Cutting Edge," 13–29.
12 For details, see Li, "Ordination, Women, and Sisterhood."
13 Mrozik, "We Love Our Nuns."
14 For information on life as a *mae chee*, see Cook, *Meditation in Modern Buddhism*, esp. chaps. 7 and 8; and Falk, *Making Fields of Merit*.
15 For a personal account of a lay meditation practitioner, see Nanayon, *Pure and Simple*.
16 For a detailed ethnography of six exceptional Thai nuns, with textual analysis, see Seeger, *Gender and the Path to Awakening*.
17 In extensive interviews with scholarly Thai *mae chee*s, Steven Collins and Justin McDaniel learned that nuns who pass the ninth level in Pāli studies receive a stipend of only 1,700 baht ($56) a month, whereas monks at the same level receive 3,000 baht ($100) a month. Collins and McDaniel, "Buddhist 'Nuns,'" 1388. This unexplained inequality, extending even to highly qualified nuns in national exams, reflects the persistence of prevailing patriarchal norms and gender bias in Thai society.
18 Bhikkhunī Dhammananda (Chatsumarn Kabilsingh) tells the story of her mother, who paved the way for her own ordination, in "Bhikkhunī Ta Tao."
19 Ajahn Brahm's account of the incident is available online: "Ajahn Brahm on Why He Was Excommunicated," *Sujato's Blog*, November 7, 2009, https://sujato.wordpress.com.
20 Heirman, "*The Discipline in Four Parts*," 11. The Dharmaguptaka School reputedly derives its name from a follower of Maudgalyāyana, a close disciple of the Buddha (12).
21 The historical background on Buddhist ordination in China is discussed in Heirman, "Vinaya"; and Heirman, "Chinese Nuns."
22 Ann Heirman discusses the early history of *vinaya* in China in her article "Can We Trace the Early Dharmaguptakas?"
23 The ten precepts of a novice monk (*śrāmaṇera*) or novice nun (*śrāmaṇerika*) are to refrain from the following actions:

1. killing (intentionally killing a human being);
2. taking what is not given (stealing something of a value that is against the law in one's society);
3. sexual intercourse (intentionally engaging in sexual intercourse and experiencing orgasm, including either heterosexual or homosexual contact);
4. lying (especially lying about one's spiritual attainments);
5. taking intoxicants (including alcohol and recreational drugs);
6. singing, dancing, and playing music;
7. wearing perfume, ornaments, or cosmetics to beautify the body;
8. sitting on a high or expensive bed or throne;

9. eating after midday; and
10. touching gold, silver, or precious objects (including money).

In the Tibetan tradition, the ten novice precepts are expanded to thirty-six.

24 In the Mūlasarvāstivāda *vinaya* lineage practiced by the Tibetans, twelve *bhikṣuṇīs* are required.

25 For example, see Chung, "Buddhist View of Women"; and Tsomo, *Sisters in Solitude.*

26 A number of the papers presented at this conference are included in Mohr and Tsedroen, *Dignity and Discipline.*

27 Jens-Uwe Hartmann, a German scholar of Indology and Tibetology, has gone on record as saying, "Sometimes I wonder if the legal problems serve only as a pretext and hide a more general and not very rational reluctance to introduce major changes in those traditions." Hartmann, "The Vinaya between History and Modernity," 24.

7. GRASSROOTS REVOLUTION

1 For example, see Starkey and Tomalin, "Gender, Buddhism and Education"; and Crookston et al., "Buddhist Nuns on the Move."

2 Walton and Hayward, *Contesting Buddhist Narratives*; Grant, *Buddhism and Ethnic Conflict*; and Jerryson, *Buddhist Fury.*

3 Wright, "Spiritual Piety."

4 Tsomo, "Khunying Kanitha."

5 Moon, "Activist Women in American Buddhism."

6 See, for example, Manuel, *Way of Tenderness*; and Manuel, *Sanctuary.*

7 Chavis, *Altars in the Street*; Chavis, *Meena, Heroine of Afghanistan.*

8 Tsomo, "Socially Engaged Buddhist Nuns."

9 Huang, *Charisma and Compassion*; and Huang and Weller, "Merit and Mothering."

10 The transformative effects of improved educational opportunities for Buddhist women are documented in Chung, "Crossing Over the Gender Boundary"; LeVine, "Dharma Education for Women"; and Tsomo, "Change in Consciousness."

11 See, for example, McGregor, "Next Dalai Lama."

12 Falk, *Making Fields of Merit*, 34.

13 LeVine and Gellner, *Rebuilding Buddhism*, esp. 76–98.

14 Tsomo, "Illustrating the Way."

15 LeVine and Gellner, *Rebuilding Buddhism*, 76–98.

16 Pachen and Donnelley, *Sorrow Mountain.*

17 Lintner, *Aung San Suu Kyi.*

18 DeVido, *Taiwan's Buddhist Nuns*, 102–10.

19 Narada, *The Buddha and His Teachings*, 284–85.

CONCLUSION

1 Tsomo, "Global Exchange."

2 For example, see Jayawardena, *Feminism and Nationalism in the Third World*; and Grewal, *Transnational America.*

3 See Omvedt, *Buddhism in India.*
4 This term is taken from the book by Cheng, *Buddhist Nuns in Taiwan and Sri Lanka.* Although Cheng's analysis makes many valuable contributions to our understanding of Buddhist women in postcolonial Sri Lanka, it tends to discount the significant contributions of Western women such as Ayya Khema in generating awareness of the depressed conditions of nuns in twentieth-century Sri Lanka and the existence of *bhikkhunī* ordination lineages in other countries that have enabled the reestablishment of the *bhikkhunī saṅgha* in Sri Lanka since 1996.
5 A number of edited compilations of writings by international Buddhist scholars and practitioners have been published in recent years, including those I have edited: *Contemporary Buddhist Women, Compassion and Social Justice, Buddhism at the Grassroots, Eminent Buddhist Women, Buddhist Women in a Global Multicultural Community, Out of the Shadows, Buddhist Women and Social Justice, Bridging Worlds, Innovative Buddhist Women, Buddhist Women across Cultures, Buddhism through American Women's Eyes*, and *Sakyadhita.*
6 Chao Hwei Shih's work is described in DeVido, *Taiwan's Buddhist Nuns*, 101–16.
7 Lee and Han, "Mothers and Moral Activists," 67–72.
8 Tsomo, "History of Japanese Nuns."
9 Meeks, *Hokkeji and the Reemergence of Female Monastic Orders.*
10 Damcho, "I Will Do It," 49–50.
11 Representative articles by Anālayo include "Mahāpajāpatī's Going Forth"; "Attitudes towards Nuns"; and "Women's Renunciation in Early Buddhism." Many of his writings can be downloaded for free from his Hamburg University webpage at https://www.buddhismuskunde.uni-hamburg.de/en/personen/analayo.html.
12 Anālayo, "Legality of *Bhikkhunī* Ordination."
13 Li, "Ordination, Women, and Sisterhood."
14 Tsomo, *Sisters in Solitude*, 26–27.
15 Rita M. Gross shared her observations about the challenging course of progress in *A Garland of Feminist Reflections: Forty Years of Religious Exploration.* From a variety of different perspectives, one hundred women share the *kōans* and stories that have inspired them along the path of Buddhist practice in Caplow and Moon, *Hidden Lamp.*
16 For trends in education, see, for example, DiPrete and Buchmann, *Rise of Women.*
17 United Nations, "Universal Declaration of Human Rights," accessed September 17, 2018, www.un.org.
18 Haas, "10 Tibetan Buddhist Women You Need to Know"; Haas, "The F Word in Buddhism"; Simmons, "Sravasti Abbey: A Dream Fulfilled for U.S. Buddhist Nuns"; and others.
19 Bibo Liang, *The Buddhist Nun of Emei Mountain* (Chengdu TV, 1995), available at https://www.youtube.com.
20 Victress Hitchcock, dir., *Blessings: The Tsoknyi Nangchen Nuns of Tibet* (Chariot Productions, 2009).
21 Heather Kessinger, dir., *In the Shadow of Buddha* (Heather Kessinger, 2010).

22 Svetlana Darsalia, dir., *Mother Sela: Artist and Buddhist Nun* (Darsalia and Three Point Landing Production, 2012), available at https://www.youtube.com.

23 Yogini Project, accessed September 18, 2018, http://theyoginiproject.org; Yogini Project, accessed September 18, 2018, https://www.facebook.com.

24 The history of this college and other advances in the education of Thai nuns is documented in Falk, *Making Fields of Merit*, esp. 193–227.

25 For examples of ethnographic studies on Buddhist women around the world, see Arai, *Women Living Zen*; Bartholomeusz, *Women under the B Tree*; Gutschow, *Being a Buddhist Nun*; LeVine, "Dharma Education for Women," 137–54; and Tsomo, "Lao Buddhist Women."

26 Changchub and Nyingpo, *Lady of the Lotus-Born.*

27 Schaeffer recounts her story in "Autobiography of a Medieval Hermitess"; and *Himalayan Hermitess.*

28 Selected papers presented at this congress have been published in Mohr and Tsedroen, *Dignity and Discipline.*

29 The seeds of this transformation have already been planted, as described in Tsomo, "Change in Consciousness."

30 Haas, *Dakini Power*; Klein, *Meeting the Great Bliss Queen.*

31 For a useful analysis of Theravāda and Mahāyāna views on this issue, see Appleton, "In the Footsteps of the Buddha?"

32 Powers, *Bull of a Man*, 13–15.

33 The names of seventy eminent Buddhist women from the time of the Buddha are recorded in the *Therīgāthā*: Khemā was extolled for her great wisdom; Uppalavaṇṇā and Paṭācārā, for their exemplary monastic discipline; Dhammadinnā, for her skill in teaching Dhamma; Nandā, for her dedication; and Soṇā, for her energetic striving. All these women are described as nuns and *arhatīs*.

34 Walters, "*Apadāna: Therī-apadāna.*"

35 Powers, in *A Bull of a Man*, presents considerable textual support for this contention.

36 On the revival of *bhikkhunī* ordination in Sri Lanka, see Mrozik, "A Robed Revolution." For Nepal, see LeVine and Gellner, *Rebuilding Buddhism*, 171–206.

37 Bonnet-Acosta, "Brave Daughters of the Buddha"; Kawanami, *Renunciation and Empowerment of Buddhist Nuns.*

38 Grant, *Eminent Nuns*; Yuan, "Chinese Buddhist Nuns."

39 Arai, *Women Living Zen*; Meeks, *Hokkeji and the Reemergence of Female Monastic Orders.*

40 Cho, *Korean Buddhist Nuns and Laywomen*; Park, *Women and Buddhist Philosophy.*

41 LeVine and Gellner, *Rebuilding Buddhism*; LeVine, "Dharma Education for Women"; Watkins, *Spirited Women.*

42 Mrozik, "We Love Our Nuns"; Mrozik, "A Robed Revolution"; Salgado, *Buddhist Nuns and Gendered Practice.*

43 DeVido, *Taiwan's Buddhist Nuns*; Yu-Chen Li, "Bhikṣuṇī Hiuwen."
44 Dhammananda, "Bhikkhunī Ta Tao"; Falk, *Making Fields of Merit*.
45 Gyatso and Havnevik, *Women in Tibet*; Makley, *Violence of Liberation*.
46 Gutschow, *Being a Buddhist Nun*.
47 See, for example, Heirman, *Rules for Nuns*; Hüsken, "Stock of Bowls"; Kabilsingh, *Comparative Study*; and Tsomo, *Sisters in Solitude*.
48 Examples include Chung, "Buddhist View of Women"; Prebish, *Buddhist Monastic Discipline*; Tsomo, *Sisters in Solitude*; and Tsomo, "Buddhist Ethics in Japan and Tibet."

WORKS CITED

Adamek, Wendy L. "A Niche of Their Own: The Power of Convention in Two Inscriptions for Medieval Chinese Buddhist Nuns." *History of Religions* 49, no. 1 (2009): 1–26.

Allione, Tsultrim. *Feeding Your Demons: Ancient Wisdom for Resolving Inner Conflict*. New York: Little, Brown, 2008.

Anālayo, Bhikkhu. "Attitudes towards Nuns: A Case Study of the *Nandakovāda* in the Light of Its Parallels." *Journal of Buddhist Ethics* 17 (2010): 331–400.

———. "The *Bahudhātuka-sutta* and Its Parallels on Women's Inabilities." *Journal of Buddhist Ethics* 16 (2009): 137.

———. "Beautiful Eyes Seen with Insight as Bereft of Beauty: Subhā Therī and Her Male Counterpart in the Ekottarika-āgama." *The Sati Journal* (2014): 39–53.

———. "Chos sbyin gyi mdo: Bhikkhunī Dhammadinnā Proves Her Wisdom." *Chung-Hwa Buddhist Journal* 24 (2011): 3–33.

———. "The Cullavagga on Bhikkhuni Ordination." *Journal of Buddhist Ethics* 22 (2015): 399–448.

———. "Karma and Female Birth." *Journal of Buddhist Ethics* 21 (2014): 109–53.

———. "The Legality of *Bhikkhunī* Ordination." *Journal of Buddhist Ethics* 20 (2013): 310–33.

———. "Mahāpajāpatī's Going Forth in the *Madhyama-āgama*." *Journal of Buddhist Ethics* 18 (2011): 268–317.

———. "Women's Renunciation in Early Buddhism: The Four Assemblies and the Foundation of the Order of Nuns." In Mohr and Tsedroen, *Dignity and Discipline*, 65–97.

Andaya, Barbara Watson. "Localising the Universal: Women, Motherhood and the Appeal of Early Theravada Buddhism." *Journal of Southeast Asian Studies* 33, no. 1 (2002): 1–30.

Anderson, Janica, and Steven Schwartz. *Zen Odyssey: The Story of Sokei-an, Ruth Fuller Sasaki, and the Birth of Zen in America*. Somerville, MA: Wisdom Publication, 2018.

Aoyama, Shundo. *Zen Seeds: Reflections of a Female Priest*. Translated by Patricia Daien Bennage. Tokyo: Kōsei Publishing, 1990.

Appleton, Naomi. "In the Footsteps of the Buddha? Women and the *Bodhisatta* Path in Theravāda Buddhism." *Journal of the Feminist Study of Religion* 27, no. 1 (2011): 33–51.

Arai, Paula Kane Robinson. "Japanese Buddhist Nuns: Innovators for the Sake of Tradition." In Tsomo, *Buddhist Women across Cultures*, 105–22.

———. *Women Living Zen: Japanese Sōtō Buddhist Nuns*. New York: Oxford University Press, 1999.

Balkwill, Stephanie. "The Sūtra on Transforming the Female Form: Unpacking an Early Medieval Chinese Buddhist Text." *Journal of Chinese Religions* 44, no. 2 (2016): 127–48.

Bartholomeusz, Tessa. *Women under the B Tree: Buddhist Nuns in Sri Lanka*. Cambridge: Cambridge University Press, 1994.

Batchelor, Martine. *Women in Korean Zen: Lives and Practices*. New York: Syracuse University Press, 2006.

Batchelor, Stephen. *Buddhism without Beliefs: A Contemporary Guide to Awakening*. New York: Riverhead Books, 1997.

Battaglia, Lisa J. "Only Skin Deep? Female Embodiment and the Paradox of Beauty in Indian Buddhism." In Tsomo, *Buddhist Feminisms and Femininities*, 183–217.

Bell, Sandra. "Scandals in Emerging Western Buddhism." In *Westward Dharma: Buddhism beyond Asia*, edited by Charles S. Prebish and Martin Baumann, 230–42. Berkeley: University of California Press, 2002.

Benn, James A. *Burning for the Buddha: Self-Immolation in Chinese Buddhism*. Honolulu: University of Hawai'i Press, 2006.

Bennage, Patricia Dai-En, and Eido Frances Carney, eds. *Zen Teachings in Challenging Times*. Olympia, WA: Temple Grounds Press, 2018.

Beyer, Stephen. *The Buddhist Experience: Sources and Interpretations*. Belmont, CA: Wadsworth, 1974.

Blackstone, Kathryn R. *Women in the Footsteps of the Buddha*. New York: Routledge, 2013.

Bode, Mabel. "Women Leaders of the Buddhist Reformation." *Journal of the Royal Asiatic Society of Great Britain and Ireland* 25, nos. 3 and 4 (1893): 517–66, 763–98.

Bonnet-Acosta, Cristina. "Brave Daughters of the Buddha: The Feminisms of the Burmese Buddhist Nuns." In Tsomo, *Eminent Buddhist Women*, 35–54.

Borup, Jørn. "Contemporary Buddhist Priests and Clergy." *Handbook of Contemporary Japanese Religions*, edited by Inken Prohl and John Nelson, 107–32. Leiden, Netherlands: Brill, 2012.

Boucher, Sandy. *Dancing in the Dharma: The Life and Teachings of Ruth Denison*. Boston: Beacon Press, 2006.

———. *Turning the Wheel: American Women Creating the New Buddhism*. New York: HarperCollins, 1988.

Butler, Judith. "Performative Acts and Gender Constitution: An Essay in Phenomenology and Feminist Theory." *Theatre Journal* 40, no. 4 (1988): 519–31.

Cabezón, José Ignacio. *Buddhism, Sexuality, and Gender*. Albany: State University of New York Press, 1992.

———. *Sexuality in Classical South Asian Buddhism*. Somerville, MA: Wisdom Publications, 2017.

Caplow, Zenshin Florence, and Reigetsu Susan Moon, eds. *The Hidden Lamp: Stories from Twenty-Five Centuries of Awakened Women*. Boston: Wisdom Publications, 2013.

Carbonnel, Laure. "On the Ambivalence of Female Monasticism in Theravāda Buddhism: A Contribution to the Study of the Monastic System in Myanmar." *Asian Ethnology* 68, no 2 (2009): 265–82.

Changchub, Gyalwa, and Namkhai Nyingpo. *Lady of the Lotus-Bọrn: The Life and Enlightenment of Yeshe Tsogyal*. Translated by Padmakara Translation Group. Boston: Shambhala, 2002.

Chavis, Melody Ermachild. *Altars in the Street: A Courageous Memoir of Community and Spiritual Awakening*. New York: Bell Tower, 1998.

———. *Meena, Heroine of Afghanistan: The Martyr Who Founded RAWA, the Revolutionary Association of the Women of Afghanistan*. New York: St. Martin's Press, 2003.

Chayat, Sherry. *Subtle Sound: The Zen Teachings of Maurine Stuart*. Boston: Shambhala, 1996.

Cheng, Wei-yi. *Buddhist Nuns in Taiwan and Sri Lanka: A Critique of the Feminist Perspective*. New York: Routledge, 2007.

———. "Luminary Buddhist Nuns in Contemporary Taiwan: A Quiet Feminist Movement." *Journal of Buddhist Ethics* 10 (2003): 39–56.

———. "Tracing Tesarā: The Transmission of Buddhist Nuns' Order along the Maritime Silk Road." *Long Yang Journal of Academic Research* 4 (2010): 19–55.

Chikusa, Masaaki. "The Formation and Growth of Buddhist Nun Communities in China." In *Engendering Faith: Women and Buddhism in Premodern Japan*, edited by Barbara Ruch, 3–20. Ann Arbor, MI: Center for Japanese Studies, University of Michigan, 2003.

Cho, Eun-su, ed. *Korean Buddhist Nuns and Laywomen: Hidden Histories, Enduring Vitality*. Albany: State University of New York Press, 2011.

———. "The Religious Life of Buddhist Women in Chosŏn Korea." In Tsomo, *Buddhist Feminisms and Femininities*, 67–83.

———. "A Resolute Vision of the Future: Hyechun Sunim's Founding of the National Bhikṣuṇī Association in Korea." In Tsomo, *Eminent Buddhist Women*, 125–42.

Chödrön, Pema. *Comfortable with Uncertainty: 108 Teachings on Cultivating Fearlessness and Compassion*. Boulder, CO: Shambhala, 2018.

———. *No Time to Lose: A Timely Guide to the Way of the Bodhisattva*. Boston: Shambhala, 2005.

———. *The Places That Scare You: A Guide to Fearlessness in Difficult Times*. Boston: Shambhala, 2002.

———. *Practicing Peace in Times of War*. Boston: Shambhala, 2007.

———. *Start Where You Are: A Guide to Compassionate Living*. Boston: Shambhala, 2001.

———. *When Things Fall Apart: Heart Advice for Difficult Times*. Boulder, CO: Shambhala, 1997.

———. *The Wisdom of No Escape*. Boston: Shambhala, 2001.

Chönam, Lama, and Sangye Khandro, trans. *The Lives and Liberation of Princess Mandarava: The Indian Consort of Padmasambhava*. Boston: Wisdom Publications, 2015.

Chung, Inyoung (Sukhdam Sunim). "A Buddhist View of Women: A Comparative Study of the Rules for *Bhiksus* and *Bhiksunis* Based on the Chinese *Pratimoksa*." *Journal of Buddhist Ethics* 6 (1999): 29–105.

———. "Crossing Over the Gender Boundary in Gray Rubber Shoes: A Study on Myoom Sunim's Buddhist Monastic Education." In Tsomo, *Out of the Shadows*, 119–28.

Collett, Alice. "Buddhism and Gender: Reframing and Refocusing the Debate." *Journal of Feminist Studies in Religion* 22, no. 2 (2006): 55–84.

———. "The Female Past in Early Indian Buddhism: The Shared Narrative of the Seven Sisters in the *Therī-Apadāna*." *Religions of South Asia* 5, no. 1 (2011): 209–26.

______. "Historio-Critical Hermeneutics in the Study of Women in Early Indian Buddhism." *Numen* 56, no. 1 (2009): 91–117.

______. *Lives of Early Buddhist Nuns Biographies as History*. New Delhi, India: Oxford University Press, 2006.

———, ed. *Women in Early Indian Buddhism: Comparative Textual Studies*. Oxford: Oxford University Press, 2013.

Collins, Steven. "The Body in Theravāda Buddhism." In *Religion and the Body*, edited by Sarah Coakley, 185–204. New York: Cambridge University Press, 1997.

Collins, Steven, and Justin McDaniel. "Buddhist 'Nuns' (*mae chi*) and the Teaching of Pali in Contemporary Thailand." *Modern Asian Studies* 44, no. 6 (2010): 1373–1408.

Cook, Joanna. *Meditation in Modern Buddhism: Renunciation and Change in Thai Monastic Life*. Cambridge: Cambridge University Press, 2014.

Crookston, Benjamin T., Kirk A. Dearden, Ketsana Chan, Theary Chan, and David D. Stoker. "Buddhist Nuns on the Move: An Innovative Approach to Improving Breastfeeding Practices in Cambodia." *Maternal and Child Nutrition* 3, no. 1 (2007): 10–24.

Dalai Lama XIV, Bstan-dzin-rgya-mtsho. "Buddhism, Asian Values, and Democracy." *Journal of Democracy* 10, no. 1 (1999): 1–7.

Damcho, Lhundup. "I Will Do It." *Buddhadharma: The Practitioner's Quarterly* (Summer 2000): 49–50.

de Jong, J. W. "Notes on the Bhiksunī-vinaya of the Mahāsāṃghikas." In *Buddhist Studies in Honour of I. B. Horner*, edited by Lance Cousins, 63–70. Dordrecht, Netherlands: D. Reidel, 1974.

Derris, Karen. "When the Buddha Was a Woman: Reimagining Tradition in the Theravāda." *Journal of Feminist Studies in Religion* 24, no. 2 (2008): 29–44.

DeVido, Elise Anne. *Taiwan's Buddhist Nuns*. Albany: State University of New York Press, 2010.

Dewaraja, Lorna. "Sanghamitta Theri: A Liberated Woman." *Colombo Daily News*, December 19, 2001.

Dhammadinnā. "Karma Here and Now in a Mūlasarvāstivāda Avadāna: How the Bodhisattva Changed Sex and Was Born as a Female 500 Times." In *Annual Report of the International Research Institute for Advanced Buddhology at Soka University for 2017*, 63–94. Tokyo: Soka University, 2018.

Dhammananda, Bhikkhuni (Chatsumarn Kabilsingh). "Bhikkhunī Ta Tao: Paving the Way for Future Generations." In Tsomo, *Eminent Buddhist Women*, 61–70.

Diemberger, Hildegard. "Female Oracles in Modern Tibet." In Gyatso and Havnevik, *Women in Tibet*, 113–68.

———. *When a Woman Becomes a Religious Dynasty: The Samding Dorje Phagmo of Tibet*. New York: Columbia University Press, 2007.

DiPrete, Thomas A., and Claudia Buchmann. *The Rise of Women: The Growing Gender Gap in Education and What It Means for American Schools*. New York: Russell Sage Foundation, 2013.

Dobbins, James C. "Women's Birth in Pure Land as Women: Intimations from the Letter of Eshinni." *Eastern Buddhist* 28, no. 1 (1995): 108–22.

Dowman, Keith. *Sky Dancer: The Secret Life and Songs of the Lady Yeshe Tsogyel*. Ithaca, NY: Snow Lion, 1996.

Downing, Michael. *Shoes Outside the Door: Desire, Devotion, and Excess at San Francisco Zen Center*. Washington, DC: Counterpoint, 2001.

Dresser, Marianne, ed. *Buddhist Women on the Edge: Contemporary Perspectives from the Western Frontier*. Berkeley, CA: North Atlantic Books, 1996.

Elverskog, Johan. "Whatever Happened to Queen Jönggen?" In *Buddhism in Mongolian History, Society, and Culture*, edited by Vesna Wallace, 3–22. New York: Oxford University Press, 2015.

Falk, Monica Lindberg. *Making Fields of Merit: Buddhist Female Ascetics and Gendered Orders in Thailand*. Seattle: University of Washington Press, 2008.

Fan, Lizhu, and James D. Whitehead. "Spirituality in a Modern Chinese Metropolis." In *Chinese Religious Life*, edited by David A. Palmer, Glenn Shive, and Philip L. Wickeri, 13–29. New York: Oxford University Press, 2011.

Faure, Bernard. *The Power of Denial: Buddhism, Purity, and Gender*. Princeton, NJ: Princeton University Press, 2003.

Findly, Ellison Banks, ed. *Women's Buddhism, Buddhism's Women: Tradition, Revision, Renewal*. Boston: Wisdom Publications, 2000.

Finnegan, Damchö Diana. "'For the Sake of Women Too': Gender and Ethics in the Narratives of the Mūlasarvāstivāda Vinaya." PhD diss., University of Wisconsin, 2009.

Friedman, Lenore. *Meetings with Remarkable Women: Buddhist Teachers in America*. Boston: Shambhala, 2000.

Gayley, Holly. *Inseparable across Lifetimes: The Lives and Love Letters of the Tibetan Visionaries Namtrul Rinpoche and Khandro Tare Lhamo*. Boulder, CO: Shambhala, 2019.

———. *Love Letters from Golok: A Tantric Couple in Modern Tibet*. New York: Columbia University Press, 2017.

———. “Revisiting the ‘Secret Consort’ (*gsang yum*) in Tibetan Buddhism.” *Religions* 9, no. 6 (2018): 1–21.
Grant, Beata. *Eminent Nuns: Women Chan Masters of Seventeenth-Century China*. Honolulu: University of Hawai‘i Press, 2009.
———. “Female Holder of the Lineage: Linji Chan Master Zhiyuan Xinggang (1597–1654).” *Late Imperial China* 17, no. 2 (1996): 51–76.
———. “Patterns of Female Religious Experience in Qing Dynasty Popular Literature.” *Journal of Chinese Religions* 23 (1995): 29–58.
Grant, Patrick. *Buddhism and Ethnic Conflict in Sri Lanka*. Albany: State University of New York Press, 2009.
Gregory, Peter N., and Susanne Mrozik, eds. *Women Practicing Buddhism: American Experiences*. Boston: Wisdom Publications, 2003.
Grewal, Inderpal. *Transnational America: Feminisms, Diasporas, Neoliberalisms*. Durham, NC: Duke University Press, 2005.
Griffin, Kevin. *One Breath at a Time: Buddhism and the Twelve Steps*. N.p: Rodale Books, 2017.
Gross, Rita M. *Buddhism after Patriarchy: A Feminist History, Analysis, and Reconstruction of Buddhism*. Albany: State University of New York Press, 1992.
———. *A Garland of Feminist Reflections: Forty Years of Religious Exploration*. Berkeley: University of California Press, 2009.
Grünhagen, Céline. “The Female Body in Early Buddhist Literature.” *Scripta Instituti Donneriani Aboensis* 23 (2011): 100–114.
Guruma, Punyawati. “Two Generations of Eminent Nepalese Nuns.” In Tsomo, *Eminent Buddhist Women*, 25–31.
Gutschow, Kim. *Being a Buddhist Nun: The Struggle for Enlightenment*. Cambridge, MA: Harvard University Press, 2004.
Gyaltsen, Sakyapa Sonam. *The Clear Mirror: A Traditional Account of Tibet's Golden Age*. Ithaca, NY: Snow Lion Publications, 1996.
Gyatso, Janet. “Down with the Demoness: Reflections on a Feminine Ground in Tibet.” In Willis, *Feminine Ground*, 33–51.
Gyatso, Janet, and Hanna Havnevik, eds. *Women in Tibet: Past and Present*. New York: Columbia University Press, 2005.
Haas, Michaela. *Dakini Power: Twelve Extraordinary Women Shaping the Transmission of Tibetan Buddhism in the West*. Boston: Shambhala, 2013.
———. “The F Word in Buddhism: ‘Daughters of the Buddha’ Discuss How Buddhist Women Can Achieve Equality.” *Huffington Post*, January 7, 2013, www.huffingtonpost.com.
———. “10 Tibetan Buddhist Women You Need to Know.” *Huffington Post*, March 20, 2013. www.huffingtonpost.com.
Haker, Hille, Susan Ross, and Marie-Theres Wacker, eds. *Women's Voices in World Religions*. London: SCM Press, 2006.
Halifax, Joan. *Being with Dying: Cultivating Compassion and Fearlessness in the Presence of Death*. Boston: Shambhala, 2009.

———. *Standing at the Edge: Finding Freedom Where Fear and Courage Meet*. New York: Flatiron Books, 2018.

Hallisey, Charles, trans. *Therigatha: Poems of the First Buddhist Women*. Cambridge, MA: Harvard University Press, 2015.

Harding, Sarah. *Machik's Complete Explanation: Clarifying the Meaning of Chöd*. Ithaca, NY: Snow Lion Publications, 2003.

Harris, Ian. *Buddhism in a Dark Age: Cambodian Monks under Pol Pot*. Honolulu: University of Hawai'i Press, 2013.

Harrison, Paul. "Women in the Pure Land: Some Reflections on the Textual Sources." *Journal of Indian Philosophy* 26, no. 6 (1998): 553–72.

Hartmann, Jens-Uwe. "The Vinaya between History and Modernity: Some General Reflections." In Mohr and Tsedroen, *Dignity and Discipline*, 23–28.

Harvey, Peter. *An Introduction to Buddhist Ethics: Foundations, Values and Issues*. New York: Oxford University Press, 1997.

Heirman, Ann. "Buddhist Nuns through the Eyes of Leading Early Tang Masters." *Chinese Historical Review* 22, no 1 (2015): 31–51.

———. "Can We Trace the Early Dharmaguptakas?" *T'oung Pao* (Second Series) 88, nos. 4–5 (2002): 396–429.

———. "Chinese Nuns and Their Ordination in Fifth Century China." *Journal of the International Association of Buddhist Studies* 24, no. 2 (2001): 275–304.

———. *Rules for Nuns according to the Dharmaguptakavinaya: The Discipline in Four Parts*. 3 vols. Delhi, India: Motilal Banarsidass, 2002.

———. "Vinaya: From India to China." In Heirman and Bunbacher, *The Spread of Buddhism*, 167–202.

Heirman, Ann, and Stephen Peter Bunbacher, eds. *The Spread of Buddhism*. Leiden, Netherlands: Brill, 2007.

Hinsch, Bret. "Confucian Filial Piety and the Construction of the Ideal Chinese Buddhist Woman." *Journal of Chinese Religions* 30 (2002): 49–75.

Hirakawa, Akira. "The History of Buddhist Nuns in Japan." Translated by Karma Lekshe Tsomo with Junko Miura. *Buddhist-Christian Studies* 12 (1992): 147–58.

———. *Monastic Discipline for the Buddhist Nuns: An English Translation of the Chinese Text of the Mahāsāṃghika-Bhikṣuṇī-Vinaya*. Patna, India: Kashi Prasad Jayaswal Research Institute, 1982.

Horner, I. B. [Isaline Blew]. *Women under Primitive Buddhism: Laywomen and Almswomen*. Delhi, India: Motilal Banarsidass, 1930. Reprint, New York: Gutenberg, 2011.

Huang, C. Julia. *Charisma and Compassion: Cheng Yen and the Buddhist Tzu Chi Movement*. Cambridge, MA: Harvard University Press, 2009.

Huang, C. Julia, and Robert P. Weller. "Merit and Mothering: Women and Social Welfare in Taiwanese Buddhism." *Journal of Asian Studies* 57, no. 2 (1998): 379–96.

Hüsken, Ute. "The Eight Garudhammas." In Mohr and Tsedroen, *Dignity and Discipline*, 143–48.

———. "The Legend of the Establishment of the Buddhist Order of Nuns in the Theravāda Vinaya Pitaka." *Journal of the Pali Text Society* 26 (2000): 43–69.

———. "A Stock of Bowls Requires a Stock of Robes: Relations of the Rules for Nuns in the Theravada Vinaya and the Bhiksuni-Vinaya of the Mahāsāṃghika-Lokottaravādin." In *Untersuchungen zur buddhistischen Literatur II, Gustav Roth zum 80. Geburtstag gewidmet*, edited by Heinz Bechert, S. Bretfeld, and P. Kieffer-Pülz, 201–38. Göttingen, Germany: Vandenhoeck & Ruprecht, 1997.

Jacobs-Stewart, Thérèse. *Mindfulness and the 12 Steps: Living Recovery in the Present Moment*. Center City, MN: Hazelden, 2010.

Jacobsen, Trude. "In Search of the Khmer *Bhikkhunī*: Reading between the Lines in Late Classical and Early Middle Cambodia (13th–18th Centuries)." *Journal of the Oxford Centre for Buddhist Studies* 4 (2013): 75–87.

Jacoby, Sarah H. *Love and Liberation: Autobiographical Writings of the Tibetan Buddhist Visionary Sera Khandro*. New York: Columbia University Press, 2016.

Jaffe, Richard M. *Neither Monk nor Layman: Clerical Marriage in Modern Japanese Buddhism*. Honolulu: University of Hawai'i Press, 2010.

———. "Seeking Sakyamuni: Travel and the Reconstruction of Japanese Buddhism." *Journal of Japanese Studies* 30, no. 1 (Winter 2004): 65–96.

Jaini, Padmanabh S. "*Padīpadānajātaka*: Gautama's Last Female Incarnation." In *Collected Papers in Buddhist Studies*, edited by Padmanabh Jaini, 367–74. Delhi, India: Motilal Banarsidass, 2001.

Jayawardena, Kumari. *Feminism and Nationalism in the Third World*. London: Zed Books, 1986.

Jayawickrama, N. A. *The Inception of Discipline and the Vinaya Nidana*. Collingwood, VIC, Australia: Trieste, 2018.

Jerryson, Michael K. *Buddhist Fury: Religion and Violence in Southern Thailand*. New York: Oxford University Press, 2011.

Jiyu-Kennett, and Daizui MacPhillamy. *Roar of the Tigress: The Oral Teachings of Rev. Master Jiyu-Kennett, Western Woman and Zen Master*. Shasta, CA: Shasta Abbey Press, 2005.

Jordt, Ingrid. *Burma's Mass Lay Meditation Movement: Buddhism and the Cultural Construction of Power*. Athens: Ohio University Press, 2007.

Jyväsjärvi, Mari Johanna. "Fragile Virtue: Women's Monastic Practice in Early Medieval India." PhD diss., Harvard University, 2011.

Kabilsingh, Chatsumarn. *A Comparative Study of Bhikkhuni Patimokkha*. Varanasi, India: Chaukhambha Orientalia, 1984.

Kawanami, Hiroko. *Renunciation and Empowerment of Buddhist Nuns in Myanmar-Burma: Building a Community of Female Faithful*. Leiden, Netherlands: Brill, 2013.

Khema, Ayya. *Being Nobody, Going Nowhere: Meditations on the Buddhist Path*. Boston: Wisdom Publications, 1987.

———. *I Give You My Life: The Autobiography of a Western Buddhist Nun*. Boston: Shambhala, 1998.

———. *When the Iron Eagle Flies: Buddhism for the West*. Boston: Wisdom Publications, 2000.

Kieffer-Pülz, Petra. "Sex-Change in Buddhist Legal Literature with a Focus on the Theravāda Tradition." In *Annual Report of The International Research Institute for Advanced Buddhology at Soka University for 2017*, 27–62. Tokyo: Soka University, 2018.

Kim, Iryop. *Reflections of a Zen Buddhist Nun*. Translated by Jin Park. Honolulu: University of Hawai'i Press, 2014.

Kim, Jinah. "Unheard Voices: Women's Roles in Medieval Buddhist Artistic Production and Religious Practices in South Asia." *Journal of the American Academy of Religion* 79 (2012): 200–32.

Kinnard, Jacob N. *The Emergence of Buddhism: Classical Traditions in Contemporary Perspective*. Minneapolis: Fortress Press, 2011.

Kirchner, Thomas Yuho, ed. *The Record of Linji*. Translated by Ruth Fuller Sasaki. Honolulu: University of Hawai'i Press, 2009.

Klein, Anne Carolyn. *Meeting the Great Bliss Queen: Buddhists, Feminists, and the Art of the Self*. Ithaca, NY: Snow Lion, 2008.

Kloppenborg, Ria. "Female Stereotypes in Early Buddhism: The Women of the Therīgātha." In Kloppenborg and Hanegraaff, *Female Stereotypes in Religious Traditions*, 151–69.

Kloppenborg, Ria, and Wouter J. Hanegraaff, eds. *Female Stereotypes in Religious Traditions*. Leiden, Netherlands: E. J. Brill, 1995.

Krey, Gisela. "Some Remarks on the Status of Nuns and Laywomen in Early Buddhism." In Mohr and Tsedroen, *Dignity and Discipline*, 39–64.

Kunga, Drime, and Yeshe Tsogyal. *The Life and Visions of Yeshe Tsogyal: The Autobiography of the Great Wisdom Queen*. Translated by Chonyi Drolma. Boulder, CO: Shambhala, 2017.

Kusuma, Bhikkhunī. "Inaccuracies in Buddhist Women's History." In Tsomo, *Innovative Buddhist Women*, 5–12.

LaMacchia, Linda. *Songs and Lives of the Jomo (Nuns) of Kinnaur, Northwest India: Women's Religious Expression in Tibetan Buddhism*. Delhi, India: Sri Satguru, 2008.

Langenberg, Amy Paris. "Female Monastic Healing and Midwifery: A View from the Vinaya Tradition." *Journal of Buddhist Ethics* 21 (2014): 152–87.

_______. "An Imperfect Alliance: Feminism and Contemporary Female Buddhist Monasticisms." *Religions* 9 (2018): 1–24.

———. "Mahāsāṃghika-lokottaravāda Bhiksunī Vinaya: The Intersection of Womanly Virtue and Buddhist Asceticism." In Collett, *Women in Early Indian Buddhism*, 81–96.

Lawergren, Bo. "Buddha as a Musician: An Illustration of a Jataka Story." *Artibus Asiae* 54, nos. 3/4 (1994): 226–40.

Lee, Chengpang, and Ling Han. "Mothers and Moral Activists: Two Models of Women's Social Engagement in Contemporary Taiwanese Buddhism." *Nova Religio: The Journal of Alternative and Emergent Religions* 19, no. 3 (February 2016): 54–77.

LeVine, Sarah. "At the Cutting Edge: Theravāda Nuns in the Kathmandu Valley." In Tsomo, *Innovative Buddhist Women*, 13–29.

———. "Dharma Education for Women in the Theravāda Buddhist Community of Nepal." In Tsomo, *Buddhist Women and Social Justice*, 137–54.

LeVine, Sarah, and David N. Gellner. *Rebuilding Buddhism: The Theravada Movement in Twentieth-Century Nepal*. Cambridge, MA: Harvard University Press, 2007.

Li, Yu-Chen. "Bhikṣuṇī Hiuwen: Enlightening Society by Institutionalizing Buddhist Education." In Tsomo, *Eminent Buddhist Women*, 101–10.

———. "From 'Vegetarian Women' to 'Female Volunteers' to 'Dharma Aunties': The Institutionalization of Buddhist Women's Affiliation with Monastic Sangha." In Tsomo, *Contemporary Buddhist Women*, 216–21.

———. "Ordination, Women, and Sisterhood: The International Full Ordination Ceremony in Bodhgaya." In Tsomo, *Innovative Buddhist Women*, 168–98.

Lintner, Bertil. *Aung San Suu Kyi and Burma's Struggle for Democracy*. Bangkok: Silkworm Books, 2011.

Littlejohn, Darren. *The 12-Step Buddhist: Enhance Recovery from Any Addiction*. New York: Simon & Schuster, 2009.

MacKenzie, Vicki. *Cave in the Snow: A Western Woman's Quest for Enlightenment*. London: Bloomsbury, 1998.

———. *The Revolutionary Life of Freda Bedi: British Feminist, Indian Nationalist, Buddhist Nun*. Boulder, CO: Shambhala, 2017.

Makley, Charlene E. *The Violence of Liberation: Gender and Tibetan Buddhist Revival in Post-Mao China*. Berkeley: University of California Press, 2007.

Manuel, Zenju Earthlyn. *Sanctuary: A Meditation on Home, Homelessness, and Belonging*. Somerville, MA: Wisdom Publications, 2018.

———. *The Way of Tenderness: Awakening through Race, Sexuality, and Gender*. Boston: Wisdom Publications, 2015.

Martin, Dan. "The Woman Illusion? Research into the Lives of Spiritually Accomplished Women Leaders of the 11th and 12th Centuries." In Gyatso and Havnevik, *Women in Tibet*, 49–82.

McGinnity, Tanya. *Lotus Petals in the Snow: Voices of Canadian Buddhist Women*. Nepean, ON: Sumeru Press, 2015.

McGregor, Jena. "The Next Dalai Lama Could Be a Woman." *Washington Post*, June 17, 2013.

Meeks, Lori R. "Buddhist Renunciation and the Female Life Cycle: Understanding Nunhood in Heian and Kamakura Japan." *Harvard Journal of Asiatic Studies* 70, no. 1 (2010): 1–59.

———. *Hokkeji and the Reemergence of Female Monastic Orders in Premodern Japan*. Honolulu: University of Hawai'i Press, 2010.

———. "Imagining Rahula in Medieval Japan: The Raun Koshiki." *Japanese Journal of Religious Studies* 43, no. 1 (2016): 131–51.

———. "In Her Likeness: Female Divinity and Leadership at Medieval Chuguji." *Japanese Journal of Religious Studies* 34, no. 2 (2007): 351–92.

———. "Reconfiguring Ritual Authenticity: The Ordination Traditions of Aristocratic Women in Premodern Japan." *Japanese Journal of Religious Studies* 33, no. 1 (2006): 51–74.

———. "Vows for the Masses: Eison and the Popular Expansion of Precept-Conferral Ceremonies in Premodern Japan." *Numen* 56, no. 1 (2009): 1–43.

Miller, Andrea, and the editors of the *Shambhala Sun*. *Buddha's Daughters: Teachings from Women Who Are Shaping Buddhism in the West*. Boston: Shambhala, 2014.

Mitchell, Matthew S. "Going with the Flow and Yet Controlling the Flow: The Early Life, Education, and Scholarship of Takatsukasa Seigyoku, Current Abbess of Zenkōji's Daihongan Convent." *International Journal of Dharma Studies* 4, no. 1 (2016): 219–35.

Miura, Isshu, and Ruth Fuller Sasaki. *Zen Dust: The History of the Koan and Koan Study in Rinzai (Linji) Zen*. Basel, Switzerland: Quirin Press, 2015.

Mohr, Thea, and Jampa Tsedroen, eds. *Dignity and Discipline: Reviving Full Ordination for Buddhist Nuns*. Boston: Wisdom Publications, 2010.

Moon, Susan. "Activist Women in American Buddhism." In *Engaged Buddhism in the West*, edited by Christopher S. Queen, 247–68. Boston: Wisdom Publications, 2000.

Mrozik, Susanne. "Materializations of Virtue: Buddhist Discourses on Bodies." In *Bodily Citations: Religion and Judith Butler*, edited by Ellen T. Armour and Susan M. St. Ville, 15–47. New York: Columbia University Press, 2006.

———. "A Robed Revolution: The Contemporary Buddhist Nun's (Bhikkhunī) Movement." *Religion Compass* 3, no. 3 (2009): 360–78.

———. *Virtuous Bodies: The Physical Dimensions of Morality in Buddhist Ethics*. New York: Oxford University Press, 2007.

———. "'We Love Our Nuns': Affective Dimensions of the Sri Lankan *Bhikkhunī* Revival." *Journal of Buddhist Ethics* 21 (2014): 57–95.

Nagao, Gadjin M., ed. *Letters of Rennyo: A Translation of Rennyo's Gobunsho*. Kyoto, Japan: Hongwanji International Center, 2000.

Nanayon, Upasika Lee. *Pure and Simple: The Buddhist Teachings of a Thai Laywoman*. Boston: Wisdom Publications, 2005.

Narada. *The Buddha and His Teachings*. 4th ed. Kuala Lumpur, Malaysia: Buddhist Missionary Society, 1988.

Nattier, Jan. *A Few Good Men: The Bodhisattva Path according to* The Inquiry of Ugra (*Ugrapartipṛcchā*). Honolulu: University of Hawai'i Press, 2003.

———. *Once upon a Future Time: Studies in a Buddhist Prophecy of Decline*. Berkeley, CA: Asian Humanities Press, 1991.

Noble, Susan. "Eastern Traditions in Western Lands." In Tsomo, *Buddhism through American Women's Eyes*, 149–54.

———. "The Monastic Experience." In Tsomo, *Buddhism through American Women's Eyes*, 125–32.

Nolot, Édith. *Règles de Discipline Des Nonnes Bouddhistes: Le Bhiksunīvinaya de L'école Mahāsāṃghika-Lokottaravādin*. Paris: Collège de France, 1991.

Norman, K. R. *Pāli Literature, Including the Canonical Literature in Prakrit and Sanskrit of the Hīnayāna Schools Buddhism*. Wiesbaden, Germany: Otto Harrassowitz, 1983.

Norsworthy, Kathryn. "Integrating Feminist Theory and Engaged Buddhism: Counseling Women Survivors of Gender-Based Violence." In Tsomo, Buddhist Women and Social Justice, 101–16.

Norsworthy, Kathryn L., and Ouyporn Khuankaew. "Bringing Social Justice to International Practices of Counseling Psychology." In *Handbook for Social Justice in Counseling Psychology: Leadership, Vision, and Action*, edited by Rebecca L. Toporek, Lawrence H. Gerstein, Nadya Fouad, Gargi Roysircar-Sodowsky, and Tania Israel, 421–41. Thousand Oaks, CA: Sage, 2005.

———. "A New View from Women of Thailand about Gender, Sexuality, and HIV/AIDS." *Feminism and Psychology* 18, no. 4 (2008): 527–36.

———. "Women of Burma Speak Out: Workshops to Deconstruct Gender-Based Violence and Build Systems of Peace and Justice." *Journal for Specialists in Group Work* 29, no. 3 (2004): 259–83.

Obeyesekere, Ranjini. *Portraits of Buddhist Women: Stories from the Saddharmaratnāvaliya*. Albany: State University of New York Press, 2001.

Ohnuma, Reiko. *Head, Eyes, Flesh, and Blood: Giving Away the Body in Indian Buddhist Literature*. New York: Columbia University Press, 2007.

———. "The Story of Rupāvatī: A Female Past Birth of the Buddha." *Journal of the International Association of Buddhist Studies* 23, no. 1 (2000): 103–45.

———. *Ties That Bind: Maternal Imagery and Discourse in Indian Buddhism*. New York: Oxford University Press, 2012.

———. "Woman, Bodhisattva, and Buddha." *Journal of Feminist Studies in Religion* 17, no. 1 (2001): 63–83.

Omvedt, Gail. *Buddhism in India: Challenging Brahmanism and Caste*. New Delhi, India: Sage Publications India, 2003.

Owen, Lisa Battaglia. "On Gendered Discourse and the Maintenance of Boundaries: A Feminist Analysis of the *Bhikkhuni* Order in Indian Buddhism." *Asian Journal of Women's Studies* 4 (1998): 8–60.

———. "Toward a Buddhist Feminism: Mahayana Sutras, Feminist Theory, and the Transformation of Sex." *Asian Journal of Women's Studies* 3 (1997): 8–51.

Pachen, Ani, and Adelaide Donnelley. *Sorrow Mountain: The Journey of a Tibetan Warrior Nun*. New York: Kodansha America, 2000.

Park, Jin Y. *Women and Buddhist Philosophy: Engaging Zen Master Kim Iryop*. Honolulu: University of Hawai'i Press, 2018.

Paul, Diana Y. *Women in Buddhism: Images of the Feminine in Mahāyāna Tradition*. 2nd ed. Berkeley: University of California Press, 1985.

Peach, Lucinda Joy. "Social Responsibility, Sex Change, and Salvation: Gender Justice in the *Lotus Sūtra*." *Philosophy East and West* 52, no. 1 (2002): 50–74.

Powers, John. *A Bull of a Man: Images of Masculinity, Sex, and the Body in Indian Buddhism*. Cambridge, MA: Harvard University Press, 2009.

Prebish, Charles S. *Buddhism: A Modern Perspective*. University Park: Pennsylvania State University Press, 1994.

———. *Buddhist Monastic Discipline: The Sanskrit* Prātimokṣa Sūtras *of the Mahāsāṃghikas and Mūlasarvāstivādins*. Delhi, India: Motilal Banarsidass, 2010.

———. "Varying the Vinaya: Creative Responses to Modernity." In *Buddhism in the Modern World: Adaptations of an Ancient Tradition*, edited by Steven Heine and Charles S. Prebish, 45–74. New York: Oxford University Press, 2003.

Rajapakse, Vijitha. "Therīgāthā: On Feminism, Aestheticism and Religiosity in an Early Buddhist Verse Anthology." *Buddhist Studies Review* 12, no. 1 (1995): 7–26; and 12, no. 2 (1995): 135–55.

Roth, Gustav. *Bhikṣuṇī-Vinaya: Including Bhikṣuṇī-Prakīrṇaka and a Summary of the Bhikṣu-Prakīrṇaka of the Ārya-Mahāsāṃghika-Lokottaravādin*. Patna, India: K. P. Jayaswal Research Institute, 1970.

Ruch, Barbara. *Engendering Faith: Women and Buddhism in Premodern Japan*. Ann Arbor, MI: Center for Japanese Studies, University of Michigan, 2003.

Salgado, Nirmala S. *Buddhist Nuns and Gendered Practice: In Search of the Female Renunciant*. New York: Oxford University Press, 2013.

Schaeffer, Kurtis R. "The Autobiography of a Medieval Hermitess: Orgyan Chokyi (1675–1729)." In Gyatso and Havnevik, *Women in Tibet*, 83–109.

———. *Himalayan Hermitess: The Life of a Tibetan Buddhist Nun*. New York: Oxford University Press, 2004.

Schireson, Grace. *Zen Women: Beyond Tea Ladies, Iron Maidens, and Macho Masters*. Boston: Wisdom Publications, 2009.

Schmidt, Amy. *Dipa Ma: The Life and Legacy of a Buddhist Master*. Birmingham, UK: Windhorse, 2005.

Schopen, Gregory. *Buddhist Nuns, Monks, and Other Worldly Matters: Recent Papers on Monastic Buddhism in India*. Honolulu: University of Hawai'i Press, 2014.

———. "Sukhavātī as a Generalized Religious Goal in Sanskrit Mahāyāna Sūtra Literature." *Indo-Iranian Journal* 19 (1977): 177–210.

———. "The Suppression of Nuns and the Ritual Murder of Their Special Dead in Two Buddhist Monastic Texts." *Journal of Indian Philosophy* 24 (1996): 563–92.

Seeger, Martin. "'Against the Stream': The Thai Female Buddhist Saint Mae Chi Kaew Sianglam (1901–1991)." *South East Asia Research* 18, no. 3 (2010): 555–95.

———. "The Changing Roles of Thai Buddhist Women: Obscuring Identities and Increasing Charisma." *Religion Compass* 3 (2009): 806–22.

———. "'The (Dis)appearance of an Author': Some Observations and Reflections on Authorship in Modern Thai Buddhism." *Journal of the International Association of Buddhist Studies* 36/37 (2013/2014 [2015]): 499–536.

———. *Gender and the Path to Awakening: Hidden Histories of Nuns in Modern Thai Buddhism*. Copenhagen: NIAS Press, 2018.

———. "Orality, Memory, and Spiritual Practice: Outstanding Female Thai Buddhists in the Early 20th Century." *Journal of the Oxford Centre for Buddhist Studies* 7 (2014): 153–90.

———. "Reversal of Female Power, Transcendentality, and Gender in Thai Buddhism: The Thai Buddhist Female Saint Khun Mae Bunruean Tongbuntoem (1895–1964)." *Modern Asian Studies* 47 (2013): 1488–1519.

Shakya, Min Bahadur. *The Life and Contribution of the Nepalese Princess Bhrikuti Devi to Tibetan History (from Tibetan Sources)*. Kathmandu, Nepal: Pilgrims Publishing, 2002.

Sharma, Arvind, ed. *Women in World Religions*. Albany: State University of New York Press, 1987.

Shaw, Miranda. *Buddhist Goddesses of India*. Princeton, NJ: Princeton University Press, 2015.

———. *Passionate Enlightenment: Women in Tantric Buddhism*. Princeton, NJ: Princeton University Press, 1994.

Shih, Pao-ch'ang. *Lives of the Nuns: Biographies of Chinese Buddhist Nuns from the Fourth to Sixth Centuries*. Translated by Kathryn Ann Tsai. Honolulu: University of Hawai'i Press, 1994.

Sidky, Homayun. "The State Oracle of Tibet, Spirit Possession, and Shamanism," *Numen* 58 (2011): 71–99.

Simmons, Tracy. "Sravasti Abbey: A Dream Fulfilled for U.S. Buddhist Nuns." Religion News Service, May 8, 2012. http://unethicalconversionwatch.org.

Skilling, Peter. "*Eṣā agrā*: Images of Nuns in (Mūla-)Sarvāstivādin Literature." *Journal of the International Association of Buddhist Studies* 24, no. 2 (2001): 135–57.

Starkey, Caroline, and Emma Tomalin. "Gender, Buddhism and Education: Dhamma and Social Transformation within the Theravada Tradition." In *Gender, Religion and Education in a Chaotic Postmodern World*, edited by Zehavit Gross, Lynn Davies, and Al-Khansaa Diab, 55–71. Dordrecht, Netherlands: Springer, 2012.

Starling, Jessica. *Guardians of the Buddha's Home: Domestic Religion in Contemporary Jōdo Shinshū*. Honolulu: University of Hawai'i Press, 2019.

———. "Rights, Centers, and Peripheries: Experimental Moves in Japanese Buddhism." *International Journal of Dharma Studies* 5, no. 9 (2017): 1–14.

Sterling, Isabel. *Zen Pioneer: The Life and Works of Ruth Fuller Sasaki*. Emeryville, CA: Shoemaker & Hoard, 2006.

Strong, John S. "Aśoka's Wives and the Ambiguities of Buddhist Kingship." *Cahiers d'Extreme-Asie* 13 (2002): 35–54.

Swearer, Donald K. *The Buddhist World of Southeast Asia*. Albany: State University of New York Press, 2010.

Symes, Michael. *An Account of an Embassy to the Kingdom of Ava in the Year 1795*. Vol. 1. Edinburgh: Constable, 1827.

Thapar, Romila. "The Householder and the Renouncer in the Brahmanical and Buddhist Traditions." In *Way of Life: King, Householder, and Renouncer: Essays in Honour of Louis Dumont*, edited by T. N. Madan, 273–98. Delhi, India: Vikas, 1982.

Toomey, Christine. *In Search of Buddha's Daughters: A Modern Journey Down Ancient Roads*. New York: The Experiment, 2016.

Trainor, Kevin. "In the Eye of the Beholder: Nonattachment and the Body in Subhā's Verse (Therīgāthā 71)." *Journal of the American Academy of Religion* 61, no. 1 (1993): 57–79.

Tsomo, Karma Lekshe, ed. *Bridging Worlds: Buddhist Women's Voices across Generations*. Taibei, Taiwan: Yuan Chuan Press, 2004.

———, ed. *Buddhism at the Grassroots*. Delhi, India: Sakyadhita, 2012.

———, ed. *Buddhism through American Women's Eyes*. Ithaca, NY: Snow Lion Publications, 2011.

———. "Buddhist Ethics in Japan and Tibet: A Comparative Study of the Adoption of Bodhisattva and Pratimoksa Precepts." In *Buddhist Behavioral Codes and the Modern World*, edited by Charles Wei-hsun Fu and Sandra A. Wawrytko, 123–38. Westport, CN: Greenwood Press, 1994.

———, ed. *Buddhist Feminisms and Femininities*. Albany: State University of New York Press, 2019.

———. "Buddhist Nuns: New Roles and Possibilities." In *Tibet: Theocracy to Democracy*, edited by Dagmar Bernstorff, 368–93. New Delhi, India: Har-Anand Publications, 2016.

———, ed. *Buddhist Women across Cultures: Realizations*. Albany: State University of New York Press, 1999.

———, ed. *Buddhist Women and Social Justice: Ideals, Challenges, and Achievements*. Albany: State University of New York Press, 2004.

———, ed. *Buddhist Women in a Global Multicultural Community*. Kuala Lumpur, Malaysia: Sukhi Hotu Press, 2008.

———. "Change in Consciousness: Women's Religious Identity in Himalayan Buddhist Cultures." In Tsomo, *Buddhist Women across Cultures*, 169–89.

———, ed. *Compassion and Social Justice*. Yogyakarta, Indonesia: Sakyadhita, 2015.

———, ed. *Contemporary Buddhist Women: Contemplation, Cultural Exchange, and Social Action*. Hong Kong: Sakyadhita, 2017.

———, ed. *Eminent Buddhist Women*. Albany: State University of New York Press, 2014.

———. "Factions and Fortitude: Buddhist Women of Bangladesh." In Tsomo, *Innovative Buddhist Women*, 42–57.

———. "Global Exchange: Women in the Transmission and Transformation of Buddhism." In *TransBuddhism: American Perspectives on the Transmission, Translation, and Transformation of Buddhism in the Global Arena*, edited by Nalini Bhushan, Jay L. Garfield, and Abraham Zablocki, 209–36. Amherst: University of Massachusetts Press, 2009.

———. "The History of Japanese Nuns." *Buddhist Christian Studies* 12 (1992): 143–58.

———. "Illustrating the Way: The Life and Times of Bhikṣuṇi Shig Hiu Wan." *International Journal of Dharma Studies* 5, no. 1 (2017): 1–10.

———, ed. *Innovative Buddhist Women: Swimming against the Stream*. Richmond, UK: Curzon, 2000.

———. "Khunying Kanitha: Thailand's Advocate for Women." In Tsomo, *Buddhist Women and Social Justice*, 173–91.

———. "Lao Buddhist Women: Quietly Negotiating Religious Authority." *Buddhist Studies Review* 27, no. 1 (2010): 85–106.
———. "Nuns, *Ḍākinīs*, and Ordinary Women: Buddhist Women of Mongolia." In Tsomo, *Eminent Buddhist Women*, 195–209.
———. "Nuns, Lives, and Rules." In *Oxford Bibliographies Online: Buddhism*, edited by Richard Payne. New York: Oxford University Press, 2012.
———, ed. *Out of the Shadows: Socially Engaged Buddhist Women in the Global Community*. Delhi, India: Sri Satguru Publications, 2006.
———. "Prayers of Resistance: Kalmyk Women's Covert Buddhist Practice." *Nova Religio: The Journal of Alternative and Emergent Religions* 20, no. 1 (August 2016): 86–98.
———. "Renunciation in Contemporary Buddhist Monasticism." In *Asceticism, Identity, and Pedagogy in Dharma Traditions*, edited by Graham M. Schweig, Jeffrey D. Long, Ramdas Lamb, and Adarsh Deepak, 49–67. Hampton, VA: Deepak Heritage Books, 2006.
———, ed. *Sakyadhita: Daughters of the Buddha*. Ithaca, NY: Snow Lion Publications, 1989.
———. *Sisters in Solitude: Two Traditions of Buddhist Monastic Ethics for Women; A Comparative Analysis of the Dharmagupta and Mūlasarvāstivāda* Bhikṣuṇī Prātimokṣa Sūtras. Albany: State University of New York Press, 1996.
———. "Socially Engaged Buddhist Nuns: Activism in Taiwan and North America." *Journal of Global Buddhism* 10 (2009): 459–85.
———. "Transition and Transformation: Buddhist Women of Buryatia." In *Buddhism in Mongolian History, Society, and Culture*, edited by Vesna Wallace, 261–79. New York: Oxford University Press, 2015.
Tworkov, Helen. *Zen in America: Five Teachers and the Search for an American Buddhism*. New York: Kodansha, 1994.
Ueki, Masatoshi. *Gender Equality in Buddhism*. New York: Peter Lang, 2001.
Usuki, Patricia Kanaya. "American Women in Jōdo Shin Buddhism Today: Tradition and Transition." *Pacific World: Journal of the Institute of Buddhist Studies*, Third Series 7 (2005): 159–75.
———. *Currents of Change: American Buddhist Women Speak Out on Jodo Shinshu*. Berkeley, CA: Institute of Buddhist Studies, 2007.
Valian, Virginia. *Why So Slow? The Advancement of Women*. Cambridge, MA: Massachusetts Institute of Technology Press, 1999.
Vargas-O'Brian, Ivette M. "The Life of dGe slong ma dPal mo: The Experience of a Leper, Founder of a Fasting Ritual, a Transmitter of Buddhist Teachings on Suffering and Renunciation in Tibetan Religious History." *Journal of the International Association of Buddhist Studies* 24, no. 2 (2001): 157–86.
Waldman, Anne. *Trickster Feminism*. New York: Penguin, 2018.
Wallis, Glenn. *A Critique of Western Buddhism: Ruins of the Real*. New York: Bloomsbury, 2018.

Walshe, Maurice. *Long Discourses of the Buddha: A Translation of the Dīgha Nikāya*. Boston: Wisdom Publications, 1995.

Walters, Jonathan S. "*Apadāna: Therī-apadāna*: Wives of the Saints: Marriage and *Kamma* in the Path to Arhantship." In Collett, *Women in Early Indian Buddhism*, 160–91.

———. "Gotamī's Story: Introduction and Translation." In *Buddhism in Practice*, edited by Donald S. Lopez Jr., 113–38. Princeton, NJ: Princeton University Press, 1995.

———. "A Voice from the Silence: The Buddha's Mother's Story." *History of Religions* 33, no. 4 (1994): 358–79.

Walton, Jeremy J., and Susan Hayward. *Contesting Buddhist Narratives: Democratization, Nationalism, and Communal Violence in Myanmar*. Honolulu, HI: East-West Center, 2014.

Watkins, Joanne C. *Spirited Women: Gender, Religion, and Cultural Identity in the Nepal Himalaya*. New York: Columbia University Press, 1996.

Wijeyaratna, Mohan. *Buddhist Nuns: The Birth and Development of a Women's Monastic Order*. Kandy, Sri Lanka: Buddhist Publication Society, 2010.

Williams, Liz. "A Whisper in the Silence: Nuns before Mahāpajāpatī." *Buddhist Studies Review* 17, no. 2 (2000): 167–73.

Willis, Janice D, ed. *Feminine Ground: Essays on Women and Tibet*. Ithaca, NY: Snow Lion Publications, 1987.

Wilson, Jeff. "Mindfully Feminine? The Role of Meditation in the Production and Marketing of Gendered Lifestyles." In Tsomo, *Buddhist Feminisms and Femininities*, 285–302.

Wright, Diana E. "Spiritual Piety, Social Activism, and Economic Realities: The Nuns of Mantokuji." In Tsomo, *Buddhist Women and Social Justice*, 205–18.

Wu Yin, Bhikshuni. *Choosing Simplicity: Commentary on the* Bhikshuni Pratimoksha. Translated by Bhikshuni Jendy Shih. Edited by Bhikshuni Thubten Chodron. Ithaca, NY: Snow Lion Publications, 2001.

Young, Katherine K. "Hinduism." In Sharma, *Women in World Religions*, 59–103.

Young, Serinity. *Courtesans and Tantric Consorts: Sexualities in Buddhist Narrative, Iconography, and Ritual*. New York: Routledge, 2004.

———. "Female Mutability and Male Anxiety in an Early Buddhist Legend." *Journal of the History of Sexuality* 16, no. 1 (2007): 14–39.

Yü, Chün-fang. *Kuan-yin: The Chinese Transformation of Avalokitesvara*. New York: Columbia University Press, 2001.

Yuan, Yuan. "Chinese Buddhist Nuns in the Twentieth Century: A Case Study in Wuhan." *Journal of Global Buddhism* 10 (2015): 375–412.

INDEX

access: to Buddhist education programs, 73, 76, 140, 156, 188n10; to education in Bhutan, 85–86; to education in Tibet, 78; to full ordination, 109, 121
accomplished Buddhist women, 19, 21–22, 26, 53, 65, 66, 70–74, 75–77, 81–82, 116–17, 190n33
acculturation, 93, 103–6
activities, charitable, 134, 137, 144
"adamantine vehicle" (Vajrayāna), 69, 71, 73, 89–90
adaptability, of Buddhism, 92–93
addictions, 104, 134
alms, 37, 41, 44, 46, 47, 50–51, 120
American Buddhism, 94–96, 99–100
Amitābha Buddha, 59, 60, 94
Anālayo, 30, 33–34, 153, 189n11; on Buddhist texts, 178n11; on *vinaya*, 31, 32, 180n50
Ānanda, 27, 28–29, 30–31, 163
Andaya, Barbara Watson, 52
antidotes, to mental afflictions, 107
arhatī (liberated women), 108
arhats (liberated beings), 4, 11, 12, 18, 23
Arunachal Pradesh, India, *80*
asceticism, 19, 22, 47, 56
Aśoka (king), 133, 180n52
āśramas (stages of life for males), 3
assumptions of Buddhist feminism, 152
attachment, 105, 115
Aung San Suu Kyi, 53, 144–45
austerities, 10, 56
Australia, 92, 97, 123–24, 153
Avalokiteśvara, 60, 71, 72. *See also* Guanyin
Awakened One (Buddha). *See* Buddha
awakening, 10–11, 16, 85, 90, 113–14, 130; the Buddha's, 19, 23; in female form, 12, 24–25, 30, 59–61, 69, 160; gender identity and, 10–11, 16, 25, 85, 161–62, 166; intersections of, 141–45, 150–53

Bangladesh, 39, 119, 134, 144
Baochang (Pao-ch'ang), 35–36, 55–56, 182n6
beauty: physical, 161; standards, 113–14
Becoming a Woman in Zanskar, 80
being good, 133–35
a being on the path to perfect awakening (*bodhisattvas*), 11, 71, 159, 183n31
bhikkhu/*bhikṣu* (monks), 7–8, 9, 20, 47, 127
bhikkhunī/*bhikṣuṇī* (nuns), 9–10, 20, 21, 42–44; lineages of, 44–45, 82–83, 119, 127, 128, 153, 165; ordination of, 117–18, 121–24; *vinaya*, 125, 186n1
bhikkhunī saṅgha (community of nuns), 13, 15, 19; in Australia, 123; founding of, 27–31, 35–37, 40, 109, 110–11; in Nepal, 163; precepts of, 110–11; restoration of, 109, 153, 163; Sinhalese, 35, 45; in Sri Lanka, 163
bhikkhu saṅgha (community of monks), 13, 35, 110, 117, 120, 121
bhikṣuṇī prātimokṣa (code of monastic conduct for fully ordained nuns), 55
Bhutan, 85–86

Bhutanese Buddhism, 85
Bhutan Nuns Foundation, 86
biases: egalitarian, 24, 90–91; gender, 108–9, 130
Biographies of Buddhist Nuns (Baochang), 35–36, 55–56, 182n6
biographies of elder nuns (*Therī-apadāna*), 20–21, 22, 161
Blackstone, Kathryn R., 19–20, 113
Bodhgaya: the Buddha in, 19; ordination in, 117, 118, 129, 153; Sakyadhita International Conferences on Buddhist Women in, 97, 117, 138, 141, 150, 165
Bodhinyana Monastery, 123, *124*
bodhisattva (a being on the path to perfect awakening), 11, 159; precepts of, 183n31; of Tibet, 71
bodhi tree, 19, *36*
Bodong Chogle Namgyal, 75–76, 77
Bŏmŏnsa Temple, South Korea, 62, *63*
bōmori (wife of a priest), 65
books, by women, 92, 185n1
Brahm, Ajahn, 123, 152
brahmacarya (the pure life), 11, 112
Brahmajāla Sūtra, 45, 65, 183n31
brāhmaṇa (prestigious social class), 3, 6, 177n1
Buddha (the Awakened One), 4, *13*, 23; history of, 17–19; Mahāpajāpatī Gotamī/Mahāprajāpatī Gautamī discourses with, 28; teachings of, 107
Buddha Śākyamuni, 3, 83, 129, 158, 163; fourfold community established by, 20–21; teachings of, 4–5, 11, 21, 107. *See also* Siddhārtha Gautama
Buddhism: adaptability of, 92–93; American, 94; Bhutanese, 85; branches of Mahāyāna Buddhism, 12; contradictions of, 58; Dharmaguptaka school of, 54; diversity within, 1, 2; feminist scholars of, 23; gender constructions of, 159–63; gender justice and, 135–39; history of, 2–5, 14–15; India transmitting, 69; institutional structures of, 143; new vision of, 15–16; psychology of, 106; sexuality and, 101–3, 111, 113–14; social activism and, 132–35; social practices of, 6–14, 34; transmitted to Western countries, 93–94; women transforming, 139–41; women transplanting, 92; Zen, 36, 63, 64–65, 95–96, 185n6. *See also specific topics*; *specific traditions*
Buddhism after Patriarchy (Gross), 164
Buddhist Churches of America Ministers' Association, 94–95
Buddhist Compassion Relief Tzu Chi Foundation, 137
Buddhist education programs, 31–32, 42, 53, 67–68; access to, 73, 76, 140, 156, 188n10; for Tibetan nuns, 80–84
Buddhist feminism, 149, 150–53; challenging assumptions of, 152; critique of, 151
Buddhist principles, 6–14. *See also specific topics*
Buddhist programs for social welfare, 133, 134, 137, 183n44
Buddhist teachers, Fourteenth Dalai Lama on, 186n22
Buddhist texts, 8–9, 21–22, 108, *138*; Anālayo on, 178n11; comparative philological analysis of, 33–34; Mahāpajāpatī Gotamī/Mahāprajāpatī Gautamī in, 179n30; Mahāyāna, 60; patriarchal norms in, 145; soteriology of, 160; *suttas*/*sūtras*, 39; women represented in early, 23–26. *See also specific texts*
Buddhist values, 133–34, 135–36, 148
Buddhist women, 89–91, *93*; accomplished, 22, 65, 66, 70, 75, 190n33; at the beginning, 20–23; in Bhutan, 85–86; changes and challenges for, 142–43; commonalities in experiences of, 9; in education, 144; as exemplars of compassion, 136; global movement of, 149,

150, 156–57, 163, 165–66; as householders, 44, 46; in Japan, 63–65; in Korea, 62–63, 182n23; of modern East Asia, 65–68; in Mongolia, 86–88; opportunities for, 140–41; pioneering, 94–100; as renunciants, 44–49; research on, 2, 14, 164–65; rights debates over, 100–101; in Russian Federation, 88–89; social activists, 136–37, 144–45; social justice and, 141–45, 148; social service of, 135; support for, 13, 84; of Tibet, 70–75; *vinaya* of, 180n53, 182n4; Western, 99–101, 103–4, 155; writings on, 189n5. *See also specific topics*
A Bull of a Man (Powers), 161
Burma. *See* Myanmar

Cabezón, José, 23, 178n14, 178n16
Candrottādārikāparipṛcchā (Buddhist text), 25
categories of nuns, 45–46
celibacy, 10, 11, 64, 102, 165; case for, 111–14; exceptions to, 177n5
centers, meditation, 39
Central Asia, 69, 86–88. *See also* Tibet
Central Institute for Higher Tibetan Studies, 78
Central Tibetan Administration, 83, 128
changes and challenges, for Buddhist women, 142–43
Chao Hwei Shih, 145, 151
charitable activities, 134, 137
charitable organizations, 137
Cheng Yen, 137, 158, 189n4
China, 35–36, 54, 124–25; female enlightenment in, 59–61; Mount Wutai, 67; patriarchal norms in, 60; Tibet occupied by, 75, 77, 79; *vinaya* in, 55
Chinese Buddhism, 54–61; modern, 66–67; ordination in early, 55; women in, 54–59
Cho, Yasmin, 84
chöd ("cutting"), 71–72, 87–88
Chödrön, Pema, 99, 155, 185n16
Chökyi, Orgyan, 70, 75, 158
Chökyi Dronma, 75–77
Chung, Inyoung, 111
City of Ten Thousand Buddhas, 122
clashes, cultural and conceptual, 103–6
code of monastic conduct for fully ordained nuns (*bhikṣuṇī prātimokṣa*), 55, 154
collective future, 146
Collett, Alice, 23–24, 178n9
commonalities in experiences of Buddhist women, 9
community of monks. *See bhikkhu saṅgha*
community of nuns. *See bhikkhunī saṅgha*
comparative philological analysis of Buddhist texts, 33–34
conceptual clashes, 103–6
conflicting ideals, 48
Confucianism, 57, 58
connections, engendering, 39–44
consciousness, 101, 160–62
consensus, 83, 129, 154, 177n7
contemplation, questions for (*kōans*), 63, 95, 185n6, 189n15
contemporary movements for ordination, 42–44, 152–53
contradictions: of Buddhism, 58; in narrative of Mahāpajāpatī Gotamī/Mahāprajāpatī Gautamī, 32; in ordination, 29–31
control, 114; of nuns, 34; of reproduction, 114; of sexual virility, 23; Soviet, 88; of women, 20, 143
Corillion, Jean-Michel, 80
critiques of Buddhist feminism, 151
cross-cultural dialogue, 159, 166
cross-cultural research projects, 165
cultural clashes, 103–6
customs, family, 6, 7, 11, 57, 58, 112
"cutting" (*chöd*), 71–72, 87–88
cycle of existence and rebirth (*saṃsāra*), 4, 5; liberation from, 49, 113, 121, 140, 160

Dakini Power (Haas), 159
Dalai Lama, Fourteenth, 73, 77, 78, 79, 83, 128–29; on Buddhist teachers, 103, 186n22; on democratic governance, 177n7; as women's rights ally, 141
Daoxuan, 56–57
Dasara, Prema, 100
dasasilmātā (ten-precept nuns), 45, 117
datsans (monasteries and temples), 87
"daughters of Māra," 12–13
debates: over Buddhist women's rights, 100–101; over ordination, 109–11, 129–31
decision-making, equity in, 154
declarations, ordination, 30
defilements, mental/destructive emotions, 4, 10, 11, 22, 49, 136; of women, 60
definitions of *saṅgha*/*saṃgha*, 179n33
democratic governance, 7, 153–54, 177n7
democratic ideals, 14
Denison, Ruth, 96
Department of Religious Affairs, Myanmar, 50
desire, 4, 102–3, 114, 115, 161; renunciation of, 8, 10, 51; sexual, 102, 111–14, 161
destructive emotions/mental defilements (*kleśas*), 10, 146, 161–62
Devasārā (Tessara), Bhikkhunī, 35–36, 151
Devendra, Kusuma, 110, 117
devotional practices, 12, 49, 87
Dewaraja, Lorna, 180n56
Dhamek Stupa, 118
Dhammachari Guruma, 116
Dhamma/Dharma: activities, 67–68; women disseminating, 34–36
Dhammadinnā, Bhikkhunī, 26
Dhammananda, Bhikkhunī, 119, 121–22, 187n18
Dhammasara Nun's Monastery, 123, 124
Dhammawati, Bhikkhunī, 116–17
Dharmaguptaka, 54, 124, 127–28, 187n20
dialectics, 84
dialogue, cross-cultural, 159, 166
Diemberger, Hildegard, 77
Dīgha Nikāya (Buddhist text), 22, 177n4
discipline, 126
discourses of the Buddha (*suttas*/*sūtras*), 39
discrimination, 21; gender, 10, 14, 94, 100, 106, 131, 140, 145, 149, 155, 159; nuns, 84, 131
disparities in education, 47–48, 137–38
dissatisfaction (*dukkha*/*duḥkha*), 103, 111, 112, 115, 132, 161
distinctions, gender, 10, 67, 85
diversity within Buddhism, 90, 115, 134
"divorce temples," 64, 135
doing good, 133–35
domestic life, rejection of, 142, 179n33
Drepung Monastery, 73
Dronma, Chökyi, 75–77
dukkha/*duḥkha* (suffering and dissatisfaction), 4, 103, 111, 115, 132, 161

East Asia, 54; Japan, 63–65, 151–52; Korea, 62–63, *63*, *157*, 182n23; modern Buddhist women of, 65–68; ordination in, 124–26; Taiwan, 66, 158–59. *See also* China
education, 41; access to, 78, 85–86; Buddhist women in, 144; disparities in, 47–48, 137–38. *See also* Buddhist education programs
egalitarian biases, 24
egalitarian ideals, 26, 40, 84, 89, 90, 109, 140, 147, 163–64
egalitarianism, 58, 60, 94, 101, 105, 143, 153–55
eight-precept nuns (*mae chee*), 119–20, 121, 187n17
"eight weighty rules" (*garudhamma*/*gurudharma*), 7, 28, 31, 110, 129, 169, 180n50
engendering connections, 39–44
enlightened transformation, 89–91

enlightenment, 12, 25, 62, 89, 161, 162–63; in female form, 59–61, 87; ideal of, 101; and social activism, 132; of women, 77, 91, 94, 140, 158
equal opportunities, 101, 155
equity, gender, 14, 37, 78, 81, 91, 104, 120, 130, 136, 138; as transnational Buddhist ideal, 153–59; transnational pathways to, 163–66
ethical ideals, 143
ethnographic research, 2, 80, 150, 156
exceptions to celibacy, 177n5
exile, freedom in, 77–80

Falk, Monica Lindberg, 142
family customs, 6, 7, 11, 57, 58, 112
female body, 11–12; enlightenment in, 59–61, 71, 100, 159–60; preconceptions of, 5, 8, 26; transforming the, 25, 67
female enlightenment, in China, 59–61
feminism, Buddhist, 149, 150–53
feminist hermeneutics, 2
feminist scholars of Buddhism, 23–24, 58
filial piety (*xiào*), 57
financial support, 80, 84
Five-Point Declaration, 123
fourfold community, 20–21, 109
freedom, 19, 50, 87, 111; in exile, 77–80; of religion, 122, 131; sexual, 11; social, 5, 104, 114–15, 121; spiritual, 5; from suffering and rebirth, 4, 21
"full of delight" (Sukhāvatī), 59, 60
the future, revolutionizing, 14–16

A Garland of Feminist Reflections (Gross), 189n15
garudhamma/gurudharma ("eight weighty rules"), 7, 28, 31, 110, 129, 169, 180n50
gender: bias in *vinaya*, 108–9, 130; Buddhist constructions of, 159–63; discrimination, 14, 94; distinctions, 10, 67, 85; equity, 37, 81, 91, 120, 130, 138; hierarchies, 7, 149–50; inequalities, 9, 22, 31, 49, 59–60, 72, 89, 100–101, 105, 129, 131, 139–40; justice, 135–39; performativity, 89; relations, 33–34; roles, 1, 7, 9, 57; shifting, 25
gendered norms, 8, 101
gender equity, 14, 37, 78, 81, 91, 104, 120, 130, 136, 138; as transnational Buddhist ideal, 153–59; transnational pathways to, 163–66
gender identities, 25–26, 140, 142; awakening and, 10–11, 16; perspectives on, 161; as social constructs, 162; as transitory, 162–63
genderless, liberation as, 101, 139, 160, 161–62
genitals, sheathed, 23, 178n16
geshe degree, 73, 74, 81, 130
globalization, 10, 14
global movement of Buddhist women, 149, 150, 156–57, 163, 165–66
good, doing or being, 133–35
government recognition, 118
great adept (*mahāsiddha*), 71
great person (*mahāpuruṣa*), 23, 160
"great vehicle." *See* Mahāyāna Buddhism
Gross, Rita M., 164, 189n15
Guanyin (goddess), 60–61, 95
gurudharma/garudhamma ("eight weighty rules"), 7, 28, 31, 110, 129, 169, 180n50

Haas, Michaela, 159
Halifax, Joan Jiko, 96
Hamburg University, Germany, 129
Harrison, Paul, 59, 60
Hartman, Blanche, 96
Hartmann, Jens-Uwe, 188n27
hereditary temples, 65
hierarchies, 15; caste, 21; gender, 7, 12, 94, 123, 149–50, 153; monastic, 45; religious, 41, 72
higher ordination (*upasampadā*), 28, 46, 122, 125
Himalayan nuns, 78–80, 82, 84, 130

Hinsch, Bret, 57
history: of the Buddha, 17–19; of Buddhism, 2–5, 14–15; of India, 20; of ordination, 108; repeating, 157–58; women practitioners throughout, 12
homeless life, 32, 33
Horner, I. B., 2, 164
householders, Buddhist women as, 44, 46
Hsi Lai Temple, 97, *98*, 117
human body, meditation on, 8
Hye Chun Sunim, 62–63

iddhi/siddhi (supernormal powers), 25
ideals: conflicting, 48; democratic, 14; egalitarian, 40, 84, 163–64; ethical, 143; gender equity as Buddhist, 153–59; liberation as theoretical, 15
identities: religious/spiritual, 42, 50, 62, 66, 120; of renunciants, 50, 52; sexual, 25–26, 101, 162; social, 42, 57. *See also* gender identities
ideologies, 15, 58, 88, 140, 143
ignorance, 162
immigrants, 94
inclusion, 145–48, 157
independent nuns' communities, 119–20
India, 24, 78, 79; Arunachal Pradesh, *80*; Buddhism transmitted from, 69; history of, 20; patriarchal norms in, 5, 9, 12–13
inequalities, 7; gender, 9, 22, 31, 49, 59–60, 72, 89, 100–101, 105, 129, 131, 139–40; of monastic life, 91; structural, 15
insight (*vipassanā*), 52, 53, 96, 97, 99
institutional status, 41
institutional structures in Buddhism, 143
integrity, 145–48
intellectual traditions, 93
international networking, 101, 157
intersections of awakening, 141–45, 150–53
issues, social justice, 134

Jaffe, Richard, 183n28
Japan, 63–65, 151–52
Jetsunma Tenzin Palmo, 98–99
Jingjian, 55, 125
Jōdo Shinshū (True Pure Land), 65, 94
justice, 14, 91, 104; gender, 135–39, 149; social, 110, 131, 134, 141–48, 165

Kālāma Sutta, 146–47
Kamalā, 72
karma (actions), 7, 8, 26
Kawanami, Hiroko, 50, 53
Khema, Ayya, 97, 185n13, 189n4
Khemā, Therī, 22, 190n33
Klein, Anne Carolyn, 159
kleśas (destructive emotions), 161
Kloppenborg, Ria, 20
kōans (questions for contemplation), 63, 95, 185n6, 189n15
Korea, 62–63, *63*, *157*, 182n23
kṣetra-śuddhi (Pure Land), 59–60
kyōshi (teachers of Buddhism), 65

lakṣaṇa (physical characteristics), 23, 178n16, 178nn13–14
lama (guru or teacher), 73. *See also* Dalai Lama, Fourteenth
lamps of liberation, 36–37
Lanka. *See* Sri Lanka
Larger Sukhāvatī-vyūha Sūtra, 59
lay meditation practice, 41–42
laymen (*upāsaka*), 20, 102
"lay novice" ordinations, 64
laywomen (*upāsikā*), 20, 37, *80*, 102, *104*
liberated beings (*arhats*), 4, 11, 12, 18, 23
liberated nuns (*arhatī*), 108
liberation (*nibbāna/nirvāṇa*), 19, 41, 121; as genderless, 101, 139, 160, 161–62; path to, 21; as theoretical ideal, 15
lineages: *bhikkhunī/bhikṣuṇī*, 44–45, 82–83, 119, 127, 128, 153, 165; *chöd*, 88; Mūlasarvāstivāda *vinaya*, 126, 127, 128, 188n24; Myanmar, 41–42; ordination, 35–36, 45–46, 52; of

Samding Dorje Phagmo, 75; of Tibetan Buddhist practices, 71–72
Ling-shou, 57
literacy, 70, 76, 144, 158; cultural, 101; religious, 38
Liu, Annette, 159
Lives of Eminent Nuns (Baochang), 35–36, 55–56
Lizhu Fan, 66
Loseling Monastery, 74
Lotus Sūtra, 25, 67
love, 8, 105, 112, 113, 115
loving-kindness (*mettā/maitrī*), 7, 105, 112
Luce, G. H., 52
luminary figures of Tibetan Buddhism, 75–77

Machig Labdrön, 71–72, 88
Madhyama-āgama (Buddhist text), 28–29, 33
mae chee (eight-precept nuns), 119–20, 121, 187n17
Mahāmāyā Gautama, 17, *18*, 143
Mahāpadāna Sutta (Buddhist text), 22
Mahapajapati Buddhist College, 156, 190n24
Mahāparinibbāṇa Sutta, 21
Mahāprajāpatī Gautamī/Mahāpajāpatī Gotamī, 3, 5, 9, 13, *27*, 143–44; in Buddhist texts, 179n30; contradictions in narrative of, 32; discourses with Ānanda, 28–29; discourses with Buddha, 28; as early feminist, 151; going forth, 26–32; social justice contribution of, 135, 147; women's liberation movement organized by, 27
mahāpuruṣa (great person), 23, 160
Mahāsāṃghika, 55, 182n4
mahāsiddha (great adept), 71
Mahāvaṃsa, 34–35
Mahāyāna Buddhism ("great vehicle"), 5, 11, 54; branches of, 12; texts of, 60; Vajrayāna branch of, 69, 71, 73, 89–90
Mahinda (prince), 35, 180n52
marriage, 6, 177n6
Matsumoto, Irene Eshin, 95
meditation, 93, 103, 114, 120, 125, 133; of the Buddha, 4–5; in Burma, 49, 50, 52, 53; in China, 35, 36, 56; foremost in, 12; as gender-free, 101; in Himalayan cultures, 81, 82; on human body, 8; in Japan (*zazen*), 64, 95; *jhāna*, 97; in Korea (Sŏn), 62, 63, 104; lay practice of, 41–42, 44, 154; on loving-kindness, 132; in North America, 96, 100; tantric, 103; Theravāda, 38, 39, 41, 48, 49, 121; Vajrayāna, 69, 103; *vipassanā*, 52, 53, 96, 97, 99
Meeks, Lori, 64, 152
Meeting the Great Bliss Queen (Klein), 159
mendicancy, 9, 31, 32, 51
mettā/maitrī (loving-kindness), 7, 105, 107, 112, 132–36, 141, 146, 148
Metta Vihar, 97
Miaoshan, 67
misconduct, 102, 103, 110, 111
modern Chinese Buddhism, 66–67
monasteries, 31, 87, 105, 125, 126; Bodhinyana Monastery, 123, *124*; City of Ten Thousand Buddhas, 122; Dhammasara Nun's Monastery, 123, *124*; Loseling Monastery, *74*; Yangchen Chöling Monastery, *138*
monasteries and temples (*datsans*), 87
monastic centers (*vihāras*), 41, 133; Dhammadharini Vihara, 97; Metta Vihar, 97
monastic codes. *See vinaya*
monastic community. *See saṅgha/saṃgha*
monasticism, 104–5
monastic life, inequalities of, 7, 49, 60, 89, 91
monastic precepts. *See* precepts
monastic universities, 81
Mongolia, 67, 72, 79, 86–88, 155
Monk, Meredith, 100
monks (*bhikkhu/bhikṣu*), 7–8, 9, 20, 47, 127

Mount Wutai, China, *67*
Mūlasarvāstivāda *vinaya* lineage, 126, 127, 128, 180n50, 182n4 188n24
Myanmar (Burma): Department of Religious Affairs, 50; lineages of, 41–42; Pagan Dynasty, 51–52; Sagaing, 51; Theravāda Buddhism in, 49–53

Namgyal, Ngawang, 85
Nandaka, 33–34
Nattier, Jan, 180n46
Nepal, 3, 18, 39, 70, 71, 73, 78, 79; *bhikkhunī saṅgha* in, 163; Theravāda nuns in, 42, 116–17
networking, international, 101, 157
new vision of Buddhism, 15–16
nibbāna/nirvāṇa. See liberation
nonviolence, 7, 133, 135
norms: gendered, 8, 101; sexist, 123; social, 12, 62, 126, 142. *See also* patriarchal norms
North America, 94
novice monks (*sāmaṇera/śrāmaṇera*), 28, 40, 187n23
novice nuns (*sāmaṇerī/śrāmaṇerika*), 28, 40, 55, 127, *157*, 187n23
nunneries, 50, 81, 84, 184n25
nuns, 7–8, 9; categories of, 45–46; eight-precept, 119–20, 121, 187n17; Himalayan, 80; at Hsi Lai Temple, 98; independent communities, 120; on Mount Wutai, China, *67*; ten-precept, 45, 117; videos about, 156; young, *138*. *See also bhikkhunī/bhikṣuṇī*; Theravāda nuns; Tibetan nuns
nyung ne fasting practice, 72

offerings, 41, 47, 49, 65, 71, 87
Ogyen Trinley Dorje, 129, 152–53
Omvedt, Gail, 150
Once upon a Future Time (Nattier), 180n46
opportunities: for Buddhist women, 62, 73, 138–41; educational, 44, 66, 70, 73, 78–79, 81, 85, 121, 158; equal, 88–89, 101, 131, 155; meditation, 44, 52; obstacles as, 106–7; ordination, 108–9, 121; secular, 38, 90; unequal, 17, 37, 115, 137
oppression, 143, 151; political, 134–35, 145; religious, 62, 77, 87
ordination, 39, 41; access to, 109, 121; of *bhikkhunī/bhikṣuṇī*, 117–18, 121–24; at Bŏmŏnsa Temple, *63*; contemporary movements for, 42–44, 152–53; contradictions in, 29–31; debates over, 109–11, 129–31; declarations, 30; in early Chinese Buddhism, 55; in East Asia, 124–26; higher ordination, 28, 125; history of, 108; in Japan, 64; "lay novice," 64; lineages of, 35–36, 45–46, 52; objections to, 128; in Theravāda Buddhism, 114–16; of Tibetan nuns, 74–75, 80, 82–84, 126–29
organizations, charitable, 134, 137

Padmāsambhāva, 71
Pagan Dynasty (Burma), 51–52
Pāli canon (Buddhist texts), 22, 26, 30, 33–34, 146, 177n4
Palmo, Karma Khechok (Freda Bedi), 97–98
Palolo Kwannon Temple, 95
past-life affinities, 162
Paṭācārā, Therī, 22, 190n33
"path of the elders." *See* Theravāda Buddhism
path to liberation, 21
patriarchal norms, 15, 38, 90, 100–101, 115; breaking, 141, 159, 163; in Buddhist texts, 145; in China, 60; in India, 5, 9, 12–13; in Korea, 62; in Southeast Asia, 116; of *vinaya*, 91
performativity, gender, 89
Phagmo, Samding Dorje, 70, 75

Phagpa, Drogön Chögyal, 86
physical beauty, 24, 76, 113, 161
physical characteristics (*lakṣaṇa*), 23, 178n16, 178nn13–14
pioneering Buddhist women, 94–100
political oppression, 134–35, 145
"possessors of virtue" (*thila shin*), 50, 52, 53
post-traumatic stress disorder (PTSD), 78, 79
Powers, John, 161
Prabhasa, Gesshin, 96
practices: Buddhist social, 6–14, 34; contemplative, 3, 4, 48, 64, 98, 114; devotional, 12, 49, 87; *nyung ne* fasting, 72
Prātimokṣa Sūtras, 55, 154, 165, 177n4
Prebish, Charles S., 186n2
preceptors, 55
precepts, monastic, 10, 19, 40, 102, 125–26; of *bhikkhunī saṅgha*, 110–11; of *bodhisattvas*, 183n31; of *śrāmaṇera* and *śrāmaṇerika*, 187n23
preconceptions: of female bodies, 8; of women, 24, 38, 58
privilege, 62, 147, 156; male, 7, 25, 49, 60, 89, 94; maternal, 20; of modern women, 70
probationer (*sikkhamāṇā/śikṣamāṇā*), 28, 126, 182n4
psychology, Buddhist, 106
PTSD. *See* post-traumatic stress disorder
publications, scholarly, 150
Pure Land (*kṣetra-śuddhi*), 59–60, 65, 94, 133
pure life, the (*brahmacarya*), 11, 112

quorums, 55, 82, 83, 127, 130

rebirth, 4, 11, 21, 25, 121; female, 26, 60, 160, 178n9; male, 5, 8, 26, 41, 60, 123, 154; recognized rebirths (*tülkus*), 75, 81–82; in Sukhāvatī Pure Land, 59, 60, 94
reform movements, 109
refugees, 78, 79, 80, 97, 144
rejection of domestic life and reproduction, 142, 179n33
relations, gender, 33–34
religion, freedom of, 122, 131
religious/spiritual identities, 42, 50, 62, 66, 120
Rennyo, 94
renunciants (*śrāmaṇas*), 3, 19; Buddhist women as, 44–49; identities of, 50, 52; symbology of, 51
renunciation, 8, 24, 51, 57, 67, 86, 113, 115–16; the Buddha's, 123, 144; depreciation of female, 142; desire as a hindrance to, 161
reproduction, rejection of, 142, 179n33
research: on Buddhist women, 2, 14, 164–65; ethnographic, 2, 80, 150, 156; philosophical, 81; projects for cross-cultural, 165
restoration of *bhikkhunī saṅgha*, 52, 109
revolutionizing the future, 14–16
risk, 145, 147
roles, gender, 1, 7, 9, 57
Roshi, Jiyu- Kennett, 95
Russian Federation, Buddhist women in, 88–89

Sagaing, Myanmar, 51, 53
Sakyadhita International Conferences on Buddhist Women, 42, 43, 44, 92, 93, 99, 101, 138–39, 140, 142, 145, 151, 163; in Bodhgaya, 97, 117, 138, 141, 150, 165; creation of, 97, 150; in Seoul, Korea, 157; in Yogyakarta, 43, 93
Sakyadhita Thilashin Nunnery School, *51*
sāmaṇera/śrāmaṇera (novice monks), 28, 40, 127, 187n23
sāmaṇerī/śrāmaṇerika (novice nuns), 28, 40, 45, 82, 117, 125, 127, 157; ordination of, 125, 128, 129, 131; precepts of, 55, 82, 109, 126, 187n23
Samding Dorje Phagmo, 70, 75

saṃsāra (cycle of existence and rebirth), 4, 5, 49, 113, 121, 140, 160
Saṅghamittā (princess), 35, 36, 151, 180n52, 180n56
saṅgha/saṃgha (monastic community), 5, 9, 13, 17–18, 20–21; definitions of, 179n35; organizational model for, 154; sociohistorical context of, 110
Sasaki, Ruth Fuller, 95
Sasana Ramsi Dhamma School, 53
scholarly publications, 150
scholarship, 14, 15–16, 31, 164–65
schools, 81; Sakyadhita Thilashin Nunnery School, 51; Sasana Ramsi Dhamma School, 53; of Tibetan Buddhism, 72
Schopen, Gregory, 31, 59, 179n38
scriptures. *See* Buddhist texts
self-reflection, 146–47
Seoul, Korea, 157
sexist norms, 7–8, 123
sexual identities, 25–26, 101, 159–63
sexuality, Buddhism and, 101–3, 111, 113–14
sheathed genitals, 23, 178n16
Shig Hiu Wan, 159
Shōtoku (prince), 63–64
Siddhārtha Gautama, 3–4, 17–18
sikkhamāṇā/śikṣamāṇā (probationer), 28, 126, 182n4
Sinhalese *bhikkhunī saṅgha*, 35
Sinhalese *bhikkhu saṅgha*, 35
sisterhood, transnational, 139–41
Sitagu International Buddhist Academy, 53
slow steps forward, 129
social activism, 132–35, 151
social activists, Buddhist women, 136–37, 144–45
social constructs, gender identities as, 162
social identities, 42, 57
social justice, 131, 145–48; Buddhist women and, 141–45, 148; issues, 134; Mahāpajāpatī Gotamī/Mahāprajāpatī Gautamī contributing to, 135, 147
social norms, 12, 62, 126, 142
social practices, Buddhist, 6–14, 34. *See also specific topics*
social service, 48–49, 86, 132, 135
social welfare, Buddhist programs for, 133, 134, 137, 183n44
sociohistorical context of *saṅgha/saṃgha*, 5, 110, 116
solitary contemplative practice, 98, 115, 132
Sŏn meditation, 62, 63
soteriology of Buddhist texts, 160
Sōtō Zen, 64, 95–96
South Asia, 38, 39, 41, 44, 85–86. *See also* Bangladesh; India; Nepal; Sri Lanka
Southeast Asia, 38, 39, 41, 44; patriarchal norms in, 116; Thailand, 38, 119–23. *See also* Myanmar
Soviet Union, 87, 88–89
śrāmaṇas. *See* renunciants
Sri Lanka, 34–35, 39, 43, 45, 55; *bhikkhunī saṅgha* in, 163; Theravāda nuns in, 117–18
stages of life for males (*āśramas*), 3
standards of beauty, 113–14
statistics on women, 155
stereotypes, 1, 19–20, 24, 44, 139, 143
stone memorials, 58
Stuart, Maureen, 96
Subhā Therī, 24
Śuddhodana Gautama, 17
Sujātā, 18, 19, 144
Sukhāvatī ("full of delight"), 59, 60
Sumedho, Ajahn, 123
supernormal powers (*iddhi/siddhi*), 25
Supreme Sangha Council of Thailand, 122
sustainable world peace, 147–48
suttas/sūtras (discourses of the Buddha), 39; *Brahmajāla Sūtra*, 45, 65, 183n31; *Larger Sukhāvatī-vyūha Sūtra*, 59; *Lotus Sūtra*, 25, 67; *Prātimokṣa Sūtras*, 55, 154, 165, 177n4; recitations, 67
Swearer, Donald, 116
symbology of renunciants, 51

Taiwan, 66, 136, 137, 144, 145, 151, 158–59
Taixu, 133
tantric meditation practices, 103
tantric texts, 69, 84
Tārā, 12, 71, 87, 100
teachings, 68, 79; access to, 70, 72; applications of, 103, 104, 132, 133, 135; of Buddha Śākyamuni, 4–5, 11, 21, 90; critical reflection on, 146–47; editing, 76; interpretations of, 106; sexist elements in, 106, 110, 149, 159, 160; tantric, 84; in Tibet, 71, 127; transmission of, 69, 73, 92, 97, 136; transnational, 15
temple guardian (*bōmori*), 65
ten-precept nuns (*dasasilmātā*), 45, 117
Tenzin Gyatso, 73
texts. *See* Buddhist texts
Thailand, 38, 119–23
Thammanuthamma-patipatti (Buddhist text), 38
Theravāda Buddhism ("path of the elders"), 5, 11, 96; ordination in, 114–16; women in, 38–44; women in Burmese, 49–53
Theravāda nuns: in Nepal, 116–17; in Sri Lanka, 117–18; in Thailand, 119–23
Therī-apadāna (Biographies of Elder Nuns), 20–21, 22, 161
Therīgāthā (Verses of the Elder Nuns), 5, 19–20, 37, 114, 115, 190n33
thila shin ("possessors of virtue"), 42, 45, 50, 52, 53
"three baskets" (*Tipiṭaka/Tripiṭaka*), 39
three bodies of a buddha (*trikāya*), 59
Tibet, 69, 126–29; *bodhisattvas* of, 71; Buddhist women of, 70–75; Central Tibetan Administration, 83, 128; China occupying, 75, 77, 79; educational access in, 78
Tibetan Buddhism, 70; lineages of practice, 71–72; luminary figures in, 75–77; schools of, 72; teachers of, 99
Tibetan nuns, 70, 77–79; Buddhist education programs for, 80–84; ordination for, 74–75, 80, 82–84, 126–29
Tipiṭaka/Tripiṭaka ("three baskets"), 39
transformation, 48, 89–91; of attitudes, 15, 89–90; of consciousness, 11; gender, 25, 61, 67; inner, 106, 132, 149; social, 48, 135, 159, 164
transitory, gender identities as, 162–63
transmission of Buddhism, 69, 73, 88; to China, 36–37; to Lanka, 35–36; to the West, 92–100, 136–37
transnational Buddhist ideal, gender equity as, 153–59
transnational pathways to gender equity, 163–66
transnational sisterhood, 139–41
transnational teachings and traditions, 15
trikāya (three bodies of a *buddha*), 59
True Pure Land (Jōdo Shinshū sect), 65, 94
Tsogyal, Yeshe, 158
tülkus (recognized rebirths of accomplished beings), 81–82

U Ba Khin, 96
United Nations Declaration of Human Rights, 155
universities: Buddhist, 144, 159; monastic, 81, 157
unwholesome actions (*karma*), 26, 60, 102, 136, 139, 146, 147
upāsaka (laymen), 20, 102
upasampadā (higher ordination), 28, 46, 122, 125
upāsikā (laywomen), 20, 37, *80*, 102, *104*
Uppalavaṇṇā/Utpalavarṇā, 25, 179n26, 190n33
Usuki, Patricia Kanaya, 94–95

Vajrayāna ("adamantine vehicle"), 12, 69, 71, 73, 89–90, 103, 156
values, Buddhist, 133–34, 135–36, 148
vegetarianism, 64, 66, 67, 125, 165
Verses of the Elder Nuns (*Therīgāthā*), 5, 19–20, 37, 114, 115, 190n33

videos about nuns, 156
vihar/vihāra (monastic center), 41, 133; Dhammadharini Vihara, 97; Dharmakirti Vihar, 18, 116; Metta Vihara, 97w
vinaya (monastic codes), 6, 21, 55, 108, 179n18, 180n41; Anālayo on, 31, 32, 180n50; *bhikkhunī/bhikṣuṇī*, 125, 186n1; of Buddhist women, 180n53, 182n4; in China, 55; early, 110; gender bias in, 108–9, 130; Mūlasarvāstivāda lineage of, 126, 127, 128, 188n24; patriarchal norms of, 91
violence, 6–7, 134; domestic, 14, 46, 64; interreligious, 135; against women, 149
vipassanā (insight), 52, 53, 96, 97, 99
virtues, 56, 61

Western Buddhist women, 92, 93–94, 99–101, 103–4, 155
Whitehead, James D., 66
Williams, Liz, 110
women's liberation movement, 27
women's rights: debate over Buddhist, 100–101; Fourteenth Dalai Lama as ally for, 141
Women under Primitive Buddhism (Horner), 2, 164
world peace, sustainable, 147–48
writings on Buddhist women, 19, 22, 23–24, 37, 56, 189n5, 190n33

xiào (filial piety), 57

Yangchen Chöling Monastery, 138
Yaśodharā, 3, 5, 18, 144
Yogyakarta, Indonesia, *43*, *93*
Young, Serinity, 25, 60, 179n27
Young Lamas' Home in Dalhousie, 98

Zen Buddhism, 36, 63, 64–65, 95–96, 185n6
Zhu, Jingjian, 55, 125

ABOUT THE AUTHOR

Karma Lekshe Tsomo, a specialist in Buddhist studies, has taught at the University of San Diego (USD) since 2000. She offers classes in Buddhist Thought and Culture, World Religions, Comparative Religious Ethics, Religious and Political Identities in the Global Community, and Negotiating Religious Diversity in India. Her research interests include women in Buddhism, death and dying, Buddhist feminist ethics, Buddhism and bioethics, religion and politics, Buddhist social ethics, and Buddhist transnationalism. She integrates scholarship and social activism through the Sakyadhita International Association of Buddhist Women and Jamyang Foundation, an innovative education project for women in developing countries, with fifteen schools in the Indian Himalayas and Bangladesh.

Made in the USA
Las Vegas, NV
18 December 2023

83090736R00135